Michael T.H. Perelaer

Ran Away from the Dutch

Or, Borneo from south to north

Michael T.H. Perelaer

Ran Away from the Dutch
Or, Borneo from south to north

ISBN/EAN: 9783337245856

Printed in Europe, USA, Canada, Australia, Japan

Cover: Foto ©Andreas Hilbeck / pixelio.de

More available books at **www.hansebooks.com**

BAPA ANDONG'S RAFT.

Ran Away From The Dutch

OR

BORNEO FROM SOUTH TO NORTH

BY

M. T. H. PERELAER

Late of the Dutch Indian Service

Translated by MAURICE BLOK, and adapted by
A. P. MENDES

LONDON
SAMPSON LOW, MARSTON, SEARLE, & RIVINGTON
St. Dunstan's House
FETTER LANE, FLEET STREET, E.C.
1887

[All rights reserved]

ILLUSTRATIONS.

	PAGE.
BAPA ANDONG'S RAFT,	*Frontispiece.*
THE NIGHT FUNERAL,	20
JOHANNES AS A PANGARERAN,	72
AN AMBASSADOR FROM THE COLONEL,	190
WIENERSDORF AND HAMADOE,	239
KIHAM HOERAS AND ITS PASSAGE,	261
MOVING THE RANGKANS OVERLAND,	302
RESCUE OF SCHLICKEISEN,	325
HUNTING FOR GOLD,	333
A SIGN OF THE ENEMY,	354

CONTENTS.

CHAPTER I.

A MILITARY REPORT—FOUR DESERTERS—BABA POETJIENG—A LETTER—A COMPASSIONATE DOCTOR, HIS REFLECTIONS—FIRST INTRODUCTION TO TOMONGGONG—THE TITIH—A CHOLERA FUNERAL—RIFLE SHOT AND CANNON SHOT . . 1

CHAPTER II.

WHISPERING—LUCULLUS MISTAKEN FOR AN ANIMAL—JOHANNES' PLAN—A GRATEFUL SMUGGLER—JOHANNES A GEOGRAPHER—A MIRACULOUS HAUL OF FISHES—LA CUEILLE'S PROMISE—DRINKING WATER—DEPARTURE 22

CHAPTER III.

A DRUNKEN MAN'S TALK—ON THE SEA—JOHANNES UP A TREE—UP THE KAHAJAN—AN ÆOLIAN HARP—THE SOENGEI TROESSAN—IN THE DAHASAN—A WOOD SPECTRE—A MOSQUITO CHARM—FURTHER PLANS—LOOK OUT FOR YOUR HEAD—SUITS OF BLACK 35

CHAPTER IV.

A STRANGE DAYAK—PAINTING A COMPLEXION—SHEIK MOHAMMED AL MANSOER—TOO HANDSOME FOR A DAYAK—IN THE FOREST MARSHES—DASSO AND DOETA—TWO BOTTLES OF DOCTORED GIN—THE BIRDS WINGED 49

CHAPTER V.

ON THE JOURNEY—A PREVENTIVE AGAINST MOSQUITOES—THE SOENGEI BASARANG—THE KAPOEAS—PAST POELOE KANAMIT—THE BOAR'S HEAD—A TRUE DAYAK MEAL—FOUND IN THE WOOD—A PANGARERAN PUTTING OUT FISHING-HOOKS—THE CAPTURE OF A CROCODILE—THE SOENGEI MANTANGEI—FIGHT WITH A BOA CONSTRICTOR—A SKIRMISH—THE JOURNEY RESUMED 59

CHAPTER VI.

THE WOUNDED GO TO KWALA KAPOEAS—THE MANTANGEI AND THE MENKATIP—THE COMMANDER IN PURSUIT—AT SEA—PURSUIT OF THE FUGITIVES—THE SCHOONER—THE RETURN—ON THE TRACK AT LAST—DEPARTURE FROM MANTANGEI—WHITE SAIL—FIRST EXPERIENCE WITH THE HEAD-HUNTERS—LA CUEILLE WOUNDED—A FUNERAL CEREMONY. 85

CHAPTER VII.

JOURNEY UP THE RIVER—POISONS, HOW THEY ARE MADE—THE SOENGEI MOEROI—THE MEETING WITH BAPA ANDONG—BEE-HUNTING—HEAD-HUNTERS AGAIN—A STRUGGLE FOR LIFE. 110

CHAPTER VIII.

THE RESULTS OF THE FIGHT—DAMBOENG PAPOENDEH'S EXPEDITION—THE MAROETAS—BACK AGAIN TO THE KAPOEAS—NIGHT FIRING—THE BEES TO THE RESCUE—ASSISTANCE IN PERIL—THE SEPARATION—CIVILIZATION AND BARBARISM. 123

CHAPTER IX.

SOLITUDE—KWALA HIANG—THE ATTACK—RIFLE AND CANNON FIRE—THE GARRISON TAKES FLIGHT—THE PILLAGE—AN ILLUMINATION—THE COMMANDER OF KWALA KAPOEAS IN PURSUIT—HIS SEARCH AT SOENGEI NANING AND SOENGEI MANTANGEI—HIS ARRIVAL AT KWALA HIANG—THE PURSUIT CONTINUED—A GIGANTIC MAP—KOTTA BAROE—OUR TRAVELLERS AGAIN ON THE WAY—THE LEGEND OF THE ELEPHANT—POENANS! POENANS! 136

CHAPTER X.

HARIMAOUNG BOEKIT'S NARRATIVE—EVENTS AT KOTTA BAROE—COUNCIL OF WAR—COALS—ARRIVAL AT KOTTA DJANGKAN—TAKING IN AMMUNITION AND PROVISIONS—A WOMAN CAGED—WIENERSDORF BECOMES DESPERATE—JOHANNES REASONS 160

CHAPTER XI.

FURTHER MEANS OF DEFENCE—THE OATH OF ATONEMENT—JOHANNES AN ORATOR—TWO GUN SHOTS—THE ATTACK—WIENERSDORF IN A FAINT—A GRATEFUL POENAN—A DAYAK BEAUTY—AN OFFER OF MARRIAGE—WIENERSDORF IS ENGAGED TO HAMADOE—AN AMBASSADOR FROM THE COLONEL—HE CARRIES BACK HIS MESSAGE 173

CHAPTER XII.

CONSULTATION—THE "BLAKO ONTONG"—A SALVO OF GUNS—THE OFFERING—A NATIONAL DANCE—DOWN WITH THE TURBAN—A CONFERENCE DISTURBED BY TWO RIFLE SHOTS—A FLOATING ISLAND—AN ATTEMPT AT SURPRISE—A FATAL SHOT—THE SIEGE RAISED—THE EPISODE OF THE CROCODILE—JOHANNES SPEAKS—A NEW CHIEF . . . 199

CHAPTER XIII.

PREPARATION FOR THE JOURNEY—AN EMIGRATION—THE FISHING—A DAYAK TRIBUNAL—THE FINGER TEST—THE PROOF WITH THE LANCE—WIENERSDORF FINDS HAMADOE A TREASURE—LA CUEILLE DISCOVERS A COAL BED—A MISUNDERSTANDING—THE GOLD FEVER 225

CHAPTER XIV.

A DAYAK IRON-FOUNDRY—A PAIR OF NATIVE BELLOWS—HARIMAOUNG BOEKIT DOWN WITH FEVER—WIENERSDORF BECOMES A PHYSICIAN—JOHANNES A MAGICIAN—NEWS FROM KWALA KAPOEAS—ONCE MORE EN ROUTE—THE WIDOW'S STONE—KIHAM HOERAS AND ITS PASSAGE—HALAMANTEK . 247

CHAPTER XV.

A DAYAK BREAKFAST—THE HALT ON THE ISLAND—THE BOEHIES—A NEW KIND OF SOUP—THE THUNDER-STORM AND ITS RESULTS—RUMORS OF WAR—A NIGHT ATTACK—THE PARABOH—KOTTA HAMEAK BESIEGED—THE BESIEGERS ROUTED . 269

CHAPTER XVI.

CREMATION — THE SLAUGHTER OF PRISONERS OF WAR — A PRISONER OF WAR SAVED — COUNCIL OF WAR — SCARCITY OF WATER — HAMADOE THIRSTY — WIENERSDORF ATTACKED BY AN ORANG OUTANG — ON THE KAHAJAN — A BLOODY BATTLE — SCHLICKEISEN LOST 295

CHAPTER XVII.

PURSUIT — A BAND OF DOESSONESE SURPRISED — ON THE TRACK OF SCHLICKEISEN — HE IS SAVED — HARIMAOUNG BOEKIT MAKES A DISCOVERY — THE JOURNEY RENEWED — GOLD HUNTING — LA CUEILLE MAKES A FIND — BARTER WITH THE OLO OTTS 318

CHAPTER XVIII.

TRAVELLING APPOINTMENTS — THE DIAMOND OF THE SULTAN OF MATAM — DIAMOND FIELDS — GEORGE MULLER'S DIARY AND SKULL — MARRIAGE CEREMONIES — AGAIN ON THE ROAD — A NOVEL BURIAL-PLACE — ON THE EQUATOR — AN INKY LAKE — THE ASCENT OF BATANG LOEPAR 343

CHAPTER XIX.

DESCENT OF THE BATANG LOEPAR — A BORNEAN WATERFALL — THE FRONTIER PASSED — SIMANGANG — PARTING — ON BOARD THE FIREFLY — A SARAWAK FORT — AT KOETSHIN — ON BOARD THE RAINBOW — AT SINGAPORE — DEPARTURE FOR EUROPE 361

RAN AWAY FROM THE DUTCH;

OR,

BORNEO FROM SOUTH TO NORTH.

CHAPTER I.

A MILITARY REPORT—FOUR DESERTERS—BABA POETJIENG—A LETTER—A COMPASSIONATE DOCTOR, HIS REFLECTIONS—FIRST INTRODUCTION TO TOMONGGONG—THE TITIH—A CHOLERA FUNERAL—RIFLE SHOT AND CANNON SHOT.

"If you please, Colonel, four men have not answered to their names at roll-call."

"Who are they?"

"Schlickeisen, Wienersdorf, La Cueille and Johannes."

"Two Swiss, a Belgian and a native," muttered the Colonel. "And has it been ascertained how late they were seen at the military kampong?"

"Impossible, Colonel, the gates close at six and after that hour may not be reopened without your permission."

"Let a corporal and three men be immediately despatched to enquire after them. Then close the gates and double the guard so that means may be at hand to send out aid if required."

"Right, Colonel."

"Let me also have a full report of the search in the kampong and its results."

"Right, Colonel! Any further orders?"

A negative being indicated by a shake of the head, the sergeant saluted and quitted the apartment.

The Colonel rose from his rocking-chair. A sudden anxiety seemed to possess him. But a few moments before his face had seemed to be cast in bronze. Not a muscle had moved. Now, however, he had become restless and perturbed. He turned up the flame of his lamp and going to a safe took down a large volume. This he placed on the table and began to read attentively. The book contained extracts from the army register, that wonderful description of the whole of the Dutch Indian force which is kept posted with the most laudable exactitude at the war office in Batavia.

"Schlickeisen," read the Colonel; "a Swiss born at Steinbach, in the canton of Glarus, twenty-one years old. Father a priest." He turned over another leaf.

"Wienersdorf, also a Swiss; born at Winterthür, in the canton of Zürich, twenty-three years old. Father a professor of natural philosophy."

"La Cueille, a Belgian, born at Cheratte, in the province of Liege, twenty-six years old. Father a miner in the coal mines of Jupille."

"Johannes, born at Padang, island of Sumatra; about thirty

years old. Father unknown. Mother the Niasian woman, Ma Troeni."

The Colonel closed the book; he could obtain from it no further information.

"A curious affair," he muttered, "and one that will cause endless trouble unless it should prove to be only a drunken brawl."

Taking another large folio from his collection of books, he turned over a few pages and read:

"Schlickeisen and Wienersdorf were recommended at the registry to be educated as officers. They were subsequently dismissed from the college for taking part in the insurrection of the Swiss at Samarang. The one was a candidate for the bar, the other had finished his curriculum at the reaalschule and had received his diploma as teacher of natural philosophy and chemistry. Both had studied at Zürich. Nothing seems to be known of La Cueille. He has said that he was once assistant to a gunmaker at Meester Cornelis, but had been dismissed for drunkenness. And Johannes, another of those Indian products of animal passion, whose birth is almost a misfortune to him."

Thus far had the Colonel read and commented when a knock was heard and the sergeant again appeared. In correct military attitude he waited until his superior officer should interrogate him.

"Well, are they found?"

"No, Colonel, we have scoured the whole of the military kampong. It is quite deserted. All we have found is this letter, addressed to you by Johannes and left by him in his hut."

The Colonel received the letter with an air of indifference, opened it and just glanced at the signature. Then dropping it carelessly on the table, he asked,

" Have you discovered whether the missing men had procured any drink ? "

" Not any, Colonel."

" Who commands the guard ? "

" Corporal Greenwood."

" Ahem ; also an old drunkard. Ascertain from him and from the sentries whether Baba Poetjieng has been in the batang." The sergeant withdrew.

Baba and Kee are used to designate the Chinese in the Dutch Indies. The former is the more complimentary. Kee is humiliating and almost a nickname.

Baba Poetjieng was a sly Chinaman who had managed to make himself indispensable to the garrison by the sale of such merchandise as tobacco, needles, thread, beer, canned meats and vegetables, paper, pens and ink, etc., all of the first quality and unmistakably cheap. His prices, compared with those of the European merchants of Bandjermasin and even of Java, could not possibly have yielded him the smallest profit. It rather seemed as if he actually lost by his transactions. This he swore by the coffin of his father and grandfather was really the case ; alleging that it was a real pleasure to him to serve his good friends the Hollanders. One day the Colonel happened to pick up outside of the fort an empty sardine box, and upon examining it became struck by its peculiar trade-mark and by an extraordinary smell which seemed to cling to it. Finding a second box on a subsequent occasion, he again detected the same odor, and the idea struck him that the boxes had contained opium. He also noticed that among both the Indian and the European soldiers of the garrison there was a certain amount of excitement whenever Baba Poetjieng was at the pier with his wares. But all efforts to entrap the sly Chinaman had proved unavailing. His tins when opened for examination were always found to contain the finest sardines or California fruits; and with a satisfied grin our Baba asked the Colonel whether he had enjoyed his purchases. He had "most carefully selected his wares for the toean." The reader will now perceive why the Colonel had expressed a wish to know whether Baba Poetjieng had been seen at the pier.

The sergeant returned with a report that nobody had seen the Chinaman that day.

Orders were then given that the sergeant and six soldiers should go to the kampong and invite the Chief of the district to visit the Commander immediately. "Proceed cautiously," said the Colonel. "The gates will be guarded until you return. The sentinels must redouble their vigilance and keep a sharp lookout. I shall presently go around myself to see how all goes on."

After the departure of the sergeant, the Colonel took up the letter, which he had thrown on the table, and read:

"HIGH-BORN AND HONORED COLONEL.—We shall be a long way off when this letter is read by you. You will undoubtedly use every effort to recapture us, but all will be in vain. Our measures have been well taken and you will never see one of us back alive. We have had enough of the Dutch service.

"We thank you most cordially, dear Colonel, for the noble treatment we have received at your hands. If any one could have reconciled us to our condition and prevented our embarking on our present dangerous enterprise, it would have been you. But who can assure us that you will remain in command over us! The time we have yet to serve is long and men's characters are not alike. We Swiss have been cruelly deceived by the recruiting officers of the Dutch army. We refrain from saying where the deceit lies. You are able to fathom our misery in all its extent. We have been enticed from our lovely valleys under the most wicked pretences; we were promised the greatest advantages, but of all these promises nothing has ever been realized.

"But why should we write all this to you—you who are entirely blameless for the miseries we suffer? We know that you have done all you could to render our fate supportable and on that account we do not wish to appear guilty in your eyes. We will be called, and we certainly are, deserters; but we do not deserve the ignominy which will cling to our names. You at least could not misjudge us. We might have considered ourselves bound to the Dutch government, but when we perceived that we were the victims of foul duplicity our contract did not appear binding upon us. In transactions of such a nature it is not fair that one side only should fulfill its duties, while the other is left free to carry out such part of its engagement as is found convenient."

"Poor wretches," said the Colonel.

"But," he continued reading, "some excuse might well be offered by us for our desertion, and on that score our consciences are easy. Necessity compels us to act as we are doing. Judge for yourself. You kindly lent us your theodolite, field-glasses, sextant and compass in order that we might keep up our knowledge of surveying. Some of those instruments we have decided to take with us. The last two are especially indispensable to us, since without them we should soon be lost in our proposed journey. The theodolite we will leave in Johannes' cabin. Pray pardon us this dishonesty. You may rest assured that we will either return the borrowed instruments or forward the cost as soon as we find ourselves once more among civilized nations. And now, dear Colonel, may God reward you for the kind treatment we have received from you. We feel that a hard chase after us is about to commence. God protect us. Farewell.

"Schlickeisen,
"Wienersdorf.

"P. S.—If we should perish in our efforts to regain our liberty our fate will not remain long concealed from you. We entreat you by everything you value, by the memory of your lamented mother, to inform our parents of our end. You will find full particulars of their addresses in our military pass-books. Once more, farewell."

"Poor devils," repeated the Colonel, wiping away a tear as if he felt humiliated by his emotion. "What a miserable fate these men have gone to encounter." He then laid the letter on the table, giving vent to a deep sigh and became wrapt in meditation. He was interrupted by the entrance of the garrison doctor, who rushed into the room with an angry and excited countenance.

The doctor was a tall, slender man, with bristly red hair and a pair of yellow mustaches, the points of which were kept well waxed so that they stood out as if trying to reach behind his ears. He also had received a letter which he held in his hand.

"Himmelskreuz! The rogue has bolted."

He was evidently a Prussian or South German.

"What? Who?" asked the Colonel.

"Der Wallon, das Vieh, and he has taken my instruments and revolvers with him."

La Cueille had likewise left a letter behind to explain the theft of the doctor's instruments and arms, which as he was a gunsmith had been entrusted to him for repair. He had also begged to be excused to the Colonel, whose two Remington rifles he had carried off.

"One cannot risk such a dangerous journey quite defenceless," the Walloon had reasoned. "The Colonel was sure to know of the dangers they would have to encounter."

The Colonel showed the doctor the letter which he had received.

"Then they have bolted together."

"Very probably."

"Poor fellows! But what will you do now?"

"I have sent to the Chief of the district. It may be that he has some information. Upon his communication will depend my course of action."

"Do you mean to pursue them?"

"Certainly," replied the Colonel.

"But the safety of the post entrusted to you?"

"Oh, my dear sir, I will not endanger that."

"How so? The garrison is not strong. You cannot take any men away from it without danger."

"Oh, I will leave the garrison intact. I will have them hunted down by a native detachment."

"That would be cruel. To be hunted down by Dayaks!"

"I must own that those fellows are not over-scrupulous; but what else can I do? As you say, I dare not take any of the garrison and I cannot very well remain inactive. However, it is impossible to decide what steps are to be taken until I have seen the Chief of the district. It may be that the deserters have already been seized by the kampong guard and that our anxieties are premature. I am now going to visit the posts, will you come with me?"

"Donnerwetter! it is no treat to grope about in that Egyptian darkness."

"Well stay behind and wait for me. The Chief may be here directly and I should like to have you present at our interview. I shall not be long."

The Colonel went out. He had only a short distance to go, the fort being very small.

The sentries were found duly posted and peering sharply into the surrounding darkness. The bridge over the moat had been let down and the gates stood ajar; but outside at the further extremity of the drawbridge there was stationed a picket of six men, whilst behind the gate the whole garrison was drawn up with shouldered rifles. The Colonel, satisfied with his inspection, was about to return to his quarters and his guest when he was accosted by a corporal.

"What is the matter?" he asked.

"The rifles of Johannes, Schlickeisen, Wienersdorf and La Cueille are missing from the gun rack and most of the men's cartridge boxes have been emptied."

"Ha! ascertain how many cartridges are lost and let the artillery sergeant replace them immediately from the magazine."

The Colonel had scarcely finished speaking when the corporal of the mess approached to report that four bags of rice and a bag of coffee were missing. These too he ordered replaced and turned away, his mind engrossed by the desertions and their consequences. The men who had deserted, thought he, did not seem to have any quantity or variety of provisions, but they were brave men who would certainly levy toll upon each kampong they passed and find food on every river they traversed. They had weapons and ammunition and could face any danger; they had also instruments whereby they could direct their course. Thus there could be no likelihood of their perishing in the virgin forests of Borneo.

"Yes," said he to himself, " we have here a job which will set both feet and pens in motion and I am afraid, with the writing mania already existing in India, pens are going to beat feet. But those poor, poor devils!"

In the meantime the doctor had stretched himself on a rocking-chair and soon became lost in deep reverie. He regretted that these men had taken so desperate a step; but he could not blame them altogether. He was full of fear for the issue of their undertaking, yet if he himself had not been bound by oath, he would have been inclined to join and become their guide and counsellor. But—he belonged to the Dutch Indian Officers' Club; he had sworn allegiance to the Dutch crown and submission to the military régime of the Dutch army.

He considered himself bound, irrevocably bound, but how had he been treated? They had told him he would be able to live and put aside from his pay a respectable fortune; that in five years he would have three thousand dollars and he had hoped then to return and marry his darling Clara. And now? His income, everything included, had never exceeded sixty dollars a month, a sum barely sufficient to maintain him, so that the fortune of three thousand dollars remained where it had been born—in his imagination. He took from his pocketbook the portrait of a young girl and looked at it until a tear rolled down his cheek. It was the portrait of his Clara.

"Thou wast tired of waiting," sighed he. Heavy footsteps approaching from without he replaced the portrait in his pocketbook just as the Colonel entered, accompanied by the Chief of the district—a Dayak of agreeable countenance, known as Tomonggong Nikodemus Djaja Nagara.

"Take a seat, Tomonggong," said the Colonel, pointing to a chair, "while I get some cigars."

The Tomonggong, however, approached the doctor, bowed his head, presented his hand and uttered the greeting,

"Tabeh toean, saja harap toean ada baik"—Good-day, sir, I hope you are well.

The doctor raised himself from his comfortable position, stepped forward to take the outstretched hand and pressed it cordially. Availing himself of the brief absence of the Colonel, he whispered to the Chief, "They must be saved, they must not be allowed to fall into the hands of the Dutch."

Tomonggong cast a penetrating look on him. Used to treason and falsehood the first feeling of an East Indian, however honest he himself may be, is one of distrust. He suspects that a snare is being laid for him.

Hence the surprise of the Tomonggong when he heard the doctor's words.

"That would be difficult, sir. The Colonel is sure to take

strong measures and I,"—after a moment's hesitation, he continued—"I must obey."

"By Mahatara! Tomonggong, save them, save them, I beseech you. If you think you owe me any gratitude, don't refuse my prayer. They are my countrymen."

The doctor stood before the Dayak with his hands pressed together in the attitude of supplication. He had a claim upon the gratitude of Tomonggong of which the Chief was not insensible. Kambang, his eldest and favorite daughter, had some years before been bitten by a very venomous snake. The father sent out for one of the antidotes of the country, but while they were seeking the plant the doctor sucked the poison out of the wound, which he then cauterized with a piece of burning charcoal. His address and promptitude saved the child's life.

The grateful father now bethought him of this and putting aside all distrust seized the doctor's hand and muttered something which was rendered inaudible by the return of the Colonel to the room. He brought a well filled cigar case from which he presented each of his guests a full flavored Manilla. He then lit one for himself and resuming his seat addressed the Tomonggong on the subject of the recent deserters.

"And not a soul in the kampong has discovered anything about their flight?"

"No, sir."

"It is strange, very strange. But, Tomonggong, they must have obtained some kind of a vessel, since flight by land was impossible."

"If any one had missed a djoekoeng the loss would undoubtedly have been reported to me. Besides the escape of white men from the garrison would when known arouse so much excitement that I must have heard of it."

The Colonel meditated for a while. He seemed to be in doubt. At length he resumed, "Tomonggong, I must recapture these men, if only to prevent the example from spreading among our troops. If those poor fellows get among the natives of the upper country they will unquestionably be attacked and perhaps killed."

"Yes, sir, they will be. The head-hunters will not spare them. But do you think they have risked going inland?"

"Their flight seaward is almost impossible," replied the Colonel. "Two cruising vessels are stationed at the mouth of the river and the whole south coast is blockaded by steamers. Suppose they manage to break through the cordon. What then? Dare they risk a voyage on an open sea in a miserable canoe, especially at this season, when the westerly gales blow with such fury? That would be tantamount to self-destruction. And then whither could they go. To Java? If they should by chance succeed in reaching the island, they would fall into the hand of the police, who are exceedingly vigilant. No: my theory is that they have gone to the interior. They will avoid all inhabited parts and try to reach Sarawak."

"Could they not do that by sea?"

"Well, yes; but they would have then to elude the cruisers and the blockading steamers. That accomplished, as soon as they rounded Cape Batoe Titi, they would fall into the line of our vessels running between Eastern Java and Singapore. Then should they reach the open Chinese Sea, at this season of the year a thousand dangers would still stare them in the face. The chances would be a hundred to one that they would either perish or be captured. Yes; they will make for Sarawak—but only straight across the island."

"But that is a very long way, sir," said the Tomonggong, "and the dangers are not slight in that direction, as you well know."

"I know all that, Tomonggong, but those are dangers which they may hope to surmount; for believe me, they are bold and brave men who will venture anything. Come, we must not delay. Every moment is precious. Return to your dwelling and summon without loss of time the chiefs of the nearest kampongs. Let them collect about fifty men provisioned for a few days. They must all be fully armed and ready to start in two hours. I will come down to inspect and will then give further instructions."

"But, sir, will they be easily captured?"

"I doubt it and that is why I am ordering arms to be taken. I wish to capture them alive and unharmed. If, however, they defend themselves and use their weapons, then—" the Colonel hesitated—he knew the weight of his words.

The doctor stood pale and with clenched fists. After a few moments of reflection the Colonel resumed in a loud voice:

"If they use their weapons you are permitted to use yours. Let one of your most influential chiefs, such as Damboeng Papoendeh, lead the expedition. Send him here at once for orders."

The Colonel spoke with decision, like one accustomed to command. His spirit seemed to infect the Tomonggong, who rose to hurry away. A look, however, at the doctor, whose face showed anxiety and despair, made him pause. He passed his hands over his sarong as if the folds of the garment were hurting him and again seated himself.

"By your leave, sir," he said quietly but firmly, "it won't do, it is already very late and such orders as you direct will cause great commotion in the kampong."

"Well! and what if they do?" asked the Colonel.

"The women and children will be alarmed and the object of these movements may be misunderstood. You know, sir, that in spite of your efforts to pacify the people, we cannot trust a great part of them. Besides there are rumors about. I mentioned yesterday that rangkans filled with head-hunters of the Doessan have been seen in our neighborhood. I cannot say that I believe in these reports, but they are not unlikely to be true because several of our families left their houses last night to seek refuge in the woods."

"But, Tomonggong," interrupted the Colonel.

"Believe me, sir," the Chief continued solemnly. "Believe me. You know that I am a faithful subject of the Dutch. The object of this night's expedition will be misunderstood by the people. They will all be alarmed and especially the families of those who are sent on this service. Besides where are they to go? You say that the fugitives have not fled seaward. You will pardon me, pardon me a thousand times when I say that I cannot share your opinion. But supposing it could be proved beyond doubt that they have gone inland, I yet repeat my question, Whither shall my Dayaks go? The island of Borneo is very large. Who will lead them on the right track in this darkness?"

"What then is to be done?" asked the Colonel with impatience.

"Wait," was the cool reply. "By to-morrow morning I shall know how your soldiers have escaped and I assure you I will soon be on their track. They could not have left the district unobserved. But while now, in the dark night and with evil reports abroad, you can only spread alarm by taking any steps, to-morrow, when the sun brightens the skies, I shall be better able to act. The natives will clearly understand the object of our expedition and all misapprehensions be rendered impossible. I shall then have no difficulty in getting the requisite number of volunteers for the service. I should also like to command the expedition myself, if you will allow me to do so, and I could not undertake to start to-night."

The Colonel reflected for a few moments. The room was in complete silence, the only sounds audible being the hurried respiration of the doctor. At length he seemed to have arrived at a decision.

"You are right, Tomonggong, perfectly right, and I thank you for your advice. Nevertheless, I should have liked to commence the search to-night, for the sooner those poor fellows fall into my hands the less they will have to suffer. They will have to pay dearly enough for this excursion; it may perhaps cost them their lives."

"Yes, sir. Hatallah only knows how dearly," said the Chief with solemnity.

"Well," said the Colonel, "till to-morrow then. I shall expect news very early. But stay, I had better come to you and thus save time. I will be with you before daybreak, Tomonggong. I will now give orders for your departure." Thus saying, he left the room.

The doctor, left alone with the chief, rushed toward him and seized his hands. "They will have a start of six hours," he said with emotion.

"It is not much," suggested the Dayak.

"Sufficient, let us hope. Oh, how can I thank you!"

The Colonel re-entered at that moment and their confidence was interrupted.

After the Tomonggong had taken his leave, the two friends remained together to empty the bottle which had been opened.

"An awkward business," observed the Colonel, "devilishly awkward for those poor fellows, but scarcely less so for me. Besides the dangers which may attend my pursuit after them, I shall have to weather the reprimands from headquarters. You know our authorities always turn these matters against us. Whenever the Dutch government has a difficulty the first impulse of all in power is to look out for a scapegoat."

"But our Commander-in-Chief is not the man to do that."

"Oh, I am not afraid of him. The bother will come from higher sources. From Batavia will go the report to the war office of the Hague, that through the negligence of a colonel four European soldiers have escaped—in war time. They will be careful to add, 'Colonel severely reprimanded.' Then the Hague authorities will be satisfied because none of them can be held responsible."

"Not responsible," said the doctor, passionately, "not responsible. Why then the whole blame rests with the Hague for——"

"Tut, tut; no politics, I beg," said the Colonel. "Even if you are right, you are wrong; that is my experience in life. Come, it is late; let us retire, for day will begin early for us to-morrow."

They shook hands and the doctor left the room to seek his couch, but the Colonel, before retiring for the night, went the rounds once more to assure himself that all was safe.

For a moment he paused at the southern bastion. This work commanded the whole expanse of water formed by the confluence of the rivers Poeloe-Petak and Kapoeas-Moeroeng, about twelve hundred yards wide at this point. The night was lovely; the stars glittered in the dark blue sky and were brilliantly reflected in the water. The woods which bordered the banks stood out boldly against the dusky horizon. On the eastern banks of the river Poeloe-Petak the outlines of the Dayak dwellings could be traced between the green herbage and here and there the flame of a lamp glittered among the trees and shrubs.

Silence reigned around, broken only by the distant barking of some watchful dog and by the soft murmur of the river.

While the Colonel stood leaning against the parapet and gazing upon this charming scene the sounds of the titih were suddenly heard. The titih is the death bell of the Dayaks. The sounds are produced by a series of strokes upon four metal basins of different sizes. The first knell is struck when a death occurs; the second when the body is coffined; the third when the corpse is being carried to the grave, and the parting knell when the grave is closed. The titih is struck continuously during the progress of the funeral, but on the other occasions there are intervals of four or five minutes between the sounds, just like our passing bell. The continuous strokes of the funeral knell are gentle at first but are interrupted every two minutes by a loud bang, and the echo of that ting, ting, toong, along the broad streams of Borneo sounds extremely mournful and disposes one to melancholy.

The Colonel pricked up his ears at the first knell and tried to recollect whether anyone had died in the kampong; but his thoughts soon returned to the deserters. When the titih continued without intermission, he knew that a funeral was in progress and this somewhat excited his curiosity. Not that it was of rare occurrence for the Dayaks to bury their dead at night. But the Colonel had recently requested the natives not to have any nocturnal funerals during war time except when absolutely unavoidable. This request, or rather command, had been hitherto respected, but now, now—it was very strange!

"Aha! I know," he said to himself, "I know. Tomonggong told me yesterday of two cases of cholera. One of the sufferers has perhaps succumbed; they are quite justified in disposing of their dead without delay."

A little while afterward two canoes were seen coming down from the kampong, decked out with bunting and illuminated by torches. As they drew nearer the hymns of the priestesses could be distinguished, accompanied by the muffled sounds of the small drums. Their elegy was borne across the river.

"Fly, soul of the departed, rise on the clouds. Fly, spirit of the dead, float upon the waters."

Everything was in the usual order. The song and the drumming proceeded from the first canoe. Immediately behind followed another boat containing the coffin. In order to be prepared for any emergency the Colonel called the guards and stationed them on the bastion, where he joined them. He also directed a non-commissioned officer to reconnoitre the approaching canoes and to be doubly watchful. His hail, "Who goes there?" was responded to and his order to land was immediately obeyed. He searched the first canoe, joked with the priestesses, but failed to discover anything suspicious. Neither did he see anything unusual on the second boat. A faint odor peculiar to the victims of cholera induced him to shorten the investigation. The canoes left the pier and soon the fort was well behind them. The Colonel followed them with his eyes for a long time and became lost in meditation when suddenly a head was seen to protrude from beneath the roof of the second boat and a voice was heard exclaiming:

"Enfoncés les Hollandais—les têtes de fromage!"

The Colonel instantly perceived how matters stood—the fugitives were hidden in the funeral cortege. He cried aloud to the oarsmen:

"Stop! Come back! Turn immediately!"

Again was heard the opprobrious epithet; this time followed by a rifle shot which wounded a Javan soldier. The Colonel ordered the four-inch gun to be turned toward the canoes, placed it himself at the proper elevation and fired; but the night hung dark and no sure aim could be taken. The shot struck the water in the rear of the second canoe, bounded over it, passed through

THE NIGHT FUNERAL.

the roof of the first boat and as it struck the water raised so great an upheaval as to nearly capsize both canoes. It was followed by a volley of rifle shot from the ramparts, which killed two of the oarsmen. But the current swept the boats rapidly away and before the soldiers had time to reload they had become lost in the intense darkness.

" That discharge has hit them," said the doctor, who had left his bed to see the cause of the commotion. " I heard a distinct cry from the canoes."

" Yes," replied the Colonel, " it has hit them, but—that is only the first part of the play. I ought not to have allowed myself to be talked over by the Tomonggong into postponing the pursuit until to-morrow. Perhaps what has just happened ought to have been prevented. Have you seen Troenosmito's wound?"

" Yes, it is only a graze."

" Well, let us retire. I know pretty well whither the deserters are bound. Early in the morning we will start in pursuit." The two men shook hands and soon a deep silence reigned through the fortress interrupted only by the regular tread of the sentry.

CHAPTER II.

WHISPERING—LUCULLUS MISTAKEN FOR AN ANIMAL—JOHANNES' PLAN—A GRATEFUL SMUGGLER—JOHANNES A GEOGRAPHER—A MIRACULOUS HAUL OF FISH—LA CUEILLE'S PROMISE—DRINKING WATER—DEPARTURE.

IT is necessary now to explain how the deserters came to be embarked in that funeral cortege and also how their project of escape had been planned and perfected. For this purpose we must go back some few days and change the scene to the dormitory of the fort of Kwala Kapoeas. The time is close upon midnight. Most of the men are wrapped in slumber and perfect silence prevails. No, not perfect silence; for in one remote corner there is a sound of suppressed conversation which challenges the notice of the officer on duty.

"Silence in that corner! What can you have to talk about so late at night! Is not the day long enough for gossip?"

This sharp rebuke was the signal for the talkers to cease, but not for long. Presently when silence reigned again, interrupted only by the loud snoring of the sleepers, a soft whispering made itself heard in that same dark corner to which the corporal had before referred.

It was Schlickeisen and Wienersdorf continuing their interrupted conversation beneath their breath.

"I repeat," observed the former, "I cannot endure this life any longer!"

"Hush!" whispered his companion. "Don't get so excited. We can't hurry, so be patient."

"That is all you can say. Patience! We have been here two months already and how far are we advanced?"

"How can we help it? One cannot break iron with his hands. You know that our enterprise is one in which we risk our necks."

"Quite so. Still if this should last much longer, I intend to take a leap into the river."

"That would be a treat for the crocodiles; but all the same it would be a poor way of gaining your liberty, unless you look upon death as your only possible liberator."

"Well I would rather be dead than remain a prisoner like this."

"But 'dead is dead.' I must own that I prefer——"

Schlickeisen had no time to finish the sentence. Some one had crept unperceived between their beds. Two hands were pressed upon their shoulders as if to compel them to remain passive. Then a voice whispered in the softest accents:

"Don't talk so loud; you fail to notice that Corporal Dunkelhof has been listening this last quarter of an hour. If he has overheard any of your talk, you may expect to be reported to-morrow morning."

"For my part," muttered Wienersdorf, "he may hear all we have said."

"You may tell that to your sister, but not to me," said the visitor, still whispering. "If the Colonel should only hear a tenth part of what you have been saying, you may be sure that you two would be under arrest before sunrise. Our Colonel is not to be trifled with."

"Oho! not quite so fast, please. Who are you? A listener can never be trusted," said Schlickeisen in a menacing though subdued voice.

"Don't fear. I wont betray you. It matters little who I am. But look how the corporal is pricking up his ears."

And indeed there came an imperative voice, "Silence there in that corner. I shan't speak any more. Those who wont hear must feel."

Wienersdorf and Schlickeisen held their breath and everything remained quiet for a while. Suddenly their mysterious visitor bent over them and whispered almost inaudibly:

"Come to the hut of Johannes to-morrow morning after breakfast."

The figure vanished under the beds and was soon lost in the darkness.

The two Swiss kept quiet for a long time. When they perceived that the corporal had dropped off to sleep, Wienersdorf whispered to his companion the enquiry:

"Who was that?"

"Perhaps Johannes himself."

"He had a brown skin and the upper part of his body was naked."

"Can we trust him?"

"Who knows? We may as well look in to-morrow morning and hear what he has to say."

"Hush! be careful; that Dunkelhof is a regular spy."

They both crept between their blankets and were soon in a sound slumber.

Next morning, after they had fetched their soup from the kitchen, they had to pass the hut of Johannes. They found him standing outside his door. Without uttering a word he moved away from the entrance as if inviting them to come in. They entered, put their pannikins on the floor and seated themselves on a bench.

On a table before them lay already spread a choice repast prepared by Johannes. In addition to the ration of soup from the barrack kitchen, there was boiled rice, snow white and well granulated, dishes of sauces made of fish and vegetables, surrounded by some smaller dishes of pepper fried in oil and pounded with shrimp. There were also plates of dried venison and cod's roe together with roasted meat. A duck, swimming in a palatable sauce, completed the cheer.

"You are a Lucullus," began Schlickeisen.

"What kind of animal is that?" demanded Johannes.

"No animal at all, but a Roman gourmand, who, however, could not compare with you."

"Laugh at me if you please, but sit down and eat. We can talk afterwards. I always find that I can reason better when I have satisfied the cravings of my stomach."

The Swiss did not wait for a second invitation but fell to and enjoyed themselves to their hearts' content. Not a word was spoken during the repast. There was nothing heard but the smacking of lips and the clatter of knives and forks.

When the last bone had been picked and the feasters had wiped their greasy fingers, Johannes produced a box of tobacco. All three having filled their pipes, he began:

"Now out with your business; you mean to bolt, don't you?"

Schlickeisen and Wienersdorf looked at each other interrogatively.

"We are quite safe here," continued Johannes. "Nobody can hear us. Come, out with it. You want to be off. Where to? Perhaps I can assist you."

The two Swiss exchanged a look of intelligence. After a while Wienersdorf said:

"Well, yes; we did talk of a plan to desert, but there is a wide distance between talking and doing."

"I should think so. But tell me your plan."

"Oh, you can scarcely call it a plan yet. We have not been here long enough to know the country and without that knowledge no attempt is possible."

"You speak," said Johannes, "like a learned man. But if you wait until you obtain the needed information you may be too old to desert. Did I hear you mention last night a Chinese craft?"

"Yes; we have been given to understand that such a vessel calls here annually and we spoke of bribing the captain to conceal us on board and carry us to China."

"Bravo! Have you any money?"

"We have about four hundred florins between us."

"Well! do you know what would happen? The Chinaman would coolly pocket your four hundred florins. He would duly receive you and hide you on board his vessel. But before leaving

Kwala Kapoeas he would drop a note to the Colonel who would despatch a cruiser after you. Your craft would be overhauled, both of you secured and the game would be up."

" But why should the captain act thus? "

" In order to pocket your four hundred florins. Perhaps also to get into the good graces of the Colonel and be enabled to sell more of his wares. No, no, you must not dream of escaping that way. Listen to me. I also have resolved to desert and have thought of it a very long time, so that I may safely say my plans are well matured. Only I don't like to enter upon such an undertaking by myself. La Cueille will go with me, but he is not sufficient. The aid of a few strong arms is what I greatly need. Now, what do you think? "

" This La Cueille is a fearful drunkard. Is he the right fellow to confide in? "

" One can't be over-particular. He has a stout heart and fears nothing. Besides we intend to take only a very small quantity of liquor which I mean to keep under my own control. I am sure he is the best fellow in the world as long as he remains sober."

" But," said Wienersdorf, " ought we not to learn your plans? What made you think of us? "

" That is very easy to understand. I observed that you two kept aloof from the other men. You were always whispering in corners and couldn't hold your tongues, even at night. I set myself to find out what was going on and I succeeded. I heard you speak together of deserting and then my heart leaped with joy, for I had found just what I wanted—a couple of sturdy fellows who like myself are burning to get away. Now are you satisfied with my explanation?"

"Quite; now tell us about your plan."

The three conspirators refilled their pipes and drew closer together. Johannes then proceeded to give a complete narrative not only of his plan, but also of the means he had provided to ensure its success.

One dark evening while he was on sentry duty outside the fort, Baba Poetjieng came up to him and offered a bundle of cigars. The Chinaman commenced a conversation in the course of which he told Johannes that in a creek near by his rangkan lay hidden and that it contained a considerable quantity of opium which he was anxious to smuggle. He had succeeded in defiance of the cruisers and coast-guards in bringing the canoe up the river. Now was to come the most difficult part of the enterprise—passing the fort; and to accomplish this he hoped his friend Johannes would help him. The sly Chinaman carefully concealed the fact that his cargo really consisted of gunpowder and salt, the two greatest necessities of the Bandjarese insurgents. He pressed a few rix dollars into Johannes' hand, who arranged with him that he would be at the same post again next evening when he would let him pass. Johannes begged for and obtained some opium, which he put by for future use in the execution of his plan. With this opium he drugged his fellow-guards and enabled the Celestial to smuggle his goods. This accomplished, the Chinaman was in his power and Johannes had no hesitation in unfolding his scheme of escape and demanding his aid and co-operation. Baba Poetjieng agreed to provide a well-fitted canoe manned by three Dayaks. Johannes then made sundry small parcels of his and La Cueille's clothing which he gave to him to convey to the canoe. The time fixed for the escape was the next change of the moon, darkness being necessary to ensure success. As it was now full moon, they had a fortnight left for making their final preparations.

"Now," said Johannes, "what do you think?"

"We think it an excellent plan," said Schlickeisen.

"It does you credit," added Wienersdorf. "But I fear there are still many difficulties to be overcome. We will get away without doubt; the fortress is not an enchanted castle—but when we shall have got away the question will be, whither are we to go?"

"Where to go? Where but down the river—seawards—that is the way. Once at sea, we direct our course westward, keeping close in shore to evade the cruisers. In the day-time we will hide the canoe in one of the creeks which abound on the south coast, but at night we shall have to row as fast as we can. When we get to Cape Batoe Titi, the southwesterly part of Borneo, our further course will be determined by the state of the weather. If everything is favorable we will run for the island of Biliton across the straits of Gaspar, and proceeding along the north of Banca reach at last the coast of Sumatra. Once there, our hardest task will be completed. We must skim along under the shadows of the thick forests until we come to Cape Basso. Thence, with a fair amount of luck, we run safely between the islands of the Riouw Archipelago and get to Singapore."

"I must own that you seem to be very well informed. Where did you learn all these particulars; from Baba Poetjieng?"

"No, no. My geography and topography come from the military school of Kedong-Kebo, where I was educated."

"But how long will it take us to reach Singapore?"

"At least three or four weeks; but mind, the slightest misadventure may upset all our calculations."

A cold shudder passed over the two Swiss and both cried out simultaneously, "Four weeks on the ocean in a nut-shell!"

"I beg your pardon; to be on the Java sea at this season is not such a dreadful affair. But you can do as you please—join or remain behind."

"Oh, no!" was the reply as both Swiss offered their hands. "We join you most certainly, even though the journey should lead to perdition."

After this emphatic ratification of their alliance the three friends separated and in order to disarm suspicion they returned by different routes to the fortress.

Now commenced a series of preparations separately conducted but all equally directed to the perfection of their arrangements. Whatever fell in their way that was likely to be useful on their voyage was taken to Johannes' hut and stored away. Thus they contrived to get together a supply of provisions and gunpowder without much difficulty. What, however, taxed their ingenuity to obtain, was a supply of rifle bullets. These they managed to smuggle during target practice, by substituting blank cartridges. Of course when a miss was proclaimed as the result of their firing, their comrades laughed and jeered, but they only looked as innocent as they could and quickly stored away the abstracted bullet. Their stock of animal food also received an important addition most unexpectedly. The garrison organized a fishing-party after the Dayak method. They closed the creeks with a kind of bamboo matting during the flood-tides which followed the full moon. At the ebb the shallow bed of the moat was left so swarming with fish that they were bailed out by basketsfull. Johannes bought up the greatest part of this catch at a price so unusually high that it attracted the Colonel's attention. When questioned by him Johannes explained that he intended to dry the fish for sale and that he had already disposed of it to Baba Poetjieng at a fair profit. This pretended speculation served also another purpose. It enabled Baba Poetjieng to visit Johannes' hut and carry away all the fish without exciting suspicion. The cleaning and curing were undertaken by Johannes with the aid of La Cueille, who had been fully recognized as one of the alliance by Wienersdorf and Schlickeisen. They were most careful to warn the intemperate Walloon against the dangers of inebriety and they made him promise not to taste gin until at least they had started on their journey.

"I faithfully promise," says La Cueille, "not to touch a drop of spirits."

"Amen," responded Johannes.

"Do you mean to keep this promise throughout?" Wienersdorf asked.

"By the sacred Lady of Scherpenheuvel," answered the Walloon.

"We can now welcome you into our brotherhood. Each of us must do his best to promote the success of our enterprise. Our motto must be 'Every one for everybody.' By the bye,

Johannes, how are we now situated in respect to provisions?"

Johannes explained that there were deposited with Baba Poetjieng five bags of rice, each weighing one hundred and twenty-five pounds.

"But we are surely not expected to live on rice?" asked Schlickeisen.

"Certainly not," answered Johannes. "What am I providing dried fish for? The Chinaman supplies us with salt, pepper and curry. We shall also have a barrel of salt beef and pork. Don't imagine, however, that you are going to fare as at your mother's table. It is enough that we shall not know want. What troubles me most is the drinking water. Supposing each man to need three pints a day that will make for a month's voyage eighty gallons or eight barrels of ten gallons each. These will take up considerable space and greatly diminish our comforts."

"Do you mean to carry water for the whole journey?"

"Well, it would be the best plan, but I am afraid it is impracticable. I therefore propose to ship only two barrels."

"That is decidedly too little," said Schlickeisen; "that is only half a pint per day."

"Listen. As long as we remain in the Lesser Dayak we need not touch our water. Nor shall we require to do so while on the coast of Borneo. We shall have to take refuge during the day in one of the many creeks in order to avoid the cruisers. Now there is no country in the world that has so many rivers opening into the sea as you find in the south of Borneo. Any of those streams will enable us to replenish our supply of water. We shall have to be careful crossing to Biliton, for there we shall be at sea. It is a little better on the north coast of Banca, but where we shall find water in abundance is on the eastern coast of Sumatra. Such streams as the Reteh and the Indragiri will furnish enough to allay our thirst."

"You are a born geographer," said Wienersdorf, "and I raise my hat in respect to your knowledge."

"What do you mean by raising your hat? I see only a shabby service cap."

"Well let us say we raise our caps; but really your explanation was so excellent that I should like you to complete it."

"Yes," said Johannes, "I know you are as inquisitive as the monkey. But come, what is it you wish to know?"

"How long will the voyage from Borneo to Sumatra occupy?"

"If the southeast monsoon continues until we reach Banca we may reckon our speed at twenty miles a day; but that will be too much to expect, so we will say fifteen miles a day. Thus the voyage, barring accidents, will take seven days."

In such conversation was the time passed during the weary days of waiting. On the second day after the new moon Baba Poetjieng arrived at the fort. He pretended that his visit was to fetch away the last of the dried fish, which concluded his contract with Johannes, but his true object was to make final arrangements and to fix the hour for departure. The time was favorable. A native had just died of cholera and no one would undertake to bury him except the three Dayaks who were to accompany the deserters. The tide would continue to flow until half-past ten and would be followed by a rapid ebb. All chances were therefore in their favor. As evening fell the four allies crept into the hut of Johannes, where they remained concealed until it was quite dark. They then stole out one by one, and passing behind the shrubs which lined the banks of the river, they reached the kampong unobserved and took their places in the canoe which was to carry the deceased to her last resting-place. About ten the coffin was taken to the boat, and at eleven o'clock came the priestesses who were to chant the hymns for the repose of the dead.

The ebb tide had already commenced when they arrived; the two canoes therefore pulled away immediately from the landing-stage and passed the fort, with the results already known.

CHAPTER III.

A DRUNKEN MAN'S TALK—ON THE SEA—JOHANNES UP A TREE—UP THE KAHAJAN—AN ÆOLIAN HARP—THE SOENGEI TROESSAN—IN THE DAHASAN—A WOOD SPECTRE—A MOSQUITO CHARM—FURTHER PLANS—LOOK OUT FOR YOUR HEAD—SUITS OF BLACK.

THE two Swiss were indignant at La Cueille's unreasonable exclamation and even Johannes was furiously angry. A single look at the Walloon, however, explained the cause. During the time they had been planning their escape he had faithfully kept his word and had not tasted a drop of spirits. He had left untouched the rations of gin which in accordance with the rules of the service had been served out to him. Deeming it a pity to leave good spirits unclaimed, he had asked the Colonel's permission to receive his daily rations and to save them up for use as a liniment for swollen feet. This permission was necessary as the regulations required every soldier to drink his allowance of gin from the hand of the sutler. The Colonel, knowing how well La Cueille liked his drop, suspected that the Walloon wished to accumulate a sufficient quantity for a regular drinking bout, and in the hope of detecting him ordered his feet to be uncovered for examination. They were found to be red and swollen, the result of a ligature which he had purposely placed above the knee. Accordingly his request was granted and he saved all his gin, which by the time it was taken on board the canoe had accumulated to about two pints. On the evening of his escape, while lying down on the boat, he produced the bottle and swallowed a couple of mouthfuls. Oh! that was delicious. How it warmed him! A second draught followed the first. "Train de plaisir de ma bouche à mon estomac," the Walloon muttered as he began to feel himself in a pleasantly excited condition. What a time they were in getting that coffin on board! He must regale himself while waiting. Then he finished the first bottle.

At length the coffin arrived. "Poeah! what an odor! enough to give one the fever! Well, the rich drink champagne as a safeguard; gin may perhaps have the same effect." So he continued imbibing until he finished the second bottle.

When the priestesses arrived the funeral cortege began to move. La Cueille sat looking on, unmoved and perfectly quiet. Trees and shrubs passed by in the midnight gloom like spectres. There stood the dark outlines of the fort. The voice of the sentry was plainly heard, crying the usual "Werda"—"Who goes there?" Presently there came the order to lay to. When the cortege stopped obedient to this command, a sergeant approached to examine the boats, but as soon as he discovered that one of them bore a case of cholera he stepped back frightened and gave the word to proceed. A few more strokes and the vessels had passed the pier. At this point the drunkard could not restrain himself and he burst out with the cry,

"Enfoncés les Hollandais, les têtes de fromage!"

"Beseai goeloeng," shouted Johannes—"Row fast," as he sprang forward to stop the Walloon's mouth. When the order to return came a second time from the fort, La Cueille, now mad with drink, repeated his salutation and before any one could interfere seized a rifle and fired in the direction of the fortification. Then came a flash, followed by the discharge of a cannon, which rent the air like a thunderbolt. The two canoes shook and darted forwards carried by the strong tide into the middle of the wide stream. In the boat of the priestesses two men were killed and one wounded, but the deserters remained unhurt. The frightened oarsmen pulled with all their force, the white foam flying up from under the prow, and their speed was maintained until daybreak, when the fugitives saw before them the open sea!

When the eastern sky became decked in purple Wienersdorf took his glasses and scoured the horizon. Two cruising canoes were seen far away, going in a northwesterly direction, as if making for the mouth of the Barito. Further off he saw the smoke of a steamer but could not determine her course. In the southwest was a trading-canoe very much like their own, going toward the Lesser Dayak river. As soon as they were clear of the mouth of the river they steered westward. One of the men advised them to land for the double purpose of burying the body and of covering their canoe with palm leaves in order to elude the observation of the cruisers. The Europeans thought it much more simple, instead of burying the body to drop it overboard, all the protests of the Dayaks notwithstanding. They, however, landed and cut a sufficient quantity of leaves to cover the canoe so that it could not be distinguished from the green herbage of the coast. They then resumed their voyage and in the hope of remaining quite unobserved kept near the shore, the rowers deftly handling their oars in such a way as to prevent any reflection on the surface of the water. They resolved to enter the mouth of the Kahajan, to conceal themselves in the first creek they should reach and to wait until evening should close in ere they continued the voyage westward. Everything succeeded precisely as they wished. The cruisers sailed away to the mouth of the Lesser Dayak, where they anchored. The other vessel observed in the southeast proved to be a trader. Our fugitives thus disembarrassed, rowed vigorously onwards and reached the mouth of the Kahajan by mid-day. They soon found a convenient creek where they concealed the canoe under some drooping shrubs; and as they were thoroughly tired out, sought repose in order to recruit their strength for the work before them.

They had been lying down perhaps a couple of hours when they were were roused by the discharge of a cannon. They all leaped to their feet and Johannes with cat-like celerity clambered into a cedar tree close at hand, which commanded an extended view seaward. What he saw was far from reassuring. A number of canoes shot out from the Lesser Dayak and signalled the cruising vessels. These immediately weighed their anchors and made sail to meet the canoes. The trader had altered her course, spread more canvas and was keeping close to the wind. She had also begun to employ her oars, endeavoring by the aid of vigorous rowing to avoid being overhauled. A wild pursuit of her now commenced; but although the cruisers carried as much canvas as they could set, the pursued vessel seemed to keep her advantage. A couple of shots danced along the tops of the waves, but the diminutive guns of the Dutch Indian cruisers could not carry far enough. Johannes at last could distinguish nothing more than a couple of dim specks on the horizon. He therefore descended and with a sigh attacked La Cueille, in reprehension of his culpable indiscretion.

"See there," he said, "the consequences of your drunken cry. Beastly sot! They are on our track already."

"But what did you see?" asked Wienersdorf.

Johannes related what he had seen. "The canoe they are pursuing," added he, "is Baba Poetjieng's smuggler. What may not happen when they overtake him? Before twenty-four hours have passed, there will be two hundred boats cruising along the coast. I wish that drunken Walloon———"

Wienersdorf stopped him, observing, "Of what use is it to rave or to reproach? We must act. Now what are we to do?"

"The whole plan has collapsed. We cannot proceed along the southern coast;—can we, Dalim?" he continued, addressing one of the Dayaks.

"No mistake about that; the way there is blocked."

He consulted for a few minutes with his countrymen and then pointing with his hand to the north, said—"There!"

"Up the Kahajan?" asked Johannes.

"No; we could not pass there. They will certainly examine the Kahajan."

"What then?"

"Through the Troessan."

"Wont they overhaul that?" asked Johannes.

"Certainly; but we must hurry on. The soengei Dahasan opens into the Troessan and communicates with the soengei Basarang, which joins the Kapoeas on the north side of the fort. Not a soul knows that region, but I noticed the fact sometime ago when I was there cutting rattan. Let us hasten: once in Kapoeas we are safe; they wont look for us in that direction."

They were all convinced of the prudence of this advice. Not an inst. nt was to be lost; even this way now projected might at any moment become impassable. No resource would then be left to them, save either to commit suicide or to throw themselves into the hands of their pursuers. They took the canoe from its hiding-place, pushed it into the swiftly flowing stream and were soon going at a rapid pace.

Suddenly the Europeans dropped their oars and the Dayaks, following their example, stopped rowing. What was that? Sounds were heard like those given forth by an æolian harp; now far away, soft and melodious, but yet distinct; then again so near that the music seemed to be suspended over the canoe. There was a perfect harmony in the sounds, which varied between the murmur of a slight breeze and the forcible rush of a hurricane through some gigantic stringed instrument. The Europeans looked aghast at each other, unable to account for these mysterious strains. La Cueille crossed himself and muttered "*Etoile de la mer, priez pour nous.*" When the Dayaks perceived the anxious, frightened looks of their white companions they burst into loud laughter. For them it was an ordinary phenomenon which they called rioeng, noise, or sometimes riwoet haroesan, breath of the stream.

Dalim related a legend which ascribes these sounds to unearthly music being played by some damsels drowned in that stream by the ire of Djata, the Crocodile God. He also added the information that the missionaries gave another explanation of the phenomenon. They attribute it to the friction of two currents—one, the advancing tide from the sea, and the other, the down-flowing water of the stream. Of course there are local conditions which influence the amount of friction. The correctness of this theory is proved by the fact that the sound is only heard at certain points where the sea meets the swift river water.

This music accompanied the fugitives into the mouth of the Troessan which they reached toward evening when nothing more was heard of the æolian harp.

"Oef!" cried La Cueille, "I feel lighter now. It seemed as if ghosts were playing music around the canoe. It would drive me mad if I had to stand it all night long."

"What are you jabbering about?" muttered one of the Dayaks; and leaning over to Johannes he whispered in his ear.

Johannes now recommended them to keep silent. In a subdued tone he proceeded to explain that they were in a narrow stream, where they were likely to meet other canoes. If their conversation, conducted in a foreign language, were to be overheard, it would certainly betray them and lead to their being pursued.

They continued rowing in silence, exerting all their might, so that by eight o'clock that evening they reached the mouth of soengei Dahasan. They still rowed on a considerable time until Dalim ordered a halt. He advised them to wait for daylight, as they might easily lose their way among the numerous rivulets found here. He, however, had other reasons for suspending the journey. They were all fatigued and needed rest. They had not partaken of any food for hours, nor had they slept.

"But," asked Wienersdorf, "is it safe to pass the night here?"

"We are perfectly safe," answered Dalim, "no Dayak will venture here and the Colonel is not likely to seek us here. He is busy following Baba Poetjieng's canoe and may be glad to find himself at the mouth of the Lesser Dayak by to-morrow night. As I said before it is impossible for them to guess that we are here, since nobody knows of this passage."

"You said no Dayak would venture here. Why is that?"

"In 1859 Pembekel Soelil was killed here by the bursting of a cannon while defending his benting against the Dutch. To save his body from the hands of the Dutchmen, his people buried him in soengei Dahasan near the spot we have just passed. Since that time this soengei is guarded by a pampahilep and woe to him who enters the forbidden territory."

"Pray, what is a pampahilep?"

"A horrible forest ghost who kills every one within his reach. But this pampahilep is a female and whenever she gets hold of a man she compels him to marry her, only to strangle him afterward."

"Brr! Quelle Canaille!" the Walloon muttered.

"But you are not afraid?" Schlickeisen asked the Dayak.

"Ah!" said he, "I invented the story myself, in order to secure a secret way for smuggling salt, powder and lead. Now everybody keeps my female pampahilep at a respectful distance."

"Do Dayaks believe everything so implicitly?"

"They are very superstitious. There are several spots in their country which they believe to be haunted and a Dayak would not venture near them for all the money in the world."

"But," said Schlickeisen, "you told us just now that in order to prevent the body of Soelil from falling into the hands of the Dutch it was buried here. Do the Dutch mutilate bodies?"

"They forbid the Dayaks to take heads, but they don't mind taking the heads of the Dayaks."

"Have you ever seen them do it?"

"No, but it is known among us. I have even heard that they put those heads in pickle!"

"Nonsense!" cried Johannes. "It certainly has happened once or twice that the head of some notorious outlaw has been forwarded to Bandjermasin for identification, but it was invariably buried afterward."

"I wish you were all further with your ghosts and dead men's heads," exclaimed La Cueille. "I shall be dreaming of them all night."

After securely mooring their boat their first care was to provide a meal, as they had scarcely tasted anything during the preceding twenty-four hours. Some dry branches were collected and they soon had a good fire to cook their food. Thanks to Baba Poetjieng, they found some green bamboo stalks in the canoe. These the Dayaks cut up into small cylinders, which after being filled with moistened rice and closed with pieces of wood were thrown on the fire. After some fifteen or twenty minutes the bamboo tubes burst asunder with a loud report. The Dayaks then withdrew them from the fire, opened them and spread the cooked rice upon large leaves.

"By Jove!" Wienersdorf said, "this is convenient. We need not fear the breaking of pots or pans, since our supply is always ready."

"Yes," laughed Johannes, "and the store is well stocked."

"I don't know that," remarked Schlickeisen, "during all our journey I have not seen a single bamboo."

"Nor will you find any in all the lower country. The bamboos require a dry soil. Later on, however, we shall meet with plenty of them."

In the meanwhile another Dayak mixed some lambok and salt in an earthen vessel and Johannes broiled some of the dried fish. The meal was now ready, its preparation had not cost much trouble and the viands were of the simplest, but hungry as they were after a day's fast, they found everything most delicious.

When they had all finished they disposed themselves to sleep. The natives were soon snoring, but our Europeans could not close an eye owing to the swarms of mosquitoes which surrounded them. The southern coast of Borneo is so low that the country is inundated at each flood. As a first result of this periodical visitation, there is a constantly-increasing formation of marshes, in which myriads of mosquitoes are hatched. Our fugitives had now to cultivate the immediate acquaintance of these insects. There had been a little trouble with them at the fort; but there, sheltered within the buildings and additionally protected by the mosquito curtains, they had been able to defy the venomous swarms and to enjoy undisturbed sleep. Here in the native woods no protection was to be found. At the imminent risk of exploding their gunpowder, the persecuted travellers kindled a large fire in their boat in the hope of repelling the aggressive insects by raising clouds of smoke. But all was in vain. Thousands upon thousands of blood-suckers came and went, and soon the faces, necks and hands of the Europeans were covered with bites, the irritation of which drove all sleep from their eyes. Finally they rose in despair, ranged themselves around the fire and endeavored by waving branches and leaves to keep their enemies at a distance.

"Ah! those cursed insects!" said La Cueille, "suppose we try a mosquito jacket."

A mosquito jacket means in the Dutch Indies getting so intoxicated that one becomes insensible to both buzz and sting. This is really the origin of that craving for drink so commonly met with among the soldiers.

"Have you already forgotten your lesson?" Wienersdorf asked in a stern voice. "Not a drop of liquor shall you have."

"I would rather throw it into the river," added Johannes.

La Cueille was silenced, but a vehement shake of his branch indicated that he was not grateful for the rebuke.

"Since it is impossible to sleep," said Schlickeisen, "we may as well review our situation which has completely changed through our being unable to escape by sea. The question now is, what are we to do next?"

Dalim pointed to the north just now," observed Johannes. "That is our way, but how are we to get through? The slightest imprudence may prove fatal to us."

"Speak. You have lived in the country longer than any of us, and must be our guide."

"You must have noticed that I was talking to Dalim this evening," continued Johannes. "Well this is the result of our conversation. We will try to get into the Kapoeas river through soengei Basarang. We then sail up that river as far as we can, cross the Kaminting mountains and make for the north coast. Don't imagine, however, that all will go as smoothly as I plan it."

"No, no, we understand that," Wienersdorf said, smiling; "still we should like to have a sketch of what we are likely to encounter."

"I really cannot tell you," proceeded Johannes, "but we have to be extremely cautious. While we are in the lower country we have everything to fear from the Dutch. Let them only suspect that we are here and we shall be hunted down like wild animals. When we get into the upper country it will be yet more dangerous, for if the natives only guess that we are Europeans we are lost. A European skull means four thousand florins."

"What do you say?" cried LaCueille, terrified, as he raised his hands to his head. "Is this then worth so much? I did not know it. It pays then to take care of it."

"You are joking, are you not?" Schlickeisen asked, impatiently.

"By no means. The skull of Colonel George Muller, who was killed in 1825, while travelling across Borneo, was actually sold for that amount and is still preserved as a valuable relic by the Olo Ot Panganese. The skulls of the Europeans belonging to the Onrust captured by the Dayaks in 1859, were all disposed of at the same rate. The skull of the commander proved a mine of wealth. After removing the flesh they filled it with dry katjang beans and immersed it in water. The beans, swelling, caused the skull to burst into numerous fragments, the smallest of which fetched two hundred reals."

"What do they do with these skulls?"

"Well you might almost call them *articles de luxe*. You will see plenty of them in the upper country. Each benting or fort is ornamented with grinning skulls fixed on the points of the palisades. There is not a house in which you will not find some skulls tied together like a rosary and affixed as an ornament to the walls. When a young man proposes for a young woman her friends do not ask how much money the aspirant has, but how many heads he can furnish. Do you understand it now?"

"I indeed perceive that it will be 'look out for your head.'"

"Quite so; that will be our motto, Look out for your head! The country abounds in head-hunters. I dare say you have heard of them."

"Certainly; but I have always thought that the reports are grossly exaggerated."

"On the contrary the narratives do not give a tenth part of the reality," continued Johannes, "for the simple reason that the natives seek to keep head-hunting a profound secret from the Dutch."

"Now then, as a first step in the direction of safety, we must part with our military attire. That alone is sufficient to betray us. Baba Poetjieng foreseeing the danger, provided us each with a suit of clothes. These we can examine when it is daylight. We shall find our new costumes suited to their purpose and the sooner we assume them the better."

"How funny I shall look," said La Cueille, "dressed in an ewah."

"It will not be in harmony with your white skin I dare say."

"It is more suited to your coffee-colored carcass," rejoined the Walloon.

"I—that reminds me. You cannot possibly retain those white skins of yours. They would at once betray you. I wish you all had my coffee-colored complexion. I must speak to Dalim, he will surely think of something."

"You will see," said the Walloon, laughing. "We shall all have to put on black suits."

"Very probably," said Johannes, drily, "and yours will become you well. So send at once for your tailor and order suits of black for three."

CHAPTER IV.

A STRANGE DAYAK—PAINTING A COMPLEXION—SHEIK MOHAMMED AL MANSOER—TOO HANDSOME FOR A DAYAK—IN THE FOREST MARSHES—DASSO AND DOETA—TWO BOTTLES OF DOCTORED GIN—THE BIRDS WINGED.

AT day-break the Europeans roused the sleeping Dayaks from their slumber. Johannes took Dalim aside and engaged with him in earnest conversation, while the others prepared to cook some rice and fish for breakfast. After Dalim had finished his conversation he went into the thick forest and in a few moments disappeared from view. Johannes produced the clothes which Baba Poetjieng had provided, selected what he required for his own use and then jumped into the river for his morning bath. Having sufficiently refreshed himself he came out, seized his bundle and retired behind some shrubs. He soon re-appeared dressed as a Dayak, mandauw in hand, and throwing himself among the other bathers, frightened them out of their wits. They were speedily re-assured, however, by hearing a well-known voice exclaiming, "Don't be afraid, Palefaces!" The strange Dayak was Johannes, who, dressed in an ewah or coarse cloth wound around his middle and with a dirty rag around his head, stood before them effectually disguised. Ere they had sufficiently looked at and admired the extemporized native, Dalim returned from the woods. He proceeded to take a pan in which he threw some leaves which he had brought from the forest, adding a little water and a few drops of a black pigment from a bottle hanging to his waist. He then placed the pan on the fire and joined the others at breakfast. By the time they had concluded the meal his mixture boiled. He then removed it from the fire and requested Schlickeisen, who sat nearest to him, to hold out his hands. He rubbed them for a little while with a rag steeped in the solution and almost instantaneously imparted to them a deep-brown color. When the hands had been tinted to his satisfaction he seized the Swiss by the neck and proceeded in the same manner to stain his face, arms and shoulders. The operation finished, Schlickeisen was unrecognizable. Johannes thought that the whole of the white men's bodies should be subjected to the treatment to ensure perfect safety. All concurring in this opinion, Dalim returned to the woods to collect such a supply of leaves as would enable him to dye wholesale. These leaves were taken from the kalampoeit, a tree of the rhododendron tribe, which also supplies the Dayaks with poison for their arrows. In the decoction they were employed only as a mordant to fix the dye, the pigment being supplied from Dalim's bottle, which contained the juice of the katiting, a tree belonging to the Rhizophora.

An hour afterward all the Europeans were beautifully bronzed and strutting about in their ewahs were fair imitators of natives. Only La Cueille failed to produce the true Dayak type. His sharply-cut features, glittering eyes, handsome whiskers and curly hair gave him rather the appearance of an Arab. In consequence, he was unanimously elected Sheik and dignified with the title of Mohammed al Mansoer. This promotion gave him the advantage of wearing a chlamyde, a kind of shirt. Around his head he wore a turban, his feet were sandaled and he was required to carry a rosary, the beads of which went gliding through his fingers in a most familiar manner.

He had great trouble with his sandals and could scarcely manage to shuffle along on the flat soles, secured to his feet by a pin between two toes. However, after diligent practice, the difficulty was overcome and he marched along stately and sanctified, muttering in bad Arabic, "There is no God but Allah," just as if he had been born in Arabia Petrea.

It was now arranged that in their meetings with natives, only Johannes and the real Dayaks were to speak. The two Swiss were to personate hirelings and to preserve a becoming silence. The Sheik would only have to mutter some Malay lingo, intermixed with an Arabic word or two and an occasional verse from the Koran, which Johannes engaged to teach him. A final operation necessary to be undergone by the other three was the coloring of their teeth. This too was effected by means of Dalim's bottle, which soon converted their ivory into polished ebony.

"You really are too handsome for Dayaks," said Dalim; nor was he wrong to think so, for though the Europeans exposed the broad chests and finely-developed arms and shoulders proper to their assumed caste, they lacked the crooked legs to which the inhabitants of Borneo owe their name. Dayak is really an abbreviation of dadajak—to totter. With very few exceptions all the natives have bandy legs, which circumstance causes their peculiar tottering gait. This physical deformity is the result of the position they are compelled to assume while sitting in their canoes. But though their natural fondness for the sea thus attenuates and deforms their lower extremities, the upper parts of their bodies become so developed as to make them fit models for the sculptor.

The disguise of the deserters being effected, they tied their military clothes in a bundle, to which they attached a heavy stone and sank it in the deepest part of the river. They then resumed their route and tried to get further up the soengei; but it proved a difficult task to accomplish. The Dahasan is nothing but one of the many side canals of an enormous marsh thickly studded with forests. Large creepers abound everywhere, bridging over the numerous rivulets, climbing the great trees and covering their tops with a dense growth of parasitical plants which forms, as it were, an elevated vegetable plateau.

The creeper most generally found among the trees of these primeval forests is the rattan, called oeai by the natives. It runs along the ground, covering everything it meets with a net-work of branches which only the powerful hatchet can clear away. It is covered with sharp thorns which make it a most formidable obstruction to all who travel through these wilds.

The seven men soon waded through the water on the bed of the soengei. Five of them, hatchet in hand, tried to remove the creepers at the cost of much laborious exertion and many painful scratches. The other two walked along the margin of the channel, pushing the boat through the tortuous passage which was in reality only a pathway made in the soft mud by some passing canoe. It was an almost superhuman labor and the united strength of the whole party was often in requisition to free the roof of their vessel from its entanglement among the overhanging branches.

At mid-day they had proceeded a few miles only, but they felt so exhausted that they were compelled to rest. The water too had been left so low by the receding tide that the boat seemed fixed in the mud. Nothing would move her, so they were compelled to wait for the next flood.

Making use of the compulsory rest, they prepared their dinner. To this meal the Dayaks brought a welcome contribution by catching some bapoejoes among the holes of the half-drained river-bed. The bapoejoe is like the perch in shape and size, only differing from it by the absence of dorsal fins. These fish are of social habits and travel in large numbers along the inundated tracks. If overtaken by the ebb-tide and left aground, they still, as if by instinct, make their way through the mud to the nearest pool. Thus they frequently remain out of the water for days together and it is really a curious sight to see hundreds of fishes struggling through the mud in a certain direction, steadily prosecuting their journey despite the difficulties interposed.

Having finished their meal the Dayaks went out to gather rattan, as provision for their possible requirements during their travels. They cut some pieces thirty or forty yards long from one species, rolled them up carefully and put them away among their stores to be employed as ropes. From other species, used in Europe for seating chairs and similar canework, they cut the usual lengths, removed the thorny bark and tied them in bundles of one hundred each. These should have been soaked in the river to prevent their speedy decay; but as time was of value they contented themselves with the crude withe and took their chance of replenishing their supply when required. While the Dayaks were thus occupied the others were resting from their fatigue and gathering strength to recommence their labors. But although their limbs rested, their tongues kept going, talking over and deliberating on their plans, Johannes continuing to remind his co-adventurers of the necessity for vigilance.

"Remember," said he, "if the Colonel gets informed of our presence in this neighborhood he would hunt us down. Aye, let him discover our track and he is the very man to follow it up. No power on earth would prevent his doing so. Shall I tell you some of his artifices? Did you ever hear of his capture of Dasso and Doeta? It is part of the history of Kwala Kapoeas."

"I have heard it spoken of," said Schlickeisen, "but I don't know the story. Who were they?"

"Listen," resumed Johannes, "and I will tell you."

"Dasso and Doeta were Dayaks of Poeloe Petak and were well connected there as well as at Kwala Kapoeas. I believe our Dalim is a half-brother of Dasso. Well both these men and the Dayaks that are now accompanying us were engaged in the coal mines of Kalangan, at the outbreak of the insurrection, and all five of them did their share in the massacre of the Europeans."

"You have introduced us to quite a select company," remarked Schlickeisen. "Can we trust these people?"

"I believe you can trust them more than you could any other natives. They are anxious to reach Singapore and need our assistance to do so. They will be very useful to us and render us good service in more ways than one. Their very presence among us will secure us from being betrayed to the palefaces by any Dayak."

"So far, so good; but suppose they betray us themselves?"

"That is not likely, with their past record and their present plan."

"Yet it will be well to be wary and prepared for everything. Now continue your narrative."

"Dasso and Doeta were reported to have committed the most horrible atrocities during the massacre of Europeans. After a time the two wretches returned to the neighborhood of the fort, where they established themselves. The Colonel became informed of this fact and was most eager to entrap them. Besides the horrible crimes of which they had been guilty it was observed that after their arrival in the district a general spirit of insubordination became manifest, which excited grave apprehensions of future trouble. You cannot imagine what marches we had to make in the effort to secure these fellows. Twice and sometimes three times a day detachments were sent off and night expeditions were organized in order to entrap them; but all without success. Dead-tired, exhausted by hunger and thirst, wet to the skin and covered with mud from wading for hours through streams and marshes we returned from our wild goose chase. All our efforts had been unavailing. When we arrived at the place where they were reported to be concealed, we found the birds had flown, though their rice was boiling over their recently kindled fires and their beds were still warm."

"But I should have thought," remarked Schlickeisen, "that with the assistance of the natives the capture of these blackguards would have been an easy matter."

"Well, so we thought; but the people actually assisted them to elude us. Nearly all the inhabitants of this district are related to them. As soon as a detachment went out in pursuit their friends signalled to them and then we might march and countermarch until further orders. One afternoon, however, I found the Commander lounging in his rocking-chair under the verandah of his house. He was in deep thought. He stared fixedly at the ground, but his nails were clenched and he pulled his moustaches as if bent upon extracting them by the roots. I thought something was brewing. Suddenly he called for an orderly and despatched him for a sailor who was on board a steamer stationed in the river. The sailor came and went. I was then summoned and ordered to bring two bottles of gin, to remove the capsules and draw the corks without disturbing the wax. I thought the Colonel wanted a dram; but instead of indulging he went to his medicine-chest and took out some morphia powders. These he put into the bottles, which he shook up well and ordered me to re-cork. He then replaced the capsules and I assure you no druggist could have done it better.

"In the evening the sailor came again and this time carried

off with him the two bottles. He stepped into a djoekoeng and rowed up the river Kapoeas. A few hours after, Sergeant Greefkes and eight soldiers took the same direction. About two o'clock in the morning, being on duty at the western bastion, I saw a boat approaching. I sang out my challenge, 'Who goes there?' and was answered by the rejoinder, 'Good friends.' At the same time a red light was displayed from the boat as a signal. When it was moored three men were lifted out who were so fast asleep that nothing seemed to disturb them. Two were immediately placed in the stocks; they were Dasso and Doeta. You should have seen their faces next morning when they woke up to find themselves in limbo.

"Now you must know that the sailor, a Bandjares by birth, had formerly been a miner at Kalangan and therefore knew them well. For a few paltry dollars he sought them out and betrayed them by the agency of the bottle. The Dayaks, like a certain friend of ours, are passionately fond of spirits and the doctored gin brought by the sailor was disposed of with so much freedom that when the sergeant arrived he had only to bind the murderers hand and foot and carry them to the boats."

"How were they punished?"

"They were tried by court-martial; but before the conclusion of the trial that famous amnesty was proclaimed which granted a free pardon to all concerned in the rebellion with few exceptions. Those exceptions were good and worthy men who had only been defending themselves against oppression, and they were denied the grace extended to robbers and murderers! Our desperadoes were liberated on the sole condition that they should report themselves once a week at the nearest military station. I never heard our Colonel curse and swear as he did when the two came the first time to report themselves to him. 'Oh!' he cried, after their backs were turned, 'if I could have foreseen this wretched farce those wretches would never have entered the fort alive.' And every well-disposed person will coincide with him."

CHAPTER V.

ON THE JOURNEY—A PREVENTIVE AGAINST MOSQUITOES—THE SOEN-
GEI BASARANG—THE KAPOEAS—PAST POELOE KANAMIT—THE
BOAR'S HEAD—A TRUE DAYAK MEAL—FOUND IN THE WOOD—A
PANGARERAN PUTTING OUT FISHING-HOOKS—THE CAPTURE OF
A CROCODILE—THE SOENGEI MANTANGEI—FIGHT WITH A BOA
CONSTRICTOR—A SKIRMISH—THE JOURNEY RESUMED.

THE journey was resumed as soon as the Dayaks had stored away the gathered rattan in their boat and the tide had sufficiently risen to float her from the mud-bed. They had at first to struggle against the same obstacles that had beset them in the morning, but at length reached a branch of the soengei Basarang; and although the difficulties in their way were still numerous, the men could now resume their places in the boat and continue their course. They rowed on all night and when next morning the sun appeared above the horizon they were entering the soengei Basarang.

Dalim proposed to stop here until night had fully set in again, when they might reach the Kapoeas in a few hours. All concurring, the travellers hid their boat among the thick shrubs overhanging the banks and prepared and ate their meal.

When they had finished the repast the Dayaks put a small

tea-pot on the fire, the contents of which they subsequently proceeded to rub over their bodies. Some also drank a few mouthfuls of the brew before disposing themselves to sleep. Johannes enquired what the liquor was and why they used it. He was informed that it was a decoction of brotoali, a species of cactus which was a safeguard against the mosquitoes. No person who drank a few cups of this mixture in the morning would be troubled by those horrible insects. Similar impunity could be secured by washing the exposed parts of the body with it. The Europeans complained of their disturbed slumbers of the preceding night and the Dayaks willingly allowed them to try the native remedy. As a consequence, sound sleep was that night enjoyed by the entire party.

About midnight Dalim, who was on guard, woke them up; the canoe was pushed in midstream and carefully guided through the soengei. Close to the mouth our fugitives observed an open space in the forest surrounded by some charred trunks of trees, which had been placed to command the soengei as well as the main stream. They were the remains of a Dayak fort built along the borders of that river. It was the first fortification raised after the outbreak of the insurrection on the south coast of Borneo.

All the while that the fugitives were sailing out of the soengei Basarang they carefully scanned the broad surface of the waters of the river. Only a few lights were visible in the southeast, and the dark outlines of the fortress at the mouth of the Kapoeas. Nothing else was perceptible to the naked eye. The river was safe and with strong efforts they pursued their journey.

But alas! after their two days' travelling they were now only at the same spot whence they had originally started. If there, where those lights shone so brilliantly, it were only known how near the reach of their guns the fugitives were! But all remained silent; the fortifications continued lost in the gloom; the midnight calm was only disturbed by two beats of a gong indicating two A.M., and the low cry of the sentries which proved that however quiet everything appeared to be, the necessary vigilance was not neglected.

A few more strokes only and the fortress was lost behind Cape Koempai, the first curve in the Kapoeas. La Cueille, who with eager eyes had been looking at his former residence, now dropped his oar and heaved a deep sigh. Johannes heard it and said:

"Are you sorry? Speak, it is not too late yet. We can land you at this corner. A pretended drunken bout will sufficiently account for your absence. You are at liberty to plead that excuse or any other you fancy as long as you do not betray us. Say—shall we land you?"

"Return to those cheeseheads? Sacré nom de tonnerre! never!" the Walloon cried energetically.

"Then stop your sighing; leave that to the women and children; men have to act."

"C'était plus fort que moi," La Cueille muttered. "The stories I have heard during the last two days come before me, and pardieu! when I saw that fortress where we might repose as safely as on our mother's lap, far away from spectres, head-hunters, blood-drinkers, and so forth—that fortress which we might have reached with only a few strokes; yes, I own it, I did feel tempted just then. But it is all over now."

And taking his oar again he vigorously assisted to make the boat spin onward as fast as possible, so that the fortification was soon altogether lost to view. The fugitives passed a group of small islets called Poeloe telloe, and at day-break found themselves near the island Kanamit.

Dalim thought it better not to continue the journey any further and advised their taking refuge in a rivulet which runs into the right bank of the Kapoeas behind the island. When the canoe entered the narrow branch of this stream Johannes pointed to a spot and said:

"Just about there we once barely escaped from the canoes of the Dayaks. Our vessel got wrecked and we were attacked by the treacherous natives. Fortunately the Montrado arrived to our aid and drove them off by firing a single gun."

"But," asked Wienersdorf, "how are the natives disposed towards us now?"

"They are very untrustworthy, and if they were to discover that we are palefaces our lives would not be worth a moment's purchase. But we are Dayaks now. Hèlo mikèh, don't fear," Johannes continued smilingly. "At all events we are seven, and we cannot do wrong in keeping our arms under our own control."

The boat now proceeded until it arrived in front of a large house. Dalim, accompanied by one of his countrymen and Johannes, went ashore, mounted a slanting notched tree, the usual kind of steps leading into Dayak houses, and entered the dwelling. All those who remained behind seized their rifles and kept themselves ready for action.

After a little while Johannes reappeared, made a reassuring sign and called out in the Dayak language that they had met with friends. It happened that a relative of one of the fugitive Dayak mutineers was living here. It was an Islamite Dayak, that is one who has embraced the Mohammedan faith; he had only done so recently and had changed his Dayak name of "Mihing" into "Ali Bahar."

The Dayaks, always ready for festivities, were only too delighted to celebrate the auspicious event of a meeting between relations and nothing seemed more natural than to welcome their kinsman and his friends with a hearty dinner and drinking bout. All, including Sheik Mohammed Al Mansoer, gave their ready consent, the latter adding that "Allah is best praised with his own gifts." Accordingly at mid-day, they took their places, seated in a circle on a mat with their legs crossed. An immensely large boar's head roasted over the fire was dished up and brought in, accompanied by a vast bowl of toeak.

Johannes bent over the Walloon and whispered something into his ear, when the latter, visibly affected, cried out in angry tones:

"May the plague choke thee, cursed animal."

The whole of the Dayak family got up, alarmed at this outburst, but Johannes pacified them, declaring that the holy descendant of the Prophet only expressed his surprise at the audacity of the newly-converted family in preparing such food and drink, and especially in offering them to him.

"See," he continued, "how the holy man trembles at the horror of seeing the unclean food so strongly forbidden by Ngabehi Mohammed."

And really the pseudo-Arab moved backwards and forwards like a maniac, muttering a curious mixture of Walloon, French and Dutch oaths. He knew too well that in deference to the character he was personating he would not be able to partake of the well-prepared boar's head and the aromatic toeak. Some time ago he had cultivated the acquaintance of the toeak, a liquor prepared from fermented rice, pepper, betelnuts and sugar, and had found its taste so agreeable that on seeing the bowl appear, he had promised himself a goodly drink of its seductive contents. But Johannes' remark effectually deprived him of any share in the potations. Meddling fellow! Why could he not keep silent? The Walloon vented his indignation on his turban, which he turned around again and again as if wishing to pitch this particular article into the soengei. However, the hostess hastened to offer the desperate Arab a fair portion of tambilok, delicately fried, seasoned and peppered, besides a few slices of liendoeng, with some nice sour egg-sauce. After the saint had said grace he peacefully set to work and finished his meal with a good dose of fried koedjang, declaring that he found this product of the art of Dayak cookery most delicious.

"I believe you," said Johannes, smiling; "it was the choicest tidbit they could offer you."

La Cueille became alarmed at his ominous smile. "In heaven's name, what did I really eat?"

"Do you mean to say you don't know, you stupid? Well,

koedjang is a kind of turnip abundantly found in lower Dayakland and which takes the place of our potatoes."

"I know I have often eaten them at Kwala Kapoeas. They are really delicious fried in thin slices. But what did they call the viands?"

"Tambilok and liendoeng, you mean?"

"Yes, what are they?"

"Have you never observed those fat white worms found in the wood which has been lying in the river for a considerable time? Well, that is what the Dayaks call tambilok and of which they make such a nice dish."

"Oh, Notre Dame de bon secours!" the Walloon shrieked, horrified.

"And the 'liendoeng,'" Johannes continued immediately, "is a kind of water-snake about three feet long and of the diameter of a man's arm. Its color is red with black stripes down the back. It has a very smooth skin and is not poisonous. It is a special favorite with the Dayaks."

"And I thought I was eating eels all the while!" La Cueille cried, with disgust on his every feature.

"But never mind," Johannes added good-naturedly, "I have wrapped a large piece of the boar's head in a leaf Dayak-fashion, and as soon as you feel hungry again you shall have food more to your mind. But mind you may have to swallow worse things than snakes or worms before you reach home."

La Cueille sighed but did not answer. He went to rest and was soon lost in a deep slumber.

While Sheik Mohammed Al Mansoer lay asleep Johannes,

Wienersdorf, Schlickeisen and Dalim, accompanied by their host, Ali Bahar, entered the forest fully armed. The two other Dayaks of the company kept watch over the canoe, rifle in hand. Nothing suspicious however occurred, and about an hour before sunset the others returned and brought with them a large quantity of spades, pickaxes and other tools, besides two small one-pounder bronze guns which they thought might be useful to them. These tools and guns they had found in an empty hut. They had belonged to a foundered vessel and had been picked up by the Dayaks. They had yet to make another journey, for there was left behind a brass powder-case such as is used on men-of-war, which still contained some gunpowder. There were also about fifty shells for the guns and some thirty fathoms of light chain which might be of immense value to them.

About eight o'clock everything was on board and La Cueille, who in the meantime had waked up again, thought they were going to continue their journey. Instead of this his companions sat down for a long chat with their host. When at last the latter had entered his house and the others had gone on board and prepared for rest, Johannes told the Walloon that they intended to stay where they were all night and the following day.

"But," asked La Cueille, "is it not running a risk to stop so near the Dutch fort longer than is absolutely necessary?"

"You see we must not be too hasty," Johannes replied. "It is contrary to Dayak custom and we must avoid exciting suspicion. You have heard our host tell us that his old priest was devoured by a crocodile. He has therefore begged us to assist him to-morrow in catching the monster. It is an invitation which no Dayak dares refuse; it might cause the most sanguinary scenes."

"What a treat! Thank God, I don't understand anything of such a hunt and will remain quietly behind."

"Wrong again; on the contrary, your presence is most urgently requested."

"I don't care as long as we are not requested to eat snakes; if we have to do so, I flatly refuse to join."

"Don't be so stupid. Listen; I have announced myself as Pangareran."

"On my word I am a descendant of the Prophet; you now turn into a Pangerang. I foresee the day when the Swiss will be converted into Rajahs. Well, as long as we reach the north-coast I am satisfied."

"You misunderstand me. I am not a Pangerang, but simply a Pangareran."

"But then I don't see of what use *I* can be."

"Well, a Pangareran never goes on his errand without being accompanied by a priest, who recites prayers; and, my dear Arab, that branch belongs to you now."

The Walloon gave a pull to his turban, meditated for a few seconds and said,

"But I thought the Dayaks were heathen. A Mohammedan prayer will be quite out of place."

"Most Pangarerans are Malays, consequently Mohammedans. You know that no Dayak is allowed to catch a crocodile."

"Why not?"

"Because Djata, brother to Mahatara, the god of Dayaks, is

the father of all crocodiles. Not for all the riches in creation would a Dayak kill one of these monsters unless compelled to do so by blood-vengeance, that is, when one of his relatives, friends or neighbors has been devoured. Then he pays a Malay to kill the culprit."

"But how do they discover the real culprit? In these waters there is no lack of crocodiles."

"It is quite certain that in such a hunt many an innocent son of Djata does perish, but the Dayaks don't seem to mind that so much. They don't abandon the hunt until they have caught one in whose interior they find some of the remains of the victim. Do you remember the time when that dear little Dayak girl, little Biengies, was taken away by a crocodile at Fort Kwala Kapoeas? I think we killed about fifty of these monsters then, until at the end of six weeks we caught a huge fellow in whose stomach was found a closely packed tuft of human hair and the brass bracelets which the girl had worn. That brought the hunt to a conclusion."

"Don't I remember it? Did I not assist the Javan soldiers to boil the fat out of their carcasses to burn in their lamps at night? And how soft that fat was, even softer than the finest lard. I meant to save a little for my chilblains."

"Well, listen now. By and by I will put out the hooks and you will have to be present. You have slept long enough, have you not?"

"Yes, I have. But why do you need my presence when you are putting out the hooks?"

"You will see that afterwards. Your duty will be light enough;

only mutter some prayers and as we shall be probably entirely by ourselves, you may even omit that for my part. But mind! in case we catch a crocodile you will have to pray properly to-morrow. You will actually have to charm the monster, lest some mishap should occur to me. Here is a well-fingered Malay sermon of Roorda van Eysinga; it will serve as a Koran—I am sure it looks dirty enough."

After this conversation both men followed the example of their companions, enveloping themselves in their blankets and went to sleep.

When the "Taloetoek," a small kind of owl with black downy feathers and red wings and tail, sounded its melancholy koekh, koekh, at midnight, Johannes signalled the Walloon and woke one of the two Swiss to look after the general safety. They then entered a djoekoeng, in which they found long rattans tied together and forming cables of thirty to forty yards long, at the ends of which there were strong iron hooks of about a foot and a half in length and about an inch thick. After having lit a small lamp they proceeded to bait the hooks with live ducks. Both hooks and ducks were fastened to a small raft of pisang trunks in such a manner that the ducks remained floating on the surface. As soon as they had finished Johannes extinguished the lamps. They then floated gently and without the least noise down the soengei, being guided by the myriads of little fire-flies which glittered on the leaves of the trees lining the banks of the rivulet like solitary bright sparks..

They put out a few hooks in the main stream of the soengei and tied the ends of the rattan cables to a heavy block of wood, which they fastened to some branches on the bank in such a manner that at the least pull they would break and set the wood floating. They also placed similar tackle in the mouth of the river and on the western shore of the island Kanamit. When all was arranged the two Europeans rowed quietly back to their starting place and went to sleep.

As soon as the sun appeared again in all its glory the inhabitants of the hut as well as the men in the boat were awakened by a couple of boys who, having gone down the soengei, had brought tidings of the disappearance of one of the decoy ducks stationed at the mouth of the rivulet. They had also observed far up the stream a piece of wood which seemed to be tugged forcibly against the running tide.

After hearing this report every man hurried forward, and as soon as breakfast had been despatched they all took to their djoekoengs and soon disappeared from the view of the two Swiss who remained behind on guard.

The bait placed at the mouth of the rivulet had disappeared, hook and rattan cable included. A sharp lookout was kept and presently a large piece of wood was seen, which from time to time was pulled forcibly against the tide to the north of the island, just as the boys had described it.

In a very short time the djoekoengs reached the log of wood. All hands grasped the cable and hauled in, when a monster at least twenty feet long became visible. When the animal was brought to the surface it gave a terrible leap, exposing the whole of its body to view, and tried to tear away or break the hook. It lashed the water fearfully with its tail and dashed forward with such force as to compel the men to let go, in order to prevent their canoes being capsized. They had barely time to throw the log of wood overboard again. They however took to their oars, and following kept it in sight. When this wild race had continued for half an hour the speed of the log began visibly to diminish, until at last it lay quite still on the surface of the water. The djoekoengs now approached again and their occupants recommenced their task of hauling the crocodile from the depths of the river to the surface. The monster renewed its struggles, turning the cable violently around and around and lashing the water into foaming spray. Then starting forward in mad fury it tried to drag the boats to the bottom. At last, however, its speed diminished and the moment drew near for the Pangareran and his acolyte to act their parts. The canoe in which they had seated themselves approached the side of the crocodile. The Pangareran had now to recite the excuses of the Dayaks for being compelled to kill a crocodile, a child of Djata, brother to Mahatara, the omnipotent. He had also to plead that they were compelled to take vengeance as one of their relations had been killed. This form was necessary to satisfy Dayak superstition.

The priest, being the Pangareran's assistant, had then to read a few chapters from the Koran, after which both were required to mount on the back of the exhausted crocodile, which was now lying motionless at the side of the canoe. The Pangareran then had to close the fearful jaws of the beast with a strong loop of rattan in order to render him harmless, the priest assisting him with prayers during the operation. As a rule, this kind of work is not dangerous if only carried out calmly and resolutely. Johannes had already jumped bare-footed on the head of the reptile and was preparing to muzzle his prey, when the Dayaks called out to him to be careful as the priest had not yet followed him. Upon this La Cueille summoned all his courage to his aid and mounted on the slippery skin of the animal. His feet went from under him and he fell, describing such awkward contortions that the Dayaks, solemn as was the occasion, could not refrain from bursting into a roar of laughter.

The crocodile, enraged by this last shock and maddened by the increased pain caused by the hook in his throat, summoned all his remaining strength and pulled the fatal cable, lashing the water violently with his tail. The Walloon endeavored in vain to keep on him, but owing to the slippery skin and prickly spine, he lost his balance and was soon in the river.

Johannes also tried to retain his seat by inserting his fingers in the sockets of the monster's eyes. Infuriated by agony the animal gave a violent tug, broke the rattan cable to which the boat was attached and disappeared with his rider beneath the water. This, however, was his last effort, for shortly afterward huge bubbles mounted to the surface of the river and the body of the crocodile was seen floating with its yellow belly upwards, exhibiting the numerous wounds which the little triangular knife had inflicted guided by the steady hand of Johannes.

When the latter reappeared on the surface he cast a rapid glance around in search of his mate, the Walloon, whom he presently discovered half-drowned. He swam to his assistance and soon succeeded in dragging him into the nearest canoe.

JOHANNES AS A PANGARERAN.

La Cueille's first action was devoutly to thank the Holy Virgin for his escape. But alas! the poor priest had lost his Koran, rosary and sandals. The sandals were fished up again a few minutes afterward, but the holy book of the Prophet and the rosary had sunk to the bottom.

The carcass of the crocodile was landed and opened. In his stomach was found a ball composed of human hair, a gold ring set with a handsome stone and a rosary. These last were relics of the devoured Hadji and proved beyond doubt that his murderer had been found and slaughtered.

Universal joy now prevailed. Vengeance was satisfied and the hunt considered to be concluded. As a token of gratitude Ali Bahar presented the courageous Pangareran with the ring, while the Arab received the rosary in compensation for the loss of his own.

Johannes seemed greatly affected and muttered to himself while minutely examining the ring,

"I will never part with this keepsake, by Heaven; it might have cost me dear. I cannot boast of my luck at Poeloe Kanamit; this is my second appearance here and both times I have had a narrow escape."

La Cueille bowed devoutly, crossed himself and solemnly promised to offer his rosary to the Holy Mother as soon as he should be restored to his native country.

"You will have made a curious collection by that time," Johannes said, "and Notre Dame will look quite gay, provided you carry your head home."

"You may laugh, you coffee-colored heathen! I was really

praying all the time, and I am quite certain that but for my presence you would have——"

"Been in the water just the same, my dear dusky Arab!" Johannes laughed good-naturedly. "However, we have both done our duty; you with your prayer and I with my knife; all is well that ends well."

Noon was long past when the crocodile-hunters returned to the house of their host. The natives occupied themselves in dissecting the captured animal, which was soon accomplished. The skeleton was elevated on four posts at a spot near the mouth of the river especially cleared for the purpose. In order to make this trophy of victory more attractive, Ali Bahar placed a human skull between the jaws of the gigantic head. Many such mementoes of victory are found in the Dayak regions, on the banks of the streams. There the bleached bones not only of crocodiles, but also of wild boars, are set up to perpetuate the history of man's prowess in destroying them; even in the burial-grounds the skeletons of such wild beasts are raised as fitting monuments to the memory of those who have successfully hunted them down.

Nor are these trophies limited to such inferior animals as crocodiles and wild boars. Even in these lower regions where the Dutch strictly interdict head-hunting, human skulls are treasured up and exhibited with pride as memorials of native prowess. When, however, a Dayak is questioned respecting their origin, he invariably pretends that he has inherited them from his father, an explanation which their appearance and condition by no means confirm.

After partaking of a hearty meal the travellers prepared for the resumption of their journey, and at sunset left to proceed further north.

When they reached the Kapoeas they found the tide running fast. They reckoned that by keeping only two oars going, sufficient speed could be obtained to enable the boat to reach soengei Mantangei against the turn of the tide. If even they should err in their calculations and ebb tide should set in before reaching the soengei, it would only be necessary to bring all oars into play and make up for lost time. They therefore proposed that two of the Dayaks should row, while a third should steer. A steersman was necessary as no rudder is ever attached to a Dayak boat.

La Cueille could not forget how shabbily he had been treated in regard to drinks and reproached Johannes for appointing him to play the part of an Arab. "I am sure," he observed, "a glass of toeak would have been welcome after my soaking."

"I dare say; but to violate the commandments of the Koran would certainly have excited suspicion, and we were not quite far enough from Kwala Kapoeas," Johannes said solemnly. "But," he continued, "now that we are unobserved, I wont grudge you a hearty pull, provided you leave the bottle in my hands. You have certainly deserved a drink to-day."

And suiting the action to the word, he produced a square bottle from beneath the seat on which he was lying, poured out a glassful of its contents and passed it to the Walloon, who took it readily and emptied it at one draught, smacking his lips.

"By Jove! that is fine toeak; I never tasted anything like it before," he sighed, regaining his breath.

"It is doubly distilled," Johannes answered.

"Do let me have another thimble full," the Walloon begged.

"Patience, dear boy. The others must also have their turn. See how the Dayaks look; ah, they are such tipplers."

"From what do they distill this toeak?" asked Wienersdorf.

"Toeak is made from rice," Johannes explained, "and especially from the Ketan rice, a species which contains much gluten and becomes thick in boiling. They manufacture it in the following manner: They first make a leaven called ragi, consisting of powdered carrots, pepper, grated pisang nuts and sugar. The Ketan rice is then carefully added to this leaven in a large earthenware vessel and the whole mixture is exposed to the heat of the sun for three days. They then pour water on it, in the proportion of one gantang of water to each gantang of rice. They now let it ferment in the heat of the sun for two days and then filter the liquor through canvas. This liquor is the toeak."

"But how is it possible for it to become as strong as that we just now tasted?" Wienersdorf asked. "According to your explanation the process is a brewing and not a distillation."

"Listen; in order to make the toeak stronger, the Dayaks boil it in a pan covered with leaves, among which a hollow bamboo has been put in a horizontal position. The steam now travels through this tube and is condensed, when the liquor is collected again in the earthen bowl. Hence it becomes distilled. The Dayaks call it arak; and one of these bottles of arak was given to me by Ali Bahar."

When our travellers had finished their pleasant conversation about toeak, Johannes repeated all the information concerning themselves and their movements which he had been obliged to give their late host. He had represented that they were on their way to the Upper Kapoeas, to trade with the Olo Ott; that Sheik Mohammed Al Mansoer was following them in order to inspect these regions, intending afterwards to return with a cargo of chintzes and prints; that the two Swiss were his servants and that Dalim and the other two Dayaks were hired as rowers for the whole of the journey. To this programme he suggested they should adhere whenever they met with strangers. It would not disturb their friendship, for Johannes was not the man to abuse the trust placed in him; while a thorough understanding would reign among them should they be respectively thrown upon their own resources.

Thus the midnight hours passed by, and at about one o'clock in the morning they reached the end of their journey for that day, the Kwala Mantangei. Long before they sighted the mouth of the stream they heard the tolling of the titih; and upon entering the soengei and approaching the dwellings built along its banks other sounds became audible which made them advance with caution.

From all sides shrieks of women and children were heard, indicating the greatest consternation. Several torch-lights were seen in the distance, and women wildly running in the direction of one of the houses, about which they congregated, uttering cries of terror. The boat was quickly hidden amongst the shrubs and Dalim landed to ascertain what was the cause of the prevailing alarm. The others remained on board, lost in conjecture as to the meaning of such a panic at such an hour. They all perceived that something important was taking place and felt some fear that they had fallen upon a party of head-hunters. This anxiety, however, was soon removed by the reappearance of Dalim, who requested his companions to land and to bring their mandauws with them. La Cueille, as the boat could not be left to the care of itself, remained behind with one of the Dayaks. The others joined Dalim and they all crept forward in the direction of the torches, advancing under the cover of the shrubs, and presently came in sight of some thirty women and children, rushing about in the greatest fear. Upon approaching nearer they saw a gigantic snake more than thirty feet long and of the diameter of a man's waist, wriggling about and displaying the most curious undulations without seeming to move from its place. It appeared as if chained within a circle. A closer inspection showed them that the snake had been caught and was attached to a rattan cable which the women had thrown around a tree. They had not dared, however, to pull the cable tight, so that the snake retained sufficient liberty to move in a large circle.

It was a boa constrictor of the largest size, and was twisting and turning about terribly, trying, alternately, to break either the cable or the tree. But its efforts were in vain. Its movements kept the women at a respectful distance; for none of them could muster sufficient courage to kill the reptile, although they all carried naked mandauws in their hands.

While our travellers stood looking on in silence, the boa again made a dart forward and grasped within its folds a little boy who had approached too near. The poor child groaned and gurgled under this fatal embrace. The women uttered horrible yells, while the unfortunate mother of the child fell on her knees, threw up her arms, and implored the animal to loosen its hold and not hurt her darling.

Lifting the child high up in the air the snake made efforts to reach the tree. These failed at first, as the cable was not sufficiently supple. At last, however, it succeeded in grasping the trunk, which it encircled two or three times. Dalim, mandauw in hand, rushed forward through the group of yelling women; but before he could reach the boa, the crunching of broken bones was heard, mingled with a single shriek of the dying victim, who was flattened against the tree as if in a mill.

Dalim advanced undismayed toward the snake and aimed a blow at it without inflicting any injury. Perceiving its new antagonist the reptile rapidly unwound itself from the child, which fell lifeless to the ground, and attacking the Dayak, encircled him with those fatal living rings and compressed him with such force that he gasped for breath. It seemed as if his chest was being screwed together by an irresistible vise. In this desperate struggle for life he dealt several blows about him without definite aim. One of these unfortunately severed the cable and set the animal at liberty, when it coiled its tail round the trunk of the tree in order to crush the Dayak as it had crushed the child.

Dalim's death would have been inevitable, had not Wienersdorf and Johannes advanced to his rescue. They threw themselves upon the boa and tried to divert its attention to them. The animal then unwound itself from Dalim and sprang at

Wienersdorf, biting him between his neck and shoulder. Johannes now cut and lacerated the snake so severely that it took flight and nearly succeeded in escaping, owing to the stupidity of the women. These, in the confusion which prevailed, had dropped their torches and left the party in complete darkness; but the time had come for Schlickeisen to act. He had also approached to Dalim's assistance, but had paused in order to lift up the mangled child. Perceiving, however, that nothing could be done for it he turned his attention to the boa, now disappearing in the gloom. He suddenly passed the child over to its mother, lifted one of the yet glowing torches from the ground, and rushed after Johannes and the boa. A few well-aimed blows with his mandauw, dealt by a vigorous arm, soon decided the contest, the head of the snake being completely severed from the body and the once powerful reptile converted into a motionless mass.

The three Europeans now shook hands together over the body of the boa and congratulated each other on the result of this extraordinary contest. Dalim also approached and thanked them cordially. He assured his companions that as he owed his life to their timely aid they might henceforth confidently trust in him; he would accompany them as far as Singapore and remain with them until they could re-enter life as free men.

After the snake had been duly skinned, the women of the kampong told the travellers that their husbands were all absent gathering rosin. On the previous night an old woman had been awakened from her sleep by a sensation of pressure on her stomach; she stretched her hands out in the dark to ascertain the cause and felt a cold and clammy object which moved at her touch. She jumped up at once, uttering horrible cries and shrieking for assistance. The neighbors were soon at hand, but the glimmer of their lamps showed them nothing but a black mass crawling along the floor and finally disappearing in the darkness. Upon entering the room in which the old woman had slept they found her husband killed by a wound under his lower ribs, large enough to receive a human head. The riddle was now solved. The kampong had been visited by a boa, an occurrence by no means frequent in these marshy regions. The women, not being able to consult their better-halves, had bethought them of setting a bait, in the shape of a live ape fastened to a hook—with the result of finding the boa caught on the following evening. Disturbed at his meal of the night before, his hunger remained unappeased and he was readily snared.

After this narrative Johannes answered the questions of the women as to whence they had come. He commenced to tell them that he was going up country for trading purposes, when a piercing "lēēēēh, lèlèlèlèlè, oeiiiit," was heard in the direction of their boat, followed by a few rifle-shots. This gave grave cause for apprehension. They hurried away as fast as possible and found La Cueille and the Dayak engaged in a fight with the occupants of several djoekoengs. Who the assailants were could not for the moment be ascertained. Our friends leaped into their boats, took their rifles and fired as if they meant to disperse a whole army. Their vigorous attack soon put the assailants to flight.

After the retreat of the djoekoengs the adventurers endeavored to discover whence the attack had proceeded.

Calling a few women who had been following them, Dalim asked whether they knew who their assailants were.

"These men are rosin-seekers who have just returned home," said one of the women. Then raising her voice she called:

"Oōōōh Mihing!!" To this summons Mihing, probably her husband, responded from the wood with a similar "Oōōōh."

They quickly obtained all particulars of the mistaken aggression. A few canoes had preceded the rosin-gatherers and on nearing the kampong had heard the cries of the women. Fearing treason they had returned to summon their mates and hence their number. They observed a canoe hidden amongst the shrubs close to the kampong and they felt quite sure that a troop of head-hunters had dropped down the Doesson and Mantangei and were busily engaged in operating upon their wives and children.

The frightened men thereupon tried to approach this boat, but were hailed by La Cueille who had observed them distrustfully. On replying to his "Who goes there?" with a shout of defiance, he had fired into the approaching mass. The Mantangese hereupon fell back frightened, but soon collected again to resume the attack. They yelled their war-cry and pushed on with their canoes, to be received by a second volley of rifle-shots. Some of their number were seriously wounded and flight again became general. Soon not a single djoekoeng remained visible; but that their occupants were not far off was proved by Mihing's ready response to his wife's call.

The Mantangese were thankful for the assistance rendered to their wives by our fugitives in the struggle with the boa. Nevertheless Demang Soerah shook his head doubtfully and thought that the travellers had better get away as soon as possible. During that fatal firing blood had been spilt, and " blood cries for blood," he said. He strongly advised them to hasten their departure in order to escape the results of the passion for vengeance which would surely be kindled among the natives.

Our fugitives saw the wisdom of this advice and left the soengei Mantangei before daybreak to pursue the journey north by the Kapoeas.

The bite of the boa in Wienersdorf's neck proved more painful than dangerous. After being attended to by Dalim, who poulticed it with leaves, the pain was assuaged and the Swiss was again fit to handle his oar next morning.

Dalim seemed to have escaped almost unscathed from the embrace of the snake: he only complained of a little stiffness in the joints and stretched out his arms and legs repeatedly, swaying his body backward and forward several times. He then asked them for a hearty drink of tocak and declared himself quite cured.

"I hope we shall have the luck to meet another boa," said Schlickeisen.

"A fine wish; and pray, what for?"

"Because I regret leaving that dead one behind."

"Upon my word! What would you do with it? We have scarcely any room as it is."

"Quite so; but we could skin it and make cigar-cases or purses out of the skin."

"If I had the skin," La Cueille said, "I should——"

"Certainly, carry it away and present it to Notre Dame," Wienersdorf interrupted.

"In addition to the rosary," Johannes went on, "I am sure that skin would be an ornament to the altar; and how it would puzzle the congregation!"

"Silence, worthless heathen! Don't joke upon sacred subjects," the Walloon exclaimed. "We shall often be in need of Heavenly aid, and I fervently pray our Holy Mother to take us under her protection."

"Amen!"

CHAPTER VI.

THE WOUNDED GO TO KWALA KAPOEAS—THE MANTANGEI AND THE MENKATIP—THE COMMANDER IN PURSUIT—AT SEA—PURSUIT OF THE FUGITIVES—THE SCHOONER—THE RETURN—ON THE TRACK AT LAST—DEPARTURE FROM MANTANGEI—WHITE SAIL—FIRST EXPERIENCE WITH THE HEAD-HUNTERS—LA CUEILLE WOUNDED—A FUNERAL CEREMONY.

ALTHOUGH the fugitives were again on their way, this was not the last they were to hear of the adventure. Several men had been wounded in the affray, and as the Dayaks were but indifferently acquainted with surgery, they resolved to take the sufferers to the fort and seek the assistance of the Dutch.

There could be no vengeance taken for the blood which had been shed, as the strangers had departed, leaving no trace of the direction they were pursuing. The Chief of the kampong, fearing that the vengeful feelings of his people would involve him in serious difficulties with the Dutch, told his people that the boat which carried our fugitives had sailed up the soengei Mantangei, in order to reach the Doesson.

When the wounded arrived at Kapoeas they were immediately attended to by the surgeon. Their wounds were found to be caused by bullets and wholly different in character from injuries inflicted by the mandauw or lance of the natives. This fact excited the greatest astonishment and suspicion. The account furnished by the wounded men also gave grounds for serious reflection. They described the incident of the boa constrictor, and related how the men of kampong Mantangei had looked upon the deliverers of their wives as head-hunters; how this mistake had led to combat and how they were wounded and put to flight by a heavy rifle-fire. The information that their assailants were Dayak merchants who were working their way to the upper Doesson by means of the Mantangei was not credited by the Colonel; on the other hand neither did he suspect the presence of the deserters in that direction. Only the day before he had returned from a journey on the Javan sea in his efforts to recapture them. He had failed, but no doubt remained in his mind of his having been upon their track.

On the morning following the desertion the Colonel had bestirred himself early. Long before sunrise he had visited the Chief of the district, Tomonggong Nikodemus Djaja Nagara. After taking some preliminary measures he had placed himself at the head of a large number of Dayaks, divided them into several canoes, and accompanied by the Tomonggong had taken his course seawards.

Passing an islet in the Lesser Dayak river they encountered the canoe which had been so terribly injured by the shots from the fortress the night before. As, however, its crew were not in the secret of the deserters no information could be gained from them. They could only show their dead and wounded and explain how the canoe carrying the coffin had disappeared in the dark down the stream. They had been terribly frightened and even now had not lost all fear. After a long palaver, however, they were convinced of their present safety and assured that they might carry their wounded to the fortress to have them surgically attended to.

Every creek, every soengei was examined, the islets thoroughly scoured, but nothing of a suspicious nature was found. The Colonel, on nearing the mouth of the Troessan, proposed to despatch part of his men through that canal with orders to rejoin him again at the mouth of the Kahajan. Had this order been executed our fugitives would have been caught. But before the division of the men had been definitely made, a canoe appeared at the mouth of the Troessan carrying the Chief of that district, a trustworthy subject, who declared that he had not met with a single canoe. It was therefore clear that the fugitives could not have escaped that way. The voyage was continued to the mouth of the Lesser Dayak. Their search in creeks and branches involved such loss of time that it was late in the afternoon before they reached the Javan sea.

The Colonel now carefully scanned the horizon and saw two cruisers lying at anchor. On the south-west a prauw was working against the wind, but as soon as it perceived the little fleet it spread all canvas and tried to get away with all speed. This strengthened the Colonel's belief that the fugitives were on board of that prauw. Even the Tomonggong declared that its appearance was not unlike that of the prauw which had borne the cholera-stricken corpse. As to who the oarsmen were he could form no conception. He knew the fear entertained by his people of this terrible malady and this fact augmented his uncertainty.

The Colonel ordered a few shots to be fired in order to attract the attention of the cruisers and displayed the national colors from his stern. Their respective commanders seemed to understand what they were required to do. They immediately weighed their anchors and made sail towards his little fleet.

The Colonel went on board one of them and ordered all sails to be set. He also directed that three blank shots should be fired as a signal for the prauw to lay to. But instead of obeying, the boat made more sail and brought as many oars into play as possible. When first observed it had appeared to carry about four oars, but now that it was in flight it seemed to be crowded with men.

The Colonel ordered the gunners to load, determined to show that he was in earnest. But the three-pound shells only rebounded on the water and burst with loud reports; the distance was too great. The number of men on board excited the suspicion of the Tomonggong also, but he declared that it could not possibly be the canoe of the fugitives and that they were on a false track. If that canoe had been manned at Kwala Kapoeas with so many oarsmen it could not have remained a secret to him, the Chief of the district.

At last the Colonel decided to despatch one of the cruisers in pursuit of the fugitive boat, while the other was to remain behind to assist him in examining the coast.

While giving his orders a cry was heard from one of the surrounding canoes that it had a box in tow. This box proved to be the coffin of the cholera patient which had been brought forth for burial on the previous evening. One of the Dayaks recognized the body, while another pretended to have himself made the coffin. The Colonel and the Tomonggong looked at each other; both measured the distance between the fugitive prauw and the mouth of the river, and as the coffin had been found near the line between these two points all doubt was removed. Even the Dayak chief now concluded that the coffin had been thrown overboard from that suspicious prauw, which must consequently contain the fugitives.

"Forward, forward!" was now in order.

All that day the pursued prauw kept its distance, now losing a little, then regaining the loss. Towards evening the south-monsoon began to drop and as is usual in those latitudes the land wind arose. The wind blew from south-east to east by north and a thick mass of clouds darkened the sky. Both cruisers, although in violation of the existing rules, carried their lights and every boat of the Dayak flotilla was also provided with a lamp. No lights however were visible from the fugitive, and it was therefore impossible to keep it in view. Nevertheless the combined fleets pursued their course west south-west during the night, to find next morning that the prauw was only visible as a dim black spot on the southern horizon. It had simply changed its course in the darkness of the night, so as not to be too near Cape Salatan.

By this manœuvre it would be enabled as soon as the wind should blow again from the south-east, to run before it.

The Dutch cruisers endeavored to regain the lost distance in the lull which generally prevails during the first hours of the morning, and as soon as the monsoon reappeared at eight they set all sail; but the result was the same as on the previous day.

About two in the afternoon a large schooner appeared on the horizon. This vessel, observing the pursued prauw, showed the Dutch colors reversed, fired a shot, and manœuvred to take the prauw in tow. This she speedily accomplished, then lying to the wind she fired another shot, the charge of which flew over the first of the cruisers, but struck the mast of the other and sent it flying overboard. Considering the distance, the result of this shot proved that she was armed with grooved guns. The Colonel, enraged at the insult of the flag and at the shot, determined to continue his pursuit; but the schooner was too fast a sailer, and within an hour she had disappeared from view.

They then began to think of the return journey. Tomonggong pointed towards the horizon and declared that the faint glimpse of land towards the north was cape Poeding and the one a little higher up to the west cape Kramat. The Colonel consulted his map and his face darkened.

"From this point we have to make about thirty-six miles against the wind. A terrible affair; the deuce take them!" he exclaimed.

Giving his orders he arranged that the two cruisers should remain together, while the dismasted one should be towed as far as the Lesser Dayak river by six canoes. Once there, she would be able to manage with her oars. This settled, the Colonel, accompanied by the Tomonggong, went on board of one of the fastest boats of the fleet, manned her with sixty picked oarsmen, and hurried on in order to regain his post at Kwala Kapoeas, which he reached late at night after an absence of four days.

He was welcomed on his arrival by the doctor who was surprised at not seeing the fugitives return with him. His look of enquiry was answered by the Colonel with the words,

"Gone, and forever! I saw them disappear on board of an armed schooner. But how could they have put themselves in communication with her? The more I think it over, the less can I make it out."

He related his experiences, the sighting of the canoes, the finding of the body, the pursuit, the fatal shot from the schooner and her reversed flag, and concluded with,

"It is a mystery to me."

"What kind of vessel was that schooner?" the doctor asked.

"How should I know? She carried European gear and I am positive that she was armed with steel-bored guns. Perhaps she was one of those British smugglers from the straits of Malacca which drive an impudent trade in contraband opium and war ammunition. However, I am going to make my report. By-the-bye, did you send off my former one during my absence?"

"The postal canoe left while you were yet in sight."

"Good; we may receive an answer to-day."

Inwardly, the doctor was glad of the escape of the deserters; but his joy would have visibly evaporated could he only have known where they were at that moment.

The day following the return of the Colonel the report was spread in the kampong at Kwala Kapoeas that Dalim and two other Dayaks, who were all three under the supervision of the police, had been seen at soengei Naning. Nobody knew that they had served as oarsmen to the funeral canoe and when the Colonel spoke of their absence to the Chief of the district he confirmed the statement that three Dayaks had disappeared. The Chief also related the whole history of the crocodile hunt at Poeloe Kanamit and declared that he had already sent out trustworthy messengers to bring those men back again. On the Colonel's enquiry whether there was any connection between the disappearance of these fellows and the desertion of the four Europeans, the Tomonggong laughed good-naturedly.

"Impossible, sir! You saw the palefaces go on board that schooner with your own eyes. What business could they have with these Dayaks, who perhaps have been taking a holiday to soengei Naning? You know that Dalim's brother lives there."

The Colonel shook his head, but remained silent.

When however two days afterwards the wounded from soengei Mantangei were brought in and with Eastern exaggeration talked about the rifle-fire as if a hundred men had been engaged—when too, the doctor imprudently declared that he was unable to say whether or not the wounds were inflicted by round bullets, but rather thought that they looked more like wounds torn by explosive balls, the Colonel began to reflect. He desired the Chief of the district to appear, talked the matter over with him and finally ordered him to keep thirty Dayaks ready. He also bade him send the Chief of the kampong, Damboeng Papoendeh, to the fort to receive further instructions.

On leaving the fort the old Tomonggong met the doctor.

"It is all over with them now," he said. "Their track is clear."

"But, Tomonggong, how is it possible that these Europeans could have fought in soengei Mantangei?"

"I cannot explain the possibility, sir, but I will swear that it was they."

"Take care," the doctor laughed, "the palefaces punish false oaths heavily."

"I am quite at ease. None such devils are found in the whole of Dayak country. First, that crocodile hunt; then the fight with a boa; afterwards the heavy fire into the boats of the approaching inhabitants of the kampong. Nobody here carries such weapons. I will lay you any wager that the repeating rifles of the Colonel have played their part in all these scenes."

"Did you tell the Colonel?"

"Not yet; he is too much taken up with the notion that the palefaces are on board that schooner. The finding of that coffin is a positive proof to him that they have chosen that direction."

"And do you not think so, Tomonggong?"

"I did think so once, sir, but not now. According to my view the fugitives have gone higher up. If the Colonel would only listen to me we should be on their track already."

"What does he intend to do?"

"To let Damboeng Papoendeh find out first what was their object in going to soengei Mantangei. But by the time he will have obtained positive reports these men will be too far away."

"Let them go, Tomonggong, let them go."

"It is all very well for you to say that; but if we do not follow them now, they will either fall a prey to the head-hunters of the upper regions, or will settle amongst the Ot Danoms and render their capture more difficult for my own people. In either case much unnecessary blood will be spilt. I will return to-night and hope to find the Colonel in a better mood for listening to my proposals."

" But could you not wait a day or two? For instance, until we receive further information? "

" My gratitude towards you, sir, begins to oppress me. I owe you the life of my child, but the lives of many human beings are now involved."

" I beseech you, have a little more patience."

" Be it so! But be sure that this is the last time that I will do anything for these fugitives. I feel that I am acting wrongly and that if I had not listened to you from the beginning we should have been saved all this trouble."

A few hours afterwards three canoes, well manned and fully armed, sailed up the Kapoeas. They were under the command of Damboeng Papoendeh, a young Dayak chief eager to gain his first spurs under the Dutch flag. When the Colonel informed him that the canoe which had given battle to the people of soengei Mantangei had sailed toward the Doesson, he smiled and said that he fully understood how to act.

A few minutes later the doctor tried to speak to him alone, but the Dayak repelled all advances and proudly stated that " he had pledged himself to bring back the fugitives, dead or alive."

The post arrived at Kwala Kapoeas next day and brought a recommendation to the Colonel not to leave any means untried to recapture the deserters.

" But what are you to do?" asked the doctor, who as usual was spending the evening with the Colonel and had witnessed the opening of the official letters.

"What am I to do? For my part, the deserters may get clean off. I will have nothing more to do with the matter. I have already exceeded my duty as military commander. It is not my fault that these cruising boats are so slow and can't get along."

While giving vent to his feelings the Colonel had almost mechanically opened the other letters and skimmed over their contents. Most of them were of an administrative nature and of little material importance. But the one which he now held in his hand seemed to rivet his whole attention. It was a communication from the Resident, that a schooner carrying reversed Dutch colors and laden with salt, opium, gunpowder and leaden and iron bullets had been captured by His Majesty's steamer Montrado, in the neighborhood of Poeloe Mangkop, south of cape Batoe Titi. Most of the men had been killed during the fight. One European only, seemingly an Englishman, appeared to have been on board. The commanders of all stations along the coast were therefore advised to be on the lookout, as similar attempts at landing contraband stores might be expected.

"By the saints! it must have been that infernal schooner," the Colonel burst out. "And the deserters were not on board after all! Where else can they be? Have we been following the wrong track? But how can we account for that coffin in the Javan sea? It is above my comprehension altogether. Old Tomonggong may be right after all that it was they who caused that fracas in the soengei Mantangei. But how did they get there?"

His excitement now became very great and he despatched a messenger to the district chief, ordering him to be present at the fort on the following morning with fifty oarsmen to accompany him to soengei Mantangei.

The fugitives continued their journey from soengei Mantangei during the night. They had now been fully seven days on their travels. The country around gradually lost its alluvial appearance, and although the elevation of the soil was not yet very important and our adventurers could still clearly distinguish in the current of the river the regular and marked appearance of ebb and flood, the riwoet haroesan, breath of the stream, had totally ceased. The highest tide never brought the sea so far up and its waters were here free from all brackishness.

About three o'clock in the afternoon the travellers reached a spot called petak bapoeti, white sail, by the natives. This consisted of a range of hills about forty feet high, formed of bluish-white sand, mingled with numerous shells of a different kind from those in the clay mud met with round the south coast of Borneo. In support of the hypothesis that once upon a time this must have been the southern coast of the island, similar hill formations are found at about the same distance from the mouths of the Doesson, Kahajan and Mantawei rivers.

To stretch their limbs a while on this white sand was a welcome relaxation to our Europeans, for to sit for days cross-legged in a canoe is exceedingly fatiguing to a person not accustomed to it. They therefore moved about freely, occupying themselves in gathering some dark red berries, not unlike our blackberries, which grew abundantly here and which supplied an agreeable relish to their monotonous meals.

After they had walked an hour or two Dalim gave the signal

for departure, telling them that where they were such multitudes of mosquitoes swarmed about at night that despite the use of any quantity of "brotoali" sleep would be impossible. According to him it was the spot where most of the mosquitoes of the island congregated; for which he accounted by relating the following legend:

"The son of Sultan Koening, the Djata—or Crocodile—King of the Batang Moeroeng, was going to be married to the daughter of Anding Maling Goena, the Crocodile King of the Kapoeas River. The marriage was to be solemnized at this spot; and the fishes, water-snakes, shrimps, frogs and other inhabitants of the stream assembled to increase the pomp of the ceremony. They brought with them some hundreds of pounds of mosquitoes as the best present they could give the young married couple in token of their affection. The present was graciously accepted; and the descendants of those mosquitoes in a most disagreeable manner impress the memory of that marriage gift upon any traveller whose ill-luck carries him thither to spend the night."

"A queer present," La Cueille remarked, "only a Dayak could suggest such a wedding gift."

"I heard Dalim speak of the island Kalimantan," said Wienersdorf. "Which island is that?"

Johannes hereupon told him that Kalimantan was the name given by the natives to Borneo, and that the European name, derived from the word Broenai, simply indicates a small division of the island situated on the north-western coast.

"Does the word Kalimantan mean anything at all?"

"Kalimantawa is the Dayak name of the dorian or jack-fruit

of Borneo, the shape of the island being similar to that of the fruit, which probably led to the adoption of the name."

"That is quite impossible," Wienersdorf rejoined. "Borneo is one of the largest islands of the world, and to define the shape of so large an island one requires a certain amount of knowledge which no people of the Indian Archipelago are likely to possess."

Dalim hereupon bent over to Johannes and whispered something in his ear.

"You may be right," the latter observed. "Dalim has just suggested Kalliintan, river of diamonds. That may be the true origin of the name, as intan means diamond."

In discourse of a similar nature time was materially shortened and our travellers soon reached kotta Towanan. This was a Dayak fortification, such as is frequently found all over the inner regions of Borneo. It consisted of a long square redoubt without projections; its parapets were made of strong wooden piles of vast size, and was ornamented here and there with life-size wooden images representing Dayak warriors in every possible attitude of war.

Approaching nearer, but still covered by the last projecting bank, Dalim advised that the kotta should be reconnoitred in order to ascertain that it was not occupied by river pirates and head-hunters. A party accompanied by Schlickeisen and La Cueille landed and penetrated into the wood. They soon returned, however, and reported that they had found nothing of a suspicious nature.

At first they proposed to pass the night in the kotta and enjoy sleep on terra firma again; but after Wienersdorf had made a careful survey, he remarked that both in the front and rear of the fort there were large apertures, which would require to be guarded. It would also be necessary to keep strict watch over their canoe, which contained all their riches. The efficient defence of these several positions would certainly be too much for their small number of men, none of whom had yet enjoyed a good night's rest. They therefore resolved to remain in their boat, and by setting one man to do duty as sentry enable the others to enjoy undisturbed repose. Evening had closed in and the Dayaks took the first watch, the Europeans arranging to succeed and relieve them later in the night.

But man proposes and God disposes. Their rest was fated to be disturbed.

It might have been about nine o'clock in the evening; the Europeans had enveloped themselves in their blankets and were already snoring. The three Dayaks were sitting together in conversation, when Dalim made the remark that their supply of wood was insufficient to keep such a fire burning as would be necessary to command a thorough survey of the territory. He ordered one of his mates to supply this want and pointed out to him a heap of dry branches which he had noticed during his examination of the fort some hours before. The Dayak made no demur whatever but proceeded on his errand. His friends saw him land and disappear through one of the apertures of the fort; when suddenly a heart-rending cry was heard which summoned the watchers as well as the Europeans to their feet. Wienersdorf and La Cueille were among the first to seize their rifles and leap on shore; Dalim followed them closely, while the others kept a sharp lookout, their rifles presented and their fingers on the trigger.

Dalim and his matès carefully entered the fort, but Wienersdorf suddenly stumbled over something, fell, and uttered a cry of horror. Dalim who was behind him hastened to his aid. He bore a lighted torch in his hand, by the faint glimmer of which they perceived the headless corpse of their native companion. The body had been decapitated after the Dayak fashion, the head having been severed from it at one blow.

As a rule, this decapitation is performed so suddenly that the victims enter into eternity before they are aware of their impending fate. In this case, however, the Dayak seemed to have realized his situation during his last moments, as was proved by the cry he had uttered. He seemed also to have clutched his assailant with his left hand, because there was the fragment of ewah in his grasp, while his right hand still held his mandauw. La Cueille perceived something lying on the grass not far from the dead Dayak; he stooped and seized it, only to give utterance to a cry of horror and dismay. Powerless to relinquish what he held in his hand he raised it up. It was the head of their companion, its eyes rolling and its jaw and lips moving in their last agonies, as if they were trying to find utterance. At this horrible sight Dalim cried out terrified as he moved backward,

"Quick, back!"

He had scarcely uttered these words when a whistling sound was heard and La Cueille with a true Walloon curse cried out that he was wounded. He shouldered his rifle without loosing his grip of the head; but Dalim took him by the arm and hurried him toward the canoe, while Wienersdorf covered the retreat, discharging the Remington into the surrounding obscurity. Upon nearing the light diffused by the boat's fire, La Cueille thought he saw something move in the bush which skirted the palisade of the fortifications. He tore himself away from Dalim, threw the yet bleeding head into the canoe, and discharged his rifle in the direction of the shrubs. The shot was quickly answered with a defiant lēēēēh, lèlèlèlèlè, ouiiiit, and at the same time some figures emerged from the darkness into the illuminated circle. Now, however, came Johannes and Schlickeisen's turn to interpose their aid. They had remained in the canoe, awaiting a favorable opportunity for action. Schlickeisen was armed with the other Remington rifle; Wienersdorf and the Walloon took their position near the canoe, and a rifle-fire was kept up which put the assailing Dayaks to rout. The first two shots fired by the Europeans from the canoe seemed almost sufficient, for these being delivered with a cool and steady aim two of their assailants were instantly hors de combat; the others soon fled.

Nothing further could be seen ashore; our adventurers therefore ceased firing and took time to recover themselves. La Cueille complained of pain in his arm, upon which Wienersdorf examined it and found that the Walloon had been wounded by a poisoned arrow. They all looked at each other dejectedly, for they had learned enough of arrow poison to be aware of its terrible consequences. Dalim took a handful of salt which he rubbed into the gums of the patient until a profuse salivation was produced. He was proceeding to rub it into the wound itself when Wienersdorf pushed him aside, and opening his pocket knife made a deep crucial incision over the small wound. He then produced a bottle of liquid ammonia and poured a few drops of the alkali into the cut.

The Walloon roared with pain, writhing terribly and mingling many forcible expletives with constant repetitions of, "Sainte Vierge, priez pour moi!"

Although the situation was grave indeed, Johannes could not refrain from pointing out to La Cueille how soon he had forgotten his part of an Arab and strongly advised him to mutter a devout, " Lā ilāha illa llāhoe," instead of invoking the Holy Virgin. The Walloon, though greatly incensed against his brown comrade, was in too much pain to give vent to his feelings. At length after many sighs and lamentations he fell into a deep slumber, which Dalim considered a favorable symptom.

It was clear that the others must not think of going to sleep. They knew that the enemy was in their immediate neighborhood. They therefore remained, rifle in hand, watching the banks from under the roof of their canoe in order to be prepared for a renewed attack. All remained quiet for a considerable time. Suddenly they heard from behind them on the river the well known but formidable lēēēēh lèlèlèlèlè ouiiiit! and a hail of small arrows dropped amongst them over the canoe and under the roof. Upon turning round sharply, they had just time to see a boat shoot by in midstream, its occupants continuing their cry of defiance. They thereupon discharged a few shots which seemed to be well aimed, for the war cry suddenly ceased and gave way to shrieks of pain. These continued to be heard for a considerable time in the stillness of the night, but they gradually grew fainter until at last they were lost in the distance.

La Cueille on first hearing the war cry and the ensuing noise of the firing had jumped up from his sleep in a great fright. Feeling about for some weapon he had seized hold of the head which a few hours ago he himself had thrown into the canoe, but had quite forgotten. Being still under the influence of the late tragedy his horror was extreme, and he at once concluded that the head-hunters were on board and busily engaged in their bloody work among his companions. Fortunately there was no weapon near, else in the intense darkness he might have wrought sad havoc among his friends. In his heedless passion of self-preservation he grasped Johannes by the neck and tried to strangle him, when the latter becoming enraged, dealt him a few smart blows in return, saying, " This diabolical Walloon means to throttle me ; I believe he is mad."

They all fancied he was suffering from a sudden fit of mania caused by the arrow poison ; but when the Walloon told them how on awakening he had taken hold of the head, they burst into hearty laughter and congratulated the pseudo head-hunter on the spoil he had secured.

"We will dissect and clean it nicely for you," said Johannes, "and you may take it with you to Jupille. It will be quite a treasure to you, and the Walloon ladies will almost besiege you when you tell them that Dayak fashion you are able to lay a skull at the feet of your lady love."

They all laughed at this suggestion except La Cueille himself, who had not yet wholly recovered from his fright. A good draught from the toeak bottle soon restored him.

After such stirring events sleep was an impossibility, although Dalim assured his companions they had nothing more to apprehend. It was, however, resolved to continue watching until the sun should appear in the heavens.

"We are getting on," Schlickeisen observed; "our little force has suffered one death and two wounded. If things continue at this rate, by the time we reach the upper country few of us will be left to tell the story of our adventures."

"Ah, bah! Did you think to escape without even a scratch?" Johannes asked. "If only half of us reach the Chinese sea we may think ourselves lucky indeed. In real fact no one of us is safe."

"Your predictions are certainly far from reassuring," Wienersdorf said.

"He is always prophesying something horrible," La Cueille muttered. "This ugly fellow tries to make our lives more insupportable than they already are."

"You will have to take life as it comes, and to face its trials fearlessly. Our position, however, is not quite so bad after all; we certainly have to lament the loss of one of our companions, but fortunately no one of us four has fallen yet. Wienersdorf's wound received from the boa has nearly healed, and since La Cueille is not quite dead yet we may laugh at his pin pricks. What a noise our Walloon made about it, did he not?" Johannes laughingly remarked.

"Since I am not dead yet you may enjoy your fun," La Cueille said. "But was I really in danger?"

"I did not entertain much hope for your life when I saw that arrow. Those weapons usually act very rapidly indeed. First, you are taken with a shivering fit, then your teeth begin to rattle, you talk at random and with the vehemence of a drunkard; and then all is over within half an hour. Since you have survived all these symptoms you may consider yourself out of danger."

The Walloon gave a sigh of relief.

"But Wienersdorf will have to be careful of that bottle of nasty smelling liquid," Johannes continued, " he has done wonders with it indeed."

"Dalim swears that his salt saved La Cueille."

"Not a bit of it," Johannes replied. "I have watched the Colonel at Kwala Kapoeas in his experiments with arrow poisons on dogs, monkeys and fowls. The salt antidote always failed; the poor animals invariably died after it, while those treated by the application of the foul smelling liquid were all cured."

Wienersdorf was sitting, lost in thought, supporting his head with his hand. "It is still a riddle to me," he said at last, " how those men came to leave a head behind them on the ground. I always thought that the head-hunter seized his victim by the hair before giving the fatal blow."

"That is what I also cannot make out," the Dayak assured him. "As a rule the grasping of the hair and the blow itself take place so rapidly that the victim has no time to utter a cry. Some instances of rapidity have been recorded where the victims actually make a few steps onward waving their arms about after decapitation. The Dayak boys of the upper regions regularly cultivate head-hunting as a fine art. They first place a cocoanut on the top of a thin post and practice until they are able to cut the post clean through just under the point where the nut rests upon it without injuring the latter. Later on, as they advance in years and their strength increases, the post is replaced by an effigy of a large boy, the neck of which is made of a piece of soft but elastic wood, and in order to complete the illusion they adorn the nut with a wig formed of the fibres of the arengpalm, which, when properly made, strongly resembles the thin hair of the natives. Hence their great dexterity."

"To which I can add," Johannes continued, " that the Dayaks of the lower country are just as great experts in the handling of their mandauws. I have witnessed at Kwala Kapoeas how, in the presence of the Colonel, any Dayak, however weak in appearance, could without visible effort divide in halves at a single blow a ripe green cocoanut, while none of the Europeans could manage to penetrate beyond the fibre."

"It seems a curious custom to offer one's lady-love these human heads," Schlickeisen continued.

"Quite so; but yet it has a meaning," Johannes answered. "Formerly it must have been a proof of his valor given by the bridegroom to his bride, to demonstrate that he was capable of protecting his wife and children. What better guarantee than the head of one of his enemies killed by his own hand could be offered by a primitive community? This custom afterwards became degraded by turning skulls into an article of luxury or of established traffic. Thus an institution originating in the best intentions became the curse of the whole population."

"But these atrocities cannot be practiced in the lower country, can they?" Wienersdorf asked of Dalim.

"The Dutch will not allow them," the latter replied.

"So that you only abandon the practice because it is prohibited. Don't you consider head-hunting an abominable occupation?"

"Who can say? Perhaps according to my views it is not," was the phlegmatic reply, proving that the perception of its horror had not greatly impressed him.

While they were conversing in this strain the night crept on and day at last reappeared, to the great delight of our travellers.

They examined the kotta carefully and found nothing but the decapitated body of their late companion. A small pool of blood was discovered at a little distance from it, while at one of the openings in the palisades some bloody finger-marks appeared on the wood-work. They therefore concluded that the enemy had also suffered loss, although to the utter disappointment of the Swiss no bodies could be found.

"Do you think those blackguards got off scot free?" Schlickeisen asked earnestly.

"Certainly not," Johannes answered, "for I could follow traces of blood as far as the river, where they took to their rangkan. We shall have to examine the ground more thoroughly. But you must not forget that the natives of the Dutch Indies consider it the greatest disgrace to leave the bodies of their fallen brethren behind."

After having examined the kotta the deserters passed outside through one of the openings to scour the neighborhood. In their explorations they reached a spot the long grass of which was trodden down. When Schlickeisen had cut a way through the thick creepers and bushes he found two bodies dressed in full war costume, with their coats of mail made of rattan chain and caps of monkey skin on their heads, their shields in their left hands and their naked mandauws in their right. According to Dalim they were Poenans, a Dayak tribe belonging to the interior of Borneo, near the sources of the Kahajan-Doesson and Kotei rivers. Both of these men must have destroyed many victims judging by the tufts of human hair which ornamented the blades and handles of their mandauws. They were young men still, and yet Dalim averred that one of them had killed four and the other seven people, facts which were proved by the number of red rattan rings round the sheaths of their mandauws.

The weapons and coats of mail of the dead were appropriated by the two Dayaks, and their bodies were then thrown into the river as an offering to Djata, the Chief of the Crocodiles. Their own fallen companion they washed carefully and painted his forehead and nails, after which they and the Europeans dug a grave and buried him, putting his head in position above his trunk. They placed a mandauw in his hand and deposited his lance beside him in the grave. Each of them then strewed a handful of raw rice over the body, saying,

"Djetoh akam," (this is for you).

They then strewed a second handful saying, "This we send to our forefathers," and finally a third one with the words, "This is for so and so"—mentioning the names of some relations who had recently died.

This ceremony of strewing rice is never omitted at funerals.

After this the Dayak companions of the dead man uttered a piercing shriek called tatoem, the lament for the dead, and then proceeded to close the grave. In order to secure the body from being interfered with, they had chosen a spot in the midst of thick herbage and had carefully cut the sods and put them aside without breaking them. They then collected the excavated earth upon a large sheet, taking care not to drop a single handful. In filling the grave they tramped the earth down as firmly as possible, planted a few short shrubs and then replaced the sods so carefully that the most searching eye could not discover where they had been divided by the spade. The remainder of the superfluous earth was carefully carried to the river, into which it was thrown, and the grave was copiously watered so as to preserve the sods and plants from withering.

When all was finished the fugitives took to their canoes again, threw out their oars, and left the spot which had nearly been their last resting-place.

CHAPTER VII.

JOURNEY UP THE RIVER—POISONS, HOW THEY ARE MADE—THE SOENGEI MOEROI—THE MEETING WITH BAPA ANDONG—BEE-HUNTING—HEAD-HUNTERS AGAIN—A STRUGGLE FOR LIFE.

"CONFOUND this stream," La Cueille muttered to himself, "one can hardly perceive that we are making any progress."

It was indeed at the cost of much labor and fatigue that any way was made through the water. The canoe seemed to glide backward and forward without advancing a single yard, though the crew used their oars with all the power at their command. This was the result of the numerous obstructions which lay in their way. It required an intimate knowledge of the river to be able to weather promontories, to cut off corners, to avoid curves, to utilize currents and to steer clear of sand-banks. But their chief danger lay in the vast quantities of dead trees that were fixed in the bed of the river. Torn away from the banks by storms or inundations, these trees are carried along by the stream a considerable distance, until they become caught by some under lying shoal or sand bank to which they attach themselves and become permanently planted. Collision with such snags is one of the greatest dangers of river navigation, as it generally proves fatal to the vessel. Dalim and his compatriots kept a sharp lookout and by their vigilance and adroitness prevented many a mishap which might have endangered their lives and involved the utter destruction of the canoe.

La Cueille found this hard rowing peculiarly irksome. He looked at his arm from time to time, but the cut made by Wienersdorf was healing well without any inflammatory symptom. There was nothing to be seen but a black circle, which Dalim informed him was always present after similar wounds by poisonous weapons, whether the wounded person died or recovered.

Upon Wienersdorf enquiring from what these poisons were made, Dalim informed him that the two principal kinds used by the Dayaks were known under the names of siren and ipoh. They were both vegetable poisons, but no specific botanical name was known for the trees from which they were obtained. About the preparation of the poisons, however, Dalim after repeated requests gave the following account.

In the interior of Borneo, and especially along the slopes of mountains and hills, there grows a tree called batang siren by the natives. Like our oak this tree reaches the age of a hundred years and more. A white milky fluid flows from it when tapped, which is collected in a little bamboo cylinder. On contact with the air, this sap soon loses its color, turns first yellow, then brown and finally black. When it leaves the tree the fluid is perfectly harmless and only acquires its poisonous properties after evaporation and admixture with other plants. The sap having been properly treated and thickened is poured into a stone jar while warm; upon cooling it soon coagulates. The Dayaks always carry this jar with them fastened to the waistband from which their mandauws depend. When required for use it is again heated in order to liquefy it. The points of their arrows are then dipped in it and speedily become covered with a thin layer of gum which dries immediately.

The first symptom shown by the wounded is a copious vomiting. This is followed by paralysis of the limbs, which continues for about ten minutes, when death ensues amid violent convulsions.

The ipoh is prepared in a similar manner, but that poison is taken from a creeper. The only difference between the effects of the ipoh and siren poisons is that the former is not attended by vomiting.

Every Dayak knows how to prepare both these poisons, but as the plants and the accessory ingredients are chiefly found in the mountainous districts, the inhabitants of the upper countries are more expert in their preparation than the natives of the coast.

About midday our travellers approached the soengei Moeroi. When trying to row past it they saw a raft coming down this broad soengei. It carried three men, who were employing all their strength in the effort to stop the course of their unmanageable craft. One of them called for assistance, and as according to the custom of the country a refusal was not to be dreamed of, Dalim steered his boat toward the raft and was soon moored alongside of it.

It was being rapidly carried away by the strong tide; therefore the first thing to be done was to make for the shore and to moor it there. Our adventurers soon produced their rattan cables, as well as the anchor chains which they had taken with them from soengei Naning. Having joined these firmly together, they fastened one end to a kind of capstan on the raft while the other end was carried ashore in a djoekoeng and tied around the trunk of a strong tree. The raft was still drifting onward with the current when the cable being drawn taut, its progress was suddenly arrested. The result was a violent shock which pitched Schlickeisen and La Cueille headlong into the river; but they were soon rescued by Dalim and some of his new friends.

The cable stood the shock admirably; it remained stretched like a cord, though the raft trembled under the pressure of the tide. Presently the unwieldy structure swung around toward the shore, when they managed by the aid of the capstan to bring it gradually nearer the tree, to which it was eventually fastened by the cable.

Our travellers now learned that the owner of the raft, a native of Kwala Kapoeas named Bapa Andong, had been collecting forest products in soengei Moeroi and had been very successful. He now was on his way to Lake Ampang, where he had various kinds of produce safely stored; but being short-handed he was unable to take his raft there against the tide. He now addressed himself to Johannes, whom he regarded as the leader of the party, and proposed that they should all help him in the navigation of his unwieldy craft. His son, with six hirelings, was awaiting his arrival at the lake, and he felt anxious about their safety. It was at length settled that our travellers should assist in taking the raft to the lake and in embarking all the goods there stored; that they should then bring the raft back again into the Kapoeas stream, after which their further assistance would be unnecessary.

Before concluding these arrangements the bargain was struck that when they should separate the two hirelings should be transferred to the canoes of our adventurers.

This contract concluded, work commenced. The raft being fastened by a second rope, the cable was loosened from the tree and carried by a djoekoeng up the stream as far as it would reach, when it was attached to another tree. The capstan was again manned and the raft thus worked further up stream against the tide. This manœuvre was repeated again and again with success. One can imagine the difficulty of the task, especially to the Europeans, who were quite unused to that kind of work; but it gave them a clear insight into the activity of the people among whom they found themselves, and exhibited the fertility of resource possessed by the children of nature.

The raft on which they now stood consisted of two hundred logs of timber of excellent quality tied firmly together by rattan cables. A floor was laid over these logs and in the centre of the raft a roomy hut was constructed. Under a roof extending from the sides of this hut the products were safely housed. The raft carried nearly four thousand trusses of rattan, a couple of thousand gantangs of rosin, a hundred pikols of bees-wax, twenty pikols of India rubber and a small parcel of birds' nests. The last two Bapa Andong had exchanged for bees-wax with some traders from the upper country. The other goods were the products of his own labor. The rattan had been cut in the surrounding soengeis, the rosin was partly gathered from the trees and partly collected along the banks of the river.

It was quite evening when the raft shot the last projection and the entrance of the channel which forms the junction between the lake and the river became visible. The crew was exhausted with fatigue, rest was accordingly absolutely necessary. As there was no earthly possibility of steering the raft through the narrow canal in the darkness they moored it to the shore, after which part of the crew landed to clear the ground for some distance, so as to command an unobstructed view of the surrounding country. The shrubs and trees thus cut down were formed into a kind of entrenchment at the edge of the clearing to prevent the possibility of a surprise. They further divided their men into two watches, who would alternately take duty and keep a lookout, Johannes taking care that he and La Cueille should remain with one party while the two Swiss would join the other division.

As soon as daylight appeared our travellers resumed their labors, and after an hour's hard toil the raft was steered into the channel. The sun had nearly risen above the horizon when they had their craft safely moored against the landing-stage to receive the rest of its cargo. The lading was executed so rapidly that by the afternoon everything was ready on board for the resumption of their journey.

But a considerable task had yet to be accomplished. Since Bapa Andong had originally begun collecting his forest products, a work which had occupied him about six months, hundreds of swarms of bees had made their nests in the trees growing on the western bank of the lake. The trees chosen by these little insects are high, with straight and smooth trunks and far spreading branches. The Dayaks call these wood-giants "tanggirang," and in favorable seasons from two to three hundred bees' nests may be found in a single tree. From the moment Bapa Andong first observed these industrious insects commencing their labor he had begun to make his preparations for collecting their produce at the proper time. He had daily driven spikes of hard wood into each tree at a distance of about a foot and a half, until these primitive ladders reached the lower branches. The task took him a long time to complete, but it could not be hastened as the continuous hammering at the spikes would undoubtedly have disturbed the bees and rendered an attack from them certain.

His hirelings now cleared the ground around the trees of every shrub and weed; and all being ready for action they awaited a favorable opportunity to commence operations. This soon came.

It was a boisterous night and the wind blew as if determined to uproot every tree; the sky was covered with thick clouds and the darkness was so great that everything seemed as if enveloped in black. They were now seventeen men in all, including Bapa Andong's son and the six hirelings found on the borders of the lake. By means of the canoe belonging to our adventurers and of the two additional djoekoengs, they crossed the foaming waters of the lake to the other side where the bee trees stood. Arrived there they stepped ashore and spread large linen sheets on four posts in such a manner that the corners being raised up they formed monster sacks. When these were ready they set fire to some previously prepared torches of green resinous wood, of which each Dayak took one and rapidly mounted the ladders. Only one man climbed each tree, while Bapa Andong with the four Europeans kept watch in the dark beneath rifles in hand.

The hirelings mounted rapidly and began to beat the numerous nests. The bees, as if determined to drown the noise of the raging storm, came out buzzing loudly to attack the intruders, but blinded by the light of the torches and suffocated by the smoke they were driven rapidly away by the violent storm and fell by hundreds of thousands on the other side of the lake. As soon as the swarms had disappeared the men, armed with bamboo knives, eagerly commenced to free the nests from the branches and to drop them into the sacks beneath. All this took but little time to accomplish and the men had already descended ere the Europeans recovered from their astonishment. The sight of those naked brown figures with flowing locks rapidly mounting the trees under the faint glimmer of their torches, their bodies bending over the branches high up in the air, the torches moving to and fro and enveloping everything in a dark smoke; the noise of the storm and the hum of the millions of bees—all these seemed so surprising, so weird, that they could fancy themselves to be dreaming but for the numerous nests dripping with honey which lay at their feet.

"They are brave fellows!" La Cueille burst forth.

"With quickness and dexterity, combined with cool calculation," remarked Schlickeisen, "not a single accident has happened to mar the undertaking."

The bees' nests were speedily stored away in the boat and the whole expedition returned long before midnight.

After all the nests had been placed upon a stage to drip, the night-watch was re-established as on the previous evening and half of the crew retired to rest.

Rest, however, seems a strange fiction in the Dayak countries. Certainly the first hours passed undisturbed, but the woodcock, which the natives call takakak from its note, had hardly sounded its morning cry about three o'clock when young Andong fancied he heard a slight noise from the side of the wood. He remained at his post as immovable as a monument, listened and signalled to his mates without making any audible sound. They all pricked up their ears and listened likewise. A movement was heard like creeping bodies trying to force a passage through the protecting wood-work and shrubs. Fortunately the storm had abated, or the suspicious sounds would not have been heard. The sleeping party was awakened with the least possible noise and preparations were made for a fight. The Europeans kept close together, having their firearms near at hand. But as these seemed almost useless in the intense darkness they, like the Dayaks whom they were impersonating, took each a strong mandauw, intending to make good use of it.

Bapa Andong, however, whispered something to Johannes which was answered with a smile and a nod; and as soon as the nature of this communication was imparted to the others the entire party prepared for action. The two Swiss took up their Remington rifles and La Cueille and Johannes their breech-loaders, while each of them was additionally provided with a revolver and the two remaining rifles were loaded for use in case of emergency.

Everything being now arranged the defenders waited with beating hearts. Nothing could be distinguished in the black darkness of the night; all they heard was a shuffling noise or the snapping of small twigs. Suddenly however about twenty figures rose as from the lake itself and jumped upon the raft, shouting their usual war cry, "Lēēēēh lèlèlèlè ouiiiit!"

The occupants of the raft knew that they were outnumbered and if their stratagem failed a fight for life or death would be unavoidable, probably resulting in their annihilation. It was a demoniacal scene to see those wild Indians leap to and fro crouched behind their shields with mandauw in hand and to hear them loudly challenging their adversaries, from whom however not a sound proceeded. This silence seemed to baffle the assailants.

Suddenly a few figures were seen to appear in the dark at the end of the raft upon which the defenders were located. These leaped into the midst of the assailants, dealt a few smart blows among them and then as quietly disappeared. The enemy again shouted their war cry, banded themselves closer together and covered by their shields ran along the planks which communicated with the raft. A couple of figures presented themselves as if they wished to dispute their passage, but these also disappeared rapidly; when suddenly a brightly burning flame ascended from the top of the heap of rattan trusses stored in the centre of the raft and at the same moment a heavy rifle fire was opened upon the now visible assailants. Wienersdorf and Schlickeisen fired their Remingtons lustily against the enemy, who had crept almost against the muzzles of their guns. La Cueille and Johannes forming the second file first discharged their rifles and then followed up with the fire of their revolvers, while it almost rained mandauw blows from the heap of rattan. It is impossible to describe the consternation amongst the enemy caused by this sudden and strong illumination and the subsequent destructive firing, very few bullets of which missed their aim. An undulating movement was observed, first backwards, then forwards; cries of rage and pain intermixed proceeded from every direction; it seemed as if the furies themselves had broken loose. At length the small number remaining divided themselves into two parties, the larger one of which took to flight, leaped ashore and disappeared in the obscurity, while the other, jumping across their own slain, made a last and desperate effort in a hand to hand fight. Shots fell uninterruptedly; the brave little band became smaller and smaller until the last remaining two of them threw themselves on the floor and by creeping along endeavored to reach their opponents with their naked mandauws. One of them was almost immediately staked to the floor of the raft by Schlickeisen. The other creeping cautiously forward raised himself and lifted his mandauw to deal a fatal blow at Wienersdorf who, seeing no chance of averting the stroke, suddenly dropped his rifle and grasped the wrists of his adversary so tightly as to compel him to relinquish his weapon. A terrible struggle now took place between the two men, who knew that the life of one of them was at stake. A few inches only separated them from the water. They were struggling breast to breast with such rapidity of movement that any interference from the others must have endangered the one as much as the other. At last the strength of the less muscular Dayak became exhausted. Wienersdorf noticing this kicked the fallen mandauw into the lake, and making a last violent effort lifted both arms of his enemy and bending them forcibly backwards compelled the panting Dayak to sink upon his knees before him.

"Blako ampoen!" I beg for mercy! cried the native.

The Swiss hearing these words uttered in a soft and imploring voice released his enemy and offered him his hand, which the native still on his knees hesitated to take. His chest heaved violently and his eyes shone like fire. At last he leaped to his feet, took the offered hand, placed it on his head and bent his proud neck as a token of submission. While doing this he gave utterance to some words which were not understood by any of his hearers.

The son of the forest remained standing thus for a few moments. He then suddenly lifted his head, took his knife, made a slight wound in the flesh of his arm, collected the flowing blood in the palm of his hand and smeared some of it upon the forehead and lips of Wienersdorf, who stood looking on as if paralyzed. He then slightly wounded the Swiss, collected his blood also and rubbed it over his own forehead and lips, after which he swallowed the remaining drops. He again took the hand of the conqueror, pressed it fervently and brought it to his lips, plainly uttering the words "Harimaoung Boekit," tiger of the mountains. Then before any one had time to prevent him he leaped into the lake, the dark water of which closed above his head.

Just at that moment, as if nature desired to contribute to the escape of the savage, a wind squall suddenly extinguished the burning flame and enveloped the occupants of the raft in total darkness.

CHAPTER VIII.

THE RESULTS OF THE FIGHT—DAMBOENG PAPOENDEH'S EXPEDITION—THE MAROETAS—BACK AGAIN TO THE KAPOEAS—NIGHT FIRING—THE BEES TO THE RESCUE—ASSISTANCE IN PERIL—THE SEPARATION—CIVILIZATION AND BARBARISM.

"I AM not sure," La Cueille said, "that it was wise in us to let that man escape."

This sentence uttered the first thing in the morning was really the continuation of the conversation held after the escape of the head-hunter.

"Morte la bête, mort le venin," was the opinion of the Walloon, given in his own language for want of knowledge of its Arabic equivalent.

When it was quite daylight the occupants of the raft counted the bodies of their assailants who had fallen under the fire of the Europeans. There were fourteen, including the one pierced by the knife of Schlickeisen. Their weapons and suits of mail became the spoils of the victors; the bodies, under pressure of necessity, were let down into the waters of the lake.

"An offering to Djata," Dalim grinned.

When this funeral was finished and mutual congratulations had been exchanged, the attention of our adventurers was drawn to three canoes visible at the junction of the canal and the river.

They were terribly alarmed when they observed the Dutch flag displayed from the stern of the first two canoes. It was certain that they were being followed and that their experience of the past was only child's play compared with what they might now expect. Breathless with alarm and anxiety they waited for further revelations.

Bapa Andong, not being able to explain the emotion of his companions, instead of seeing danger, saw certain help from those canoes in the event of the reappearance of the Poenans. He therefore, assisted by his son, cried out lustily three times, "Come this way, quick! ahoy!"

The reader will certainly have divined who had brought those canoes into the lake. It was Damboeng Papoendeh, whom he saw depart from Kwala Kapoeas and who now appeared on the scene. The young chief in his intense eagerness had set out for soengei Mantangei, and had employed the utmost expedition in his pursuit of the deserters. There he had heard of the struggle with the snake and the subsequent firing at the male inhabitants and became convinced that the fugitives had sailed up the Mantangei in order to reach the Doesson.

Although inclined at first to disbelieve this statement, the people were so positive and circumstantial that he could not doubt further. He therefore resolved to sail for the same destination.

After travelling on the Mantangei for a whole day he arrived at a small kampong called Takisan. Here he was obliged to stop in consequence of the place being under the ban of the maroetas.

Maroetas means unclean, and a house, a village, or even a whole district may be proscribed and pronounced unclean in consequence of being the scene of death, infectious disease or any contaminating influence. When a house has become maroetas it is simply closed and the ladder removed from it. Its inhabitants dare not leave it nor may they receive visitors. If a village or district has become maroetas all its roads and pathways are blocked and may not be opened under penalty of death.

Thus it happened that Damboeng Papoendeh found the soengei Mantangei closed by a double rattan cable, the ends of which were guarded on shore by armed men. He knew that force would be useless here, so he at once gave orders for the route to be reversed, his canoes were turned around and the backward journey commenced with the utmost speed. In order to make up for lost time they rowed onwards night and day without intermission, until they arrived in the neighborhood of lake Ampang. Here they rested, wholly unconscious of their proximity to the objects of their pursuit.

The wind was blowing hard from the north-west and considerably impeded and endangered their journey; Damboeng Papoendeh was therefore obliged to give way to the remonstrances of his men and consent to pass the rest of the night moored in one of the creeks. After this repose he intended to proceed to kotta Baroe with all possible despatch to seek news of the fugitives. His plan was to row past them and by lying in ambush further on capture them easily, with the assistance of the natives. The plan seemed very feasible and its simplicity might have given him every chance of success, but for an accident which intervened and upset all his calculations.

It might have been about three in the morning when suddenly

a piercing lēēēh lèlèlèlèlè ouiiiit was heard very close by, coming from a westerly direction. This was followed by a sharp rifle fire. Damboeng now knew that the men he was seeking were near and fighting either with the inhabitants of the kampong, as had been the case at soengei Mantangei, or with head-hunters, who might be expected to infest this locality.

The night was passed in intense impatience, and as soon as daylight appeared he perceived the mouth of the canal leading to the lake. He was now positive that the drama played on the preceding night must have taken place there and he did not lose a moment in speeding in that direction.

Nothing remarkable or suspicious was found in the channel; but upon arriving at the lake they saw far away on the eastern shore a large raft covered by rattan trusses, whose occupants seemed to invite them to approach, their cry being distinctly audible.

Damboeng ordered one of his canoes to remain behind to guard the mouth of the channel, with strict injunctions to suffer nothing to pass. He then sailed with the other two canoes along the western bank of the lake in order to examine every angle and creek while making this circuitous progress towards the raft on the eastern shore.

Bapa Andong, foreseeing the danger of this manœuvre, wished to signal the canoes to return; but Dalim imperatively closed his mouth and whispered something into his ear, giving him at the same time a taste of a small dagger between his ribs. The Dayak looked frightened at his compatriot; he observed how Dalim's companions, rifle or mandauw in hand, surrounded him with anxious faces while his own mates remained almost indifferent to the scene. He could not understand it at all, but it became evident to him that for the present he had better remain silent.

The two canoes on the other side still kept close to the western bank. Suddenly a fearful cry came forth from both vessels and their occupants were seen to throw up their arms and wave them about desperately. Some of them jumped into the lake and tried to save themselves by swimming as fast as they could, diving repeatedly and crying out, "badjanji! badjanji!" the bees, the bees.

They had been furiously attacked by the insects whose nests had been so mercilessly robbed the night before. Stifled by the smoke and carried onward by the storm the bees had fallen to the ground stupefied. On the following morning they had returned to their old haunts in search of the nests whence they had been so rudely driven, and finding them all removed became infuriated. This is always the case; for several days after the ingathering of these harvests of wax and honey, it is extremely dangerous to approach the trees where the nests formerly hung, and of this fact Damboeng Papoendeh and his followers now received forcible confirmation. They had innocently approached the spot when suddenly clouds of bees swarmed down upon them and furiously attacked them with their envenomed stings.

The Europeans on the raft looked on in speechless astonishment at the panic which seemed to have overtaken the occupants of the advancing canoes, but by reason of the distance had not the slightest idea of what had happened. When, however, they saw Dalim jump with delight and heard what kind of enemies had attacked their pursuers a selfish sensation of gratitude took possession of them. They could not help rejoicing at the denouement which had thus prevented a sanguinary encounter. When, however, they began to realize the danger to which their pursuers were exposed their hearts melted and they felt almost ashamed at idly looking on while their fellow-creatures were in their death struggles. Already the two Swiss had sprung into a djoekoeng to assist the unfortunates, in whom they no longer beheld enemies but suffering brethren. The Dayak, however, conjured them to remain where they were unless they wished to rush into certain death. The wisdom of this counsel soon became manifest, for the wild hordes of bees, not satisfied with their primary revenge on the occupants of the canoes, began to disperse about the lake and to assail every living thing they encountered.

Wienersdorf and Schlickeisen had already received some painful stings on their hands and faces which sent them flying back to the raft. Any assistance to the sufferers was consequently out of the question. They, themselves, in order to escape further attacks were compelled to light fires and envelope themselves in dense smoke.

Nothing further was heard from aboard the two canoes which, carried on by the current of the lake, quietly drifted towards the mouth of the channel beyond the reach of the revengeful insects. As soon as Dalim and Bapa Andong perceived that the fury of the bees was abated and that they were flying back to the tree, they resolved to approach the drifting boats in order to learn what could be gathered from their appearance and appointment. Johannes, Wienersdorf, and the three hirelings accompanied them. These last carried an abundance of green branches wherewith to kindle a fire in the event of its becoming necessary to protect themselves with smoke.

The spectacle presented when they approached the canoes was heartrending. Four of the occupants were found struggling in the last agonies of death and exhibiting strong symptoms of delirium; while the others had their arms, hands, faces, nay, every part of their body which had been exposed to the fury of the bees, swollen to such a degree as to render their aspect quite unlike that of human beings. All were senseless from the intense pain caused by the innumerable poisonous stings.

In order to be safe from a renewed attack the boats were taken into mid-channel. When safely there they all, and especially the two Europeans, set to work to render assistance. They gave the sufferers water to drink, rubbed their swollen faces and limbs with cocoanut oil and used every effort to lessen their agony. While they were thus occupied, the boat which had been left behind by Damboeng Papoendeh to guard the canal came to the aid of their fellow voyagers. Medical assistance seemed to be the first necessity. To secure this the return journey was immediately decided upon. The twelve occupants of the sentinel canoe were divided among the three boats and the flotilla started homewards.

Dalim proposed to accompany them as far as the Kapoeas, thus assisting them through the intricate navigation of the canal. Ere the outlet was reached four of the sufferers died and the condition of the three others, including Damboeng Papoendeh, had become extremely dangerous. Dalim therefore strongly advised the natives to row with all despatch to the nearest kampong, where they would be sure to obtain further assistance.

Before parting, Wienersdorf attended once more to the wounded and supplied them each with a cocoanut shell filled with water to quench their burning thirst. Johannes in the meantime took possession of the Dutch flags carried by the two largest boats, protesting that he should make excellent use of them. He also secured the written instructions entrusted to Damboeng Papoendeh. These he found, with the official seal duly attached, safely stowed away in a bamboo box under the cushion of the chief. The boats were then left to the current and rapidly disappeared.

The first thing to be done after their departure was to bring the raft, which now carried its full cargo, from the lake into the river. This done they shook hands cordially and the clumsy craft, separated from its moorings, soon drifted away, carried along by the swift current. Our adventurers then took to their own boat, planting one of the Dutch flags on it, sent a lusty hurrah after the raft, dipped their oars in the water and soon disappeared from the view of the friends whose labors and troubles they had so bravely shared.

Johannes now reminded his comrades that since their track had become known everything depended upon speed. They owed their present deliverance to the merest accident, a second one might not perhaps occur so opportunely. He calculated that they would have an advantage of five days, in which they might with a little more exertion cover a large distance and perhaps get beyond the reach of the Dutch. They therefore resolved to keep to the oars days and night.

The boat with which the Chinaman Baba Poetjieng had furnished the deserters was a splendid vessel. It was slenderly built and had a sharp bow which enabled it to glide smoothly and easily over the water.

"Thank goodness! that is over," La Cueille said, when they were resting in the afternoon during the preparation of their dinner. "Events follow each other rapidly I must say. The day before yesterday we had one dance and last night another similar entertainment. It seems to me that all the head-hunters of Borneo are following us."

"Nonsense," Johannes replied. "Those of last night were the same ones that attacked us before. Do you imagine that they ever lost sight of us? Not a bit of it."

"But who invented the stratagem of enticing them into that narrow passage, and whence came that light so suddenly? It seemed almost like a miracle."

"For all this you may offer a prayer on behalf of Bapa Andong," Johannes answered. "He had pounded a large quantity of rosin during the day and spread it on a sieve of rattan above a layer of oil contained in a plate. This he kept in readiness to light up with a little flame which I contributed in the shape of a box of matches."

"But oh!" Wiernersdorf cried, "what a destruction of human lives! This is a dreadful journey and who knows when and how it will end yet!"

"Pray don't let us dwell upon that subject just now," said Johannes. "We are in the boat and must sail with her."

Schlickeisen now tried to give the conversation a different turn. "What a beautiful lake that seemed," said he, "into which we guided the raft. I felt enraptured at the first view. That smooth, unrippled surface, reflecting the surrounding landscape and the sky above it so pure and blue; those curves and creeks which appeared almost lost beneath the dark verdure of the virgin woods; those capes and promontories which seemed longing to meet in the transparent fluid; and though last, not least, that wild forest, like a frame around a mirror, with its fantastic creepers and winding plants, the wood-giants defining their dark yet shining foliage against that lovely sky and intermingling with wonderful orchids and beautiful flowers—all these presented such a charming picture that I almost remained spellbound for the moment."

Wienersdorf, who had been seated, lost in meditation, seemed greatly attracted by this description. He gradually lifted his head, looked at the speaker and listened attentively. He appeared to have taken leave of his melancholy thoughts and his face reflected the truth of the words spoken by his companion.

"Oh, yes! that lake was indeed lovely," he said, when the other had ceased speaking. "Especially lovely in its solitude. Everything shone and glittered under the rays of the tropical sun like diamonds just escaped from the hands of the Creator."

"Ha! ha! ha!" laughed Johannes.

"What are you laughing at?" Wienersdorf asked, somewhat vexed.

"Continue, continue!" Johannes said, still laughing. "Pray don't allow your poetical strains to be disturbed by prosaical me. I like to listen to you."

"I felt exalted," Wienersdorf continued, "especially as those shores are not poisoned by the smoke of factories; no steamboats ruffle the smooth surface of the lake; no steam-whistle breaks the calm and holy silence of its banks, and no human crowd pursuing gain and practising usury. One felt there alone, alone under the eye of God."

"All very fine! and I wish I could speak like that," Johannes interrupted sharply. "How blind man becomes when he is indulging in poetical rhapsody, or rather how differently he views things from what they really are. True, we have neither seen the smoke of factories nor heard the whistle of flying locomotives or steamboats on the lake; no industrious manufacturers are there pushing their way amid restless merchants; but those are subjects more for lamentation than for rapture. Instead of them, what did we find? In place of the dense smoke of factories we saw the spiral wreaths of wood fires, at which the murderer was roasting the captured heads of human beings in order to remove their flesh. Instead of a steam-whistle we heard the war cry of those fiends as they sprang upon their sleeping prey, that cry which serves as a warning of death, from which the attacked can only escape by becoming a murderer himself. And you dare compare all this to a diamond just escaped from the hands of the Creator and say that you felt yourself as if in the presence of God? Is that all the glory you give the Almighty? What about the savages who came against us with their naked sword? What about the Dayaks who surrounded us on the raft? Were they not human beings? Alone, and alone with God! No, we were undoubtedly brought into contact with men, and men of the lowest type. Some of them brutes, eager for murder; men who delight in the sound of the death-rattle and the gurgling of blood."

"Stop, stop!" interrupted Wienersdorf. "I don't wish to defend head-hunting. I fully endorse your abhorrence of it. But the other Dayaks whom we have seen are surely men who do their share in the labor of life. Those people are content with an existence passed, for months together, in a wilderness where they toil to rob the forest of its treasures—men like Bapa Andong."

"Bapa Andong and his class have their faults, as I could show you," said Johannes; "but even they are an exception to the general rule. You will find few rich Dayaks, and this fact, considered with the abundant resources of their forests, will serve to prove what a poor, improvident race they are. Look at their dwellings; they are the most miserable hovels on earth; notice their dress which, when a Dayak is in full costume, consists only of dirty and miserable rags mostly woven from bark and scarcely different from the skin which an animal has for its sole covering. You will have ample opportunities of seeing this in the upper countries."

"What you tell me is very deplorable," Wienersdorf remarked somewhat bitterly. "Man is almost a curse to this beautiful island."

"On the contrary, the country is the curse of man," Schlickeisen answered vehemently. "The country is too rich, it yields its treasures without compelling man to fixed labor. He has only to stoop to pick them up. This makes him lazy; and laziness, as you know, is the root of all evil."

This was touching the wound which gnaws at the existence of human beings in this, the loveliest, richest and largest of Holland's possessions. During all the years that the Dutch have held Borneo and have jealously tried to keep other nations away from it, they have done nothing whatever to stimulate the population into activity.

In the meantime dinner being concluded and the hour for rest gone by, the men resumed their oars with renewed energy and the journey was continued.

CHAPTER IX.

SOLITUDE—KWALA HIANG—THE ATTACK—RIFLE AND CANNON FIRE—THE GARRISON TAKES FLIGHT—THE PILLAGE—AN ILLUMINATION—THE COMMANDER OF KWALA KAPOEAS IN PURSUIT—HIS SEARCH AT SOENGEI NANING AND SOENGEI MANTANGEI—HIS ARRIVAL AT KWALA HIANG—THE PURSUIT CONTINUED—A GIGANTIC MAP—KOTTA BAROE—OUR TRAVELLERS AGAIN ON THE WAY—THE LEGEND OF THE ELEPHANT—POENANS! POENANS!

THREE days and two nights passed without any incident. It seemed as if the island had been depopulated. Not a single human being had they encountered during all this time, not a boat had been noticed, not even a cloud of smoke to indicate the presence of a hut in which some native was struggling for bare life. Now and then a troop of monkeys emerged from the borders of the forest, to disappear again immediately amidst the green foliage, uttering cries of terror and making the most horrid grimaces. Occasionally, too, a large fish disturbed the smoothness of the water and rose to view. These were all they saw to assure them that animal life had not fled from Borneo.

They had rowed on without stopping. The canoe steered by Dalim had passed through several cut-offs, and by thus avoiding many curves of the river had made considerable headway. The third night was half spent when the travellers approached Kwala Hiang.

This fort had been built at the mouth of the Hiang by order of the Dutch government, to prevent marauding expeditions into the Kapoeas country. It was armed with four small cannon and garrisoned by fifty Dayaks of Kwala Kapoeas.

Dalim had repeatedly conversed in whispers with Johannes in reference to the danger which was to be apprehended at this place. It was doubtless quite impossible that the garrison could be already informed of the escape of the four European soldiers. Yet they all knew that Dalim and his Dayak companions were under police supervision. Everybody at Kwala Hiang would recognize them; and if so discovered, the chief, Tomonggong Patti Singa Djaja, would certainly arrest them and send them back to Kwala Kapoeas. To avoid the fort and thus elude discovery was also impracticable, as no cut-off existed at this part of the river by which they might diverge and reach the stream at some point further up.

Johannes was lost in meditation. At last he proposed to make for Kwala Hiang during the night at as late an hour as possible. The Dayak garrison would then be sound asleep and the canoes might probably succeed in passing unobserved.

This resolution was adopted; but to prepare for emergencies, Johannes and La Cueille occupied themselves in attaching the two small cannon taken from soengei Naning to a couple of solid pieces of wood, their muzzles pointing landwards. They were both charged with blank cartridges.

It was intensely dark when they reached the fortifications.

The oars were carefully and almost noiselessly handled. Dalim steered the canoe close to the covered bank on which the fort was situated. They proceeded slowly and had nearly reached the borders of the wood when suddenly a voice was heard, crying,

"Hullo, what do these people want here?" and before any answer could be given a shot was fired which went through the roofing of the canoe.

The die was cast.

"They are firing on the Dutch!" Johannes cried out loudly in the Dayak language. "This kotta is now occupied by insurrectionists! Forward, attack these marauders! Fire, fire into them!"

La Cueille, at his command, fired both guns which, without doing any harm, illuminated the dark night with a long ray of light and sounded like thunder as the reverberations echoed among the thickly-studded banks. Johannes and Dalim, having four rifles at their disposal, discharged them in the direction of the fortification and almost immediately reloaded them. The two Swiss opened a smart fire with their repeating rifles, which inspired the Dayaks with the belief that a considerable force, ten times stronger than it really was, had entered into action.

Our adventurers kept up the firing with vigor until about a hundred charges had been spent, when Johannes gave the order to cease. Not a sound was heard. The Dayak garrison had been aroused from their sleep by the firing, but these gentry are never remarkable for bravery when exposed to fire-arms. So instead of seeking their own weapons they had become panic-stricken and had fled through the gate in the rear of the fortification, whence they escaped into the forest. So hurried was the departure of these courageous defenders that several of them nearly broke their necks in descending the ladder leading to the exterior, their flight being hastened by hearing Johannes issue his commands in Dutch. This made them imagine that they were attacked by Dutchmen; a fear confirmed by the sentries, who positively declared that they had seen the Dutch flag flying in the foremost canoe.

Perfect silence reigned in the fortification. A few cries of terror only were heard from the forest in the distance. La Cueille now charged both guns with a handful of rifle bullets and discharged them in the direction whence the sounds came. The bullets flew whistling through the forest and lent wings to the retreating fugitives.

Johannes then stepped on shore while the others sat ready, rifle in hand, to cover the retreat of their friend. He soon returned to inform them that the fortification was empty. With the exception of two Dayaks left behind to guard the boat the whole party now leaped ashore. The Europeans immediately closed and barred the gate at the back of the fortification. Three of them kept a sharp lookout so as to prevent a possible return of the garrison; while Johannes, accompanied by Dalim and the others, made a thorough survey of the place. They confiscated the cartridges and powder which they found, and assisted by their hirelings carried them to the canoe. They also took possession of the four small guns and forty rifles which formed the armament of the garrison.

After the fortification had been thoroughly examined and a

few more trifles had been seized, including some baskets of tobacco, Johannes took a piece of burning wood and thrust it among a heap of fagots stowed away under a shed. In a short time the fire spread and our adventurers had to make all haste in order to reach their boat and convey it out of danger into the middle of the stream. A few djoekoengs belonging to the fort, which they found moored in a neighboring creek, were incontinently scuttled and sunk. They then resumed their journey, leaving the fortification burning fiercely, the flames illuminating the stream and converting night into day.

"Aha!" Johannes said cheerfully, "this is an illumination in honor of our escape."

"But is not that illumination an act of folly?" Wienersdorf asked. "Was this attack upon the garrison necessary? I think we could have passed on without hindrance or molestation, and that incendiarism might have been avoided."

"Incendiarism!" Johannes said angrily. "You express yourself rather strongly! No, it was impossible to avoid it; the point of concentration of these people had to be removed and they themselves compelled to fly. No, I adhere to my assertion that under the circumstances the capture of this fortification and its destruction were comparatively necessary."

Although Johannes spoke with earnest conviction, he could not know that this raid would have another and more direct influence upon their escape. He only realized the immediate results of his calculations; but at that very moment another danger greater than the one just overcome was preparing for them.

Our readers will remember that on the day after the departure of Damboeng Papoendeh, the commander at Kwala Kapoeas ordered the chief of the district to be ready with fifty armed Dayaks to accompany him on an expedition to the upper Kapoeas.

The state canoe belonging to the fort, a handsome, fleet and roomy vessel, was made ready and provisioned; and at the appointed hour the Colonel set out. His parting instructions to the doctor urged the necessity of being always on the alert, and of keeping him continually informed of every important event occurring during his absence.

His first visit was to soengei Naning, but he failed to obtain any trustworthy information. At the approach of the handsome kaloeloes, as the state barge is called in the Dayak tongue, carrying the Dutch flag on its bow and manned by a large number of oarsmen, Ali Bahar flew to the wilderness. His wife was duly interviewed, but she was so terrified at this visit that all the kind and conciliating language addressed to her by Tomonggong Nikodemus Djaja Nagara failed to elicit any important information. She, however, persisted in declaring that no whitefaces had been seen by her.

An attempt was then made to hunt up Ali Bahar in the wilderness, but this proving unsuccessful the Colonel resolved to continue his journey.

At soengei Mantangei the reports gained were just as unsatisfactory. The natives knew nothing and could tell nothing beyond describing the visits which had been made there. At last, after long deliberation, it was resolved to row up the

Kapoeas as far as Kwala Hiang, to seek information there, and afterward, assisted by part of the garrison of that fort, to take such further measures as might be found advisable.

"You will see, sir," the old Tomonggong said, "that we shall do best by going there. The fugitives would not possibly endeavor to escape by the Doesson, where their lives would not be safe for a moment."

"I sincerely hope you are right," the Colonel replied, "for I am heartily tired of this groping in the dark."

The journey was then continued and presently the first important information was gained. Damboeng Papoendeh's canoe was met, but the sufferers were still in such a critical condition that nothing positive could be learned from them. They told all they knew; that they had heard a heavy rifle fire during the night, which induced them to pay a visit to Lake Ampang. They gave an account of their being attacked by the bees, and finally described the assistance rendered to the sufferers by Bapa Andong and the occupants of the raft. But all this threw very little light upon the subject, as they persistently declared that they had seen no white men. The only part of their narrative which struck both the Tomonggong and the Colonel as being remarkable was the statement that a strongly-built Dayak, after having carefully treated the patients, had taken away the two Dutch flags. Diligent search was made for the written instructions which had been given to Damboeng Papoendeh, but they could not be found, although nobody could positively assert that the document had been stolen.

The Colonel and the Tomonggong looked at each other for a

few minutes. Neither of them could give shape to his thoughts, nor did they seek to interchange their impressions. The Colonel, however, decided to continue the journey as far as Kwala Hiang, feeling convinced that he would obtain further intelligence there.

About one in the morning they sighted the mouth of the soengei Hiang; but nothing was to be seen of the fortification which used to be situated at that opening.

"What has become of the kotta?" the Colonel asked, surprised.

"I was also looking for it," was the Tomonggong's answer. "I cannot understand; it used to be on that spot."

Whilst uttering these words he pointed with his finger in the direction in which he expected to find the fort.

Upon a nearer approach the travellers discovered the charred remains of what had once been the kotta. It was now clearly evident that the benting had been burned down. But was that demolition the result of an accident? or did it mean anything else?

While the Colonel and the district chief were discussing the matter a few shots were fired at them from behind some bushes, the whistling bullets causing a perfect panic among the Dayak occupants of the state barge. The Tomonggong took his hunting rifle, the Colonel his revolvers, and both prepared for action. The rowers, however, without being ordered to do so reversed their oars, so that the boat almost immediately swung around and commenced a hasty retreat. But as everything remained quiet on shore their panic was soon calmed down. Cool as ever, but yet cautious, the old chief stepped ashore alone and unarmed. He raised his voice and shouted aloud to the hidden assailants that there was no danger; no one should receive any injury. His cries remained unanswered for some time, but at length a reply was heard, and after a long interval the chief of the burned kotta issued from the thick foliage. He broke out with the bitterest expressions of hate against the Dutch, called them betrayers, assassins, marauders, etc. No words seemed forcible enough to give expression to his indignation.

The calm Nikodemus let him rave on; but as soon as want of breath compelled him to pause he was made to understand that he had been duped and that no blame rested with the Dutch. The Tomonggong then told him that the commander of Kwala Kapoeas was on board the state barge and would be glad to receive full information of what had occurred at the fort.

The chief thereupon related all that had happened, with a considerable amount of exaggeration. The fortification had been attacked with cannon and rifle fire, and the garrison had fled only after the palisades had been destroyed. The Colonel smiled when the word cannon was mentioned. The deserters were possessed of rifles, but whence could they have procured cannon? Yet all the witnesses brought forward verified the statemen that they had been repeatedly fired upon by large guns, and that after their flight a hailstorm of heavy shot was sent after them which could only have been accomplished by cannon. The Colonel frowned and shrugged his shoulders, not knowing what to believe. He felt certain that he was now on the right track of the deserters, for all confirmed the assertion that their assailants had used the Dutch language in giving commands. How should he act?

Duty and honor, thought he, demanded some effort from him.

He would attempt impossibilities, trusting to some lucky accident for success.

Consulting with the district chief as well as with the Tomonggong, they finally concluded to row as far as kotta Baroe, where they would summon the population to arms. They could at least reckon upon a couple of hundred men. Such a force combined with those they could get here, a few of whom carried rifles, would enable them to make a vigorous attempt at capturing the deserters.

Meanwhile the fugitives had not remained inactive. They knew that danger was at hand. Their object was to reach the upper country, as the further they could get away from the Dutch, the safer they would be. They therefore rowed on vigorously and when daylight appeared in the heavens the rising smoke of the burning fort was no longer discernible.

They landed on one of the numerous sand banks which encircle the projecting angles formed at this part of the river, and while preparations were being made for their meal they refreshed and fortified themselves with a dip in the cool transparent stream.

After this bath and while the rice was cooking the Dayaks seated themselves in a circle to discuss the events of the last few days. They had learned to look with a certain amount of awe on those four men, who, though as brown as they were, and equally simple in their demeanor, yet bore themselves like devils whenever they encountered any difficulties. The fight on board the raft and the assault of the fort had left a deep impression upon the natives. They laughed right heartily when they remembered how their countrymen had fled, and they repeatedly referred to some ludicrous incidents which had characterized that attack.

The Europeans stretched themselves at full length in a little group on the bright white sand, delighted at being able to exercise their limbs again after the cramping confinement of the narrow boat. The recent events furnished them also with food for conversation, but only for a short time.

Their attention was soon diverted by the beauty of their surroundings. The morning light was gilding the skies and the edges of the wood, and gave the river under the reflection of this golden flood the appearance of a stream of liquid gold. The aurora, rising from the east, at first an insignificant stripe of the softest rose color, had gradually covered the whole firmament with a lovely tint, which grew more intense as the god of day approached nearer to the horizon. Nature assumed a calm splendor which, although occurring daily in these regions, is yet so rarely enjoyed by civilized and reflecting beings. Not a breath of air was felt, not a leaf rustled; only the soft murmur of the river was heard, as if offering up an exalted and grateful morning prayer. The vaulted heavens became gradually clad in glittering purple. A moment more and in the midst of this splendor a clearly defined spot was distinguished in the east. This gradually grew larger until it reached the size of a fiery ball and mounted above the horizon—the glorious sun! Not only the tops of the trees were now gilt by its rays; its radiance penetrated between the leaves and branches, dispersing the darkness of the night and diffusing light and life in the most sombre corners of the wood. In glowing colors the sky depicted these wonders of wonders and spoke to man in that impressive language which can only be heard and understood in the midst of a tropical forest.

As the sun rose higher the purple diminished. Its rays gradually bathed everything in a clear white light, while the heavenly vault arrayed itself in the purest azure, the hue of infinite space. Amid the perfect calm which generally accompanies the first hours of the day in tropical climates, there appeared in the blue sky a phenomenon which, though not rare in Borneo, is nevertheless not of daily occurrence. Just above their heads our adventurers saw a band of the minutest feathery clouds, extending from south to north and delineating every curve of the river. It was as if a gigantic map unrolled itself in the heavens, upon which the stream was vividly depicted as if painted on a blue ground; the silver hue increasing in intensity as the purple disappeared. In this reflection the banks of the Kapoeas were distinctly defined; every soengei was indicated, even the lakes and marshes along the banks of the river were plainly visible. The river decreased in width toward the north and increased toward the south, until next to the horizon it reached the border of the forest and became lost in ethereal space. Nothing could be more perfect than this hydrographic drawing, one corner of which might have truly recorded in large characters, "Scale of natural size," while the other corner might have borne the imprint, "Deus sculpsit."

Our travellers were lost in deep admiration. "Gloriously beautiful," Schlickeisen avowed, adding enthusiastically, "The heavens declare the glory of God and the firmament sheweth His handiwork."

"What is the cause of such reflection?" La Cueille asked.

"I'm just considering," Wienersdorf answered, "and will try and explain my opinion respecting its formation. The enormous evaporation to which the mass of water is exposed, on a marshy soil like Borneo and under the influence of a tropical sun, causes more clouds to be formed here than anywhere else on the globe. I imagine that with a very dry and perfectly calm atmosphere these vapors formed above each sheet of water rise perpendicularly, and arrived in higher regions, concentrate into these feathery clouds now seen by us up there. If it is equally calm in those upper regions these clouds will concentrate above the waters from which they have originated and present their exact counterpart."

"Beautifully explained," Schlickeisen remarked, "but one more explanation before I propose a vote of thanks to our comrade. You said that feathery clouds rise after evaporation formed from every sheet of water. Now, as the whole of that part of marshy Borneo in which we now are may be considered as forming a coherent sheet of water, if the formation takes place in the manner described by you, how is it that only the image of one river or stream is given? And why is not the whole firmament covered with a similar network of clouds?"

"So it would be," Wienersdorf replied, "if the evaporation could take place undisturbed above these marshy grounds; or in other words, if what takes place above rivers and lakes could occur everywhere. But the dense foliage of the virgin forest is spread out over these marshes and forms as it were a roof difficult to penetrate. At night radiation takes place, the branches and leaves cool down and the rising mist condenses against them in the same manner as the particles of moisture are deposited against the window of a heated room. See for yourself whether the trees are covered with an abundant dew or not. This dew would have formed the feathery clouds if only allowed to rise. It will evaporate fast enough as soon as the branches and leaves have acquired the same temperature as the surrounding atmosphere. The forest, therefore, in regard to the evaporation, forms a horizontal roof, a plain which is only intersected above the rivers, soengeis, lakes, etc., and allows the evaporated atoms of water to escape during the first hours of the morning. Elsewhere those atoms are held bound down. I trust I have given you a satisfactory explanation. To myself these reasons suffice to explain the origin of the magnificent air-picture which we just now admired, but which has disappeared, dispelled by the south-eastern wind."

"I am perfectly satisfied and delighted with your mode of explanation," Schlickeisen replied.

"I also," said Johannes; "I tender you my sincerest thanks for your clear and interesting lecture; but the rice is ready and, divided into rations by our Dayaks, stands there invitingly spread out on large leaves. We shall presently have time to consume it, but for the present I order every one back to the canoe to resume his oars. No time must be lost in trying to reach kotta Baroe."

The sun was nearly setting when our travellers reached kotta Baroe. Dalim and Johannes went ashore. The inhabitants, who had seen the approach of a canoe under Dutch colors, were full of curiosity. Jóhannes, producing the written orders taken from Damboeng Papoendeh, demanded twenty oarsmen to row the canoe into the upper river. Of course none of them could read the document; as, however, it was provided with the Dutch coat of arms, duly impressed upon red wax, it had some influence. Much greater weight was however exercised by the promised remuneration of a rix-dollar a day and a present of tobacco. The latter was especially irresistible, and when Johannes produced a basketful of the nicotian herb and presented a packet to the chief, all arrangements were speedily made. Loud applause followed. Stalwart fellows fought to be enlisted, and no sooner were they approved of than they brought their little mats and pillows into the canoe, seized the oars, and were ready to commence the journey. Johannes did some good business here. He exchanged two baskets of tobacco for five pikols of rice and a bag of salt. They were now, he thought, fully provisioned for their entire journey, especially as the twenty oarsmen engaged here would be discharged in ten days. The four hirelings of Bapa Andong were entrusted to the chief of the kotta, to be sent back to Kwala Kapoeas at the earliest opportunity. Johannes in one of his liberal moods presented each of them with a rix-dollar in remuneration of their voluntary services and expressed his entire satisfaction with their conduct. All these negotiations were concluded, be it remembered, on behalf of the Dutch Indian Government. The beflagged canoe and the stamped paper were so many proofs that Johannes was an agent of the white men, officially charged to open communication with the Olo Ott, and to report upon their disposition towards the government. The liberal payment of the oarsmen and the presents of tobacco just distributed strengthened the general belief, and the people became impressed with the conviction that they were dealing with representatives of the Dutch Government.

As no coin is current above kotta Baroe, and nothing can be procured in the interior of Borneo except by barter, Johannes exchanged all the money of the travellers for chintz, linen goods and gold dust. This precious metal is found in small quantities in the alluvial sand of the river at other places, but at kotta Baroe it is found in quantities which render the search remunerative, so that gold dust appears here as a regular article of commerce. Johannes, as a functionary of the Dutch Government, was liberally treated and received for fifty-five guilders a thaël of gold of which the value at Bandjermasin is from sixty to seventy guilders.

After a stay of two hours the canoe, impelled by six-and-twenty pairs of oars, shot onward with lightning speed and soon disappeared on its course up the river.

It was now arranged that during the night twenty oarsmen should be continually kept at work while the remaining six should rest for two hours and thus relieve six others who would in their turn enjoy two hours repose. The canoe, with its resources thus husbanded, went on quietly and expeditiously.

The conversation of the Europeans, which never flagged however vigorously they were rowing, now turned upon the fauna of the country they were traversing.

" With the exception of some crocodiles and a few troops of

monkeys climbing the trees like wild boys, we have as yet seen very little of animal life on this island," Schlickeisen remarked. " And yet animals must be strongly represented in a country like this."

" By no means," Johannes answered. "In fact, Borneo is much worse supplied in this respect than any of the larger islands of the Indian Archipelago. We have no rhinoceroses, elephants or tigers, not even a native horse. The island abounds in snakes, the cause of which may be found in its marshy soil. This over-population of snakes is in its turn the cause of the paucity of birds observable in the lower regions, as these reptiles creep up the trees to get at the nests and either suck the eggs or devour the broods."

" It seems curious that this central island of the Indian Archipelago only is totally deprived of its share of animals."

" Totally deprived is not the right expression," Johannes interrupted. "We have not seen very much as yet of the great central island, as Wienersdorf calls it. We shall find that the monkeys are quite as numerous as they are anywhere. We are now in the paradise of the orang-outang, the homo silvarum, which Darwin must certainly have had in view when, advancing his theory of the descent of our forefathers, he paid the monkeys the poor compliment of having us for their progeny. Herds of deer rove about the forests and higher plateau, in quantities and varieties that would give you quite a different opinion and confute your statement that there is a total dearth of the animal kingdom."

" A saddle of venison would not be unwelcome," La Cueille suggested, smacking his lips; "only one single morsel out of all this abundance is, I am sure, not asking too much."

"Have patience, my friend! All in good time. But to return to our subject. Do you not consider this a happy country where on land man has only to fear his fellow man, and in the water that other insatiable monster, the crocodile?"

"But to what may be ascribed this absence of large animals in Borneo, while in other islands they are so abundantly met with?"

"I once read that the series of islands which commence at the gulf of Pegu in Farther India was probably connected with New Guinea. In the course of time, by the agency of convulsions and earthquakes, the various straits were formed which now separate those islands and admit the waters of the Indian Ocean into the Chinese sea. If this theory can be believed it will account for the existence in those islands of so many of the animals which since the creation have been distributed over Hindostan and Farther India."

"That account is all very well for the islands mentioned; but for Borneo the reason remains still a mystery."

"Patience; I have not quite finished yet. At the time when this series of islands was still one continent Borneo did not exist. Its site was occupied by a large sea reaching from what is now Java to the Chinese coast, being bounded on the west by Sumatra, Malacca, and Cochin China, and on the east by Celebes and the Philippian Archipelago."

"Beautifully explained," La Cueille observed; "it stands to reason that neither elephants, rhinoceroses nor tigers were swimming about in this sheet of water."

Johannes looked disdainfully at the Walloon, but not noticing the interruption, continued,

"In the midst of this large basin, sundry small coral reefs raised their flat tops above the surface of the water. By gradual elevation of the base, the stone and clay layer upon which these coral reefs rested gradually appeared above the water. The shape obtained by this rise defined the future range of mountains running from north-east to south-west, with a few lateral spurs branching out from it. Borneo thus acquired its present form, which however it will lose again sooner or later."

"And why?" Schlickeisen asked.

"Because it has not yet arrived at its full formation. Whether this elevation of soil is still going on I cannot say. I leave that for others to determine, and a series of observations will have to be made in order to establish the fact. But the alluvial deposits still continue and it is curious to notice how clearly visible the withdrawal of the sea and the projection of the mainland are at the south coast. The Tjemara forest especially offers a certain measure. Small trees scarcely a couple of inches high are found close to the borders of the sea; the rows behind these are a little higher and this graduation continues until, about one or two hundred yards away from the water, we come to the high woods, where trees of thirty feet high are found. The gradual increase in the height of the trees is hardly noticeable, only that the foliage seen from the sea forms a kind of smooth slope of the purest green."

"All this is certainly cleverly explained," Wienersdorf said, lost in thought. "But on what is the hypothesis of this gradual elevation based? Is it only a theory invented by European savants in their own studies, or is it proved by facts?"

"By positive facts, my dear Swiss! Perhaps we may pass the borders of the chalk formation to-morrow, if we make a little haste. Then,—in the corals which you collect, in the accumulations of broken shells, etc., which you will see, you will find positive proofs that the sea once rolled its waves there. But don't fancy that in the Kapoeas only these breccia of coral and shells are to be found. You find the same formation on the banks of every river running parallel with that stream. The most remarkable coincidence of all is, that if you draw a line along the chalk formations, that undeniable proof of the former existence of a coast, this line will pretty nearly coincide with the course of the central mountain range and serve as it were for its base."

"Is there nothing to be found in the traditions of the country indicating such a condition?" Schlickeisen asked.

"Certainly. Many legends and stories exist among the different Dayak tribes who inhabit the banks of these rivers."

"Do you know whether the absence of the larger carnivora has been noticed by the natives also?" asked Wienersdorf, "and do their traditions throw any light upon the subject?"

"Their traditions, as far as I know, do not mention anything of the kind; perhaps they do not even suspect the presence of those animals in other parts of the globe. And yet a legend is told which, while indicating some notion of large animals, illustrates one of the characteristics of this people, namely, the use of stratagem against violence. The legend goes:

"In the times when animals were still possessed of speech, a huge elephant arrived at the south coast of Borneo from the other side and swam up the Kahajan. The animals residing there saw with astonishment how this monster was making its way up their stream. A large crocodile was sent to enquire into the intentions of the stranger. This crocodile not very diplomatically began to grasp part of the body of the intruder between his teeth and thought to gain an easy victory. The elephant, however, took him up in his powerful trunk, raised him like a ball in the air, and shattered his spine against a floating tree. Enraged by this cowardly attack, the visitor stepped ashore, called to a deer grazing in the vicinity, and commissioned him to declare war against all the animals in Borneo. He sent a couple of tusks by this ambassador in order to convey an adequate impression of the size and strength of the challenging party.

"Although this defiance was rather boastful, the elephant correctly foresaw what would happen. The animals became frightened and were astounded on seeing these colossal teeth; while the fate of the crocodile, described by the deer, did not tend to abate their terror. In the midst of all this consternation, the little porcupine appeared as their saviour. She advised them to send a few of her quills, bidding the stranger compare the hair of his future opponents with his own, and thence form some idea of the size of the teeth of animals which possessed such colossal bristles. The stratagem succeeded perfectly. The elephant, by no means anxious to enter into a contest with such powerful opponents, asked for his teeth to be returned, and swam back as fast as he could to the country whence he had come. Up to the present date, the spot where the pachyderm stepped ashore is called rantau gadjah oendoer, or the bend of the river where the elephant returned."

"By the saints! that was cleverly done," La Cueille observed, "such bristles would make a sapper feel ashamed of his beard, and they truly conveyed the warning, 'qui s'y frotte, s'y pique.'"

"The legend is not bad," Schlickeisen said, "but I do not find what I inquired after. This flight of the elephant I fancy points more to some foreign attack, perhaps of Hindoos, in former times, which was baffled by the cunning of the natives. It does not indicate any knowledge of wild animals like the elephant. It is not unlikely, however, that if the assailants were really Hindoos, they had armed elephants with their army."

"Possibly," Johannes answered phlegmatically, "but I have told you all I know, and I am quite certain that with the exception of a few Cingalese who have here and there settled as traders, nothing Hindoo is found in Borneo."

In conversation of this kind the night passed tranquilly. Our travellers did not care to sleep. When day began to break they commenced to recognize undoubted traces of the presence of man. They had travelled for days together without having seen either human beings or any indication of their presence. Here it was quite different. They often found plantations of maize, sugarcane, etc., and fruit trees, such as cocoanuts, pisangs, doerians, etc., etc., planted along the borders of the primitive forest. Dwellings were observed at various distances and they felt gladdened to see human beings engaged in their various occupations. But the same peculiarity was here observed that had struck them at kotta Towanan and kotta Baroe. Each house in the upper regions was surrounded by heavy palisades and was thus transformed into a kind of fortress. With very little vigilance on the part of the inhabitants, it would be impossible for any foe to enter the enclosure, while only hunger or cowardice could compel the defenders to surrender such a stronghold. This is the result of the terrible passion for collecting human skulls. Everybody defends himself against possible massacre, and only finds security behind strong walls and barricades.

The altered aspect of the country considerably increased the interest of our travellers. In a single night they had arrived as it were at quite a new world. Their first thought was to utilize their opportunity by augmenting their stock of provisions or at least by effecting a change in their fare. They therefore stopped near a garden, presented the watchman with some tobacco, and in return were allowed to gather as many roots and vegetables and as much maize as they liked. They had also some cocoanuts and other fruit given to them. The watchman further told them that a band of Poenans had been in the neighborhood during the last few days and advised them to be cautious. Again the old warning, " Look out for your head."

After taking in sufficient provisions our fugitives resumed their journey, and by noon they had reached the mouth of soengei Koeatan, the principal river on this side of the Kapoeas. This soengei is navigable for some days for canoes of medium size. It originates in a marshy tract of land having communication with the Doesson by the soengei Lemo.

Johannes proposed to pursue their journey along the Koeatan

as the Doesson continues navigable much longer than the Kapoeas; and they would thus sooner reach the central mountains, across which their course lay. The other three Europeans concurred in his proposal; but Dalim and the Dayaks strongly opposed it. The way was certainly easier, but they, as inhabitants of the Kapoeas regions, would land among their bitterest enemies, from whom they could not possibly hide themselves or escape, and who would show them no mercy or compassion. A journey in that direction was like a sentence of death to them. While they were still deliberating a rangkan impelled by twenty oars was observed in the rear of the travellers. The appearance of this vessel, coming around a sharp corner, was so sudden that the oarsmen in the canoe became paralyzed with terror.

"Poenans! Poenans!" they cried, taking their mandauws.

The Europeans seized their guns and a heavy rifle fire would have soon welcomed the visitors if Dalim had not stopped them, crying out, "Halt, don't fire!"

A Poenan in full war costume, but quite unarmed, was standing on the bow of the rangkan, nodding and waving his arms about like a maniac.

When the vessels were a little nearer to each other, the travellers recognized the head-hunter. It was Harimaoung Boekit—the Poenan whose life had been spared by Wienersdorf at Lake Ampang. He was now returning to his tribe, but having reason to believe that his new friends were in some peril he had come to aid them. Thus it was that on approaching our travellers, he and his companions had laid aside their weapons, in token of friendship.

CHAPTER X.

HARIMAOUNG BOEKIT'S NARRATIVE—EVENTS AT KOTTA BAROE—
COUNCIL OF WAR—COALS—ARRIVAL AT KOTTA DJANGKAN—TAK-
ING IN AMMUNITION AND PROVISIONS—A WOMAN CAGED—WIEN-
ERSDORF BECOMES DESPERATE—JOHANNES REASONS

WHEN the rangkan came alongside the canoe, the Poenan chief told our adventurers that upon the arrival of his party at kotta Baroe on the preceding night, they had found everything in the greatest confusion. There was a state barge moored to the shore and a throng of people assembled, as if some important enterprise was in progress. Impelled by curiosity, Harimaoung Boekit had gone ashore and learned that a white officer from Kwala Kapoeas, whom he described as carrying a long mandauw, had called the populace together and ordered them to pursue a canoe which contained some escaped fugitives. He had made a requisition for two hundred and fifty armed men, with the necessary complement of canoes—a demand which caused no little dissatisfaction. The Poenan, upon hearing all this, immediately concluded that they meant to capture the very men who had so generously spared his own life, and he at once determined to warn and if necessary to assist them. He therefore crept back to his rangkan as quietly as he had left it, and upon regaining it beckoned to some of his mates and at once repeated his information.

When Harimaoung Boekit had ended his narrative, the fugitives looked at each other in anxious amazement. They had never expected to be followed by the Dutch so closely and so quickly. They had in fact calculated that they were at least ten days in advance of their pursuers. What was now to be done?

"On, on!" Wienersdorf cried, "our only safety is in flight."

"No," Johannes said, "since the Colonel is so close upon us flight can be of little use. He has decidedly left kotta Baroe by this time, and having impressed a sufficient number of natives into his service, he will have a larger complement of oarsmen than we."

"But what else can we do?"

Johannes did not answer, but addressing the Poenan chief, he asked,

"Were there any white men among the Commander's crew?"

"I looked most carefully," said the Poenan, "but could not discern a single paleface except the one you call the Colonel."

"No white soldiers among them; that is worth knowing. But perhaps he has an escort of Javan soldiers, who are even less easy to deal with," Johannes muttered to himself. "Were any of them armed?" he further asked.

"The paleface carried a small gun in his hand and a slave bearing a rifle was continually following close behind him. The rest were armed with their mandauws and most of them had a blow pipe for poisoned arrows or a lance. The chief of Kwala

Kapoeas, whom I know well, was the only one who carried a rifle. But—"

The Poenan now whispered something to Johannes.

"That can be tried," the latter answered, his face brightening, and addressing his companions, he said,

"If we can only reach kotta Djangkan, our chances will be better and we may hope again. Now, row on!"

Loud acclamations followed. The rangkan was taken in tow and the roof of the canoe was lowered. Harimaoung's companions placed themselves among the oarsmen, so that the vessel, now impelled by forty-four oars, shot along with the speed of lightning, rivalling the fastest steamer. The Poenans stood up, as they usually do in their canoes, between the seated oarsmen, and in this position used their long oars without any hindrance to the others. They were fine men, tall head-hunters with great broad chests and muscular arms. They were dressed in full war costume, ornamented by two long plumes of the rhinoceros bird and wore coats of mail fastened over thick jackets of beaten bark. Both garments were open in front and displayed their bodies handsomely tattooed with designs as beautiful as if limned by the pencil of an artist. Their shields, painted with the oddest arabesques, were borne against the lower parts of their bodies, while from their waists depended their mandauws, proudly ornamented with numerous locks of hair.

As soon as the canoe was in full progress, Johannes called the two Swiss, the Walloon, and Harimaoung Boekit to the stern of the boat, where Dalim was already seated in charge of the tiller. They then proceeded to concoct measures to be adopted at kotta Djangkan. This was a strongly palisaded fort built on the Kapoeas River, in a very commanding position.

Five hundred souls, including nearly eighty warriors, lived within the walls of this kotta, which thus formed what almost every kotta in the interior of Borneo really is, a strongly fortified kampong. Its chief was an old man named Amai Kotong, who also commanded the kotta Mawat and Brobok, situated on the soengei Mawat.

Amai Kotong was a Poenan by birth. As the son of a great chief residing at soengei Miri, he had married an Ot Danom wife and afterward established himself on the banks of the Kapoeas. He had seen his riches increase by the spoil of several marauding expeditions, but his fortune had been chiefly made by gold digging. He was uncle to Harimaoung Boekit and had always held the son of his elder brother in great esteem. The Poenan chief therefore looked forward to a favorable reception and hoped for valuable assistance at kotta Djangkan.

Such was the information now briefly conveyed by Johannes to his audience.

"And what is the purpose of all this detail?"

"The purpose is simply this," was the rather angry reply, "that we take up our residence in kotta Djangkan and quietly await the result. If we should be attacked, we will not fail to defend ourselves bravely."

"I really believe it safer to continue our flight; no vessel afloat can overtake us at our present speed."

"But can we keep up that speed?" Johannes interrupted vehemently. "We may consider ourselves lucky if we can do so until to-night, when we may perhaps reach kotta Djangkan. If we could change oarsmen from time to time it would be different, but we cannot do so. Our pursuers, I will lay any wager, have before this taken in fresh men. But courage! let us face the situation like men; we have nothing to do but to defend ourselves. You will see that a favorable result will crown our efforts."

"God grant it," Wienersdorf sighed.

"Amen!" cried La Cueille, "and now I think we had better give a hand at the oars. Four pair of European arms like ours are not to be despised, and the greater the distance between those cheese-heads and us the better."

The journey was now continued with increased energy. While rowing the four Europeans observed between the white sand of the various projecting angles some large lumps of a black substance. La Cueille's attention had been especially drawn to them, but he had not been able to distinguish their nature on account of the rapidity with which the canoe was proceeding. But arriving at one of the projections, just as their boat approached the objects, he leaped into the shallow water, grasped some of them and reappeared in the canoe again before it had rounded the point.

"Nom d'un chien!" he cried, enthusiastically showing his prize, "real coal and of the best sort I can assure you. And this is found here along the banks of the river?"

"Keep cool," Johannes laughed, "you will see plenty more and may gather it if you like. But I am heartily glad to see it here. It is a sure sign that we are approaching kotta Djangkan. Three or four considerable strata of coal run through the hill upon which the kotta is situated and the deepest of these is said to yield capital fuel."

"That is indeed a treasure," La Cueille observed.

"Yes, it would be if properly used. But the Dayak never troubles himself about coal. His forests produce sufficient wood to render coals superfluous to him. And in many places the use of it is prohibited to him as rendering him unclean. As for the Dutch——"

Johannes was here interrupted by one of the oarsmen calling out that kotta Djangkan was in sight ahead. Truly enough, there lay the fortification high on the hill. The numerous tall masts, reaching above the palisades, all of them ornamented with bleached skulls, considerably increased the impression produced upon the Europeans by their first glimpse of this formidable place. Near the bank of the river a tomoi was erected, from which a ladder descended to the water. The canoe halted there and the Poenan chief stepped on shore. After a short time Harimaoung reappeared, accompanied by his uncle Amai Kotong, a stolid elderly Dayak, who informed our friends that the kotta was altogether at their disposal. He had hardly spoken his welcome when the oarsmen sprang ashore and commenced, under supervision of Dalim, to unload the canoe.

After a preliminary introduction to their host the Europeans also set to work. The day was already far gone and the appearance of the pursuers might be hourly expected. La Cueille and Schlickeisen undertook to put the six guns in position, to pack away the ammunition and to look after the armament of the garrison. To Wienersdorf the defence was entrusted, the construction of all necessary work in the fort and the surrounding territory being left to him; while Johannes was charged with the commissariat and general command.

On overhauling the fort, our artillerists found a few useless small guns and a fair quantity of gunpowder which, added to their own supply, removed all fear of insecurity. After all the ammunition had been stored away, the Europeans, assisted by some Dayaks, placed two small guns upon the ramparts on the land side and removed a few palisades in order to afford a wider range. Another piece was placed on each of the ramparts commanding the stream.

Wienersdorf in the meantime carefully reviewed the interior of the fortification. The footways running along the palisades he strengthened here and there with strong planks. He made loopholes in the centre of the four walls, but especially near the ramparts, so as to secure the free use of their rifles; and finally he collected from amongst the lumber in the fort some boards and beams, with which he constructed upon one of the highest buildings a kind of covered sentry-box whence the whole neighborhood might be surveyed without danger.

Johannes soon completed his task. He warehoused all his provisions and at the same time enquired into the resources of kotta Djangkan. The result of his inspection was eminently satisfactory. There was not only an abundant supply of rice, but a large quantity of dried meat, besides two very large deer, fresh killed. He also found twenty pigs, a number of fowls, geese and ducks. Thoroughly satisfied, the commander-in-chief, at the head of a strong escort of Dayaks, sallied out of the fort to clear the surrounding territory from tall grass and all shrubs behind which an enemy might creep up to the works unnoticed. That accomplished, he removed the ladder which afforded access from the river up the steep bank.

On re-entering the fortification he encountered Amai Kotong, who had returned with some of his men from the gardens and adjacent woods. They had gone out to gather a large quantity of wild Spanish pepper, cocoanuts, bamboo tops, etc., all of which would serve them as delicacies during the impending siege. The Amai had also despatched one of his sons up the soengei Mawat to summon his subjects to war.

Harimaoung's companions occupied themselves in scraping the points of their arrows and in dipping them in fresh arrow poison. Meanwhile their chief joined his uncle and engaged in earnest conversation with him.

Having thus taken every possible precaution our deserters were seated together to enjoy the delightful evening. The sky was clear and now that the sun had gone down the heat was replaced by that fresh and agreeable coolness which renders these evening hours the most delightful in tropical lands. Thus bathed in the soft moonlight they sat engaged in conversation about the incidents of the last few days, and the probability of future encounters.

"How I wish they could be avoided," Wienersdorf said. "Blood, always blood! Ours is a horrible journey."

"Don't worry," Johannes answered angrily. "You should have stayed at home if you are so tenderly disposed. Besides, we only defend ourselves. Not a shot has been fired or a blow given except when enforced. Defence, not defiance has been our rule and so it must continue to be as long as may be possible."

While they were thus conversing they suddenly heard a soft sob, as if uttered by a woman. They looked at each other, not knowing how to account for the sound. They had seen all the women in the kampong. Those not constrained by the jealousy of their lords and masters had moved about freely among the strangers and many had made merry at the awkwardness of the pretended Dayaks. Johannes alone, by virtue of his turban, had commanded their respect. There were old and young, handsome and ugly ones amongst them; but they all displayed a peculiar tendency to mirth, if not frivolity, quite irreconcilable with the sobbing now heard.

La Cueille, the most polite of the four, got up, resolved to discover the meaning of that strange sound. He returned in a few moments and informed his comrades that yonder, near the high building where Amai Kotong resided, he had found a large cage in which a woman was imprisoned. He had addressed her and received a reply, but what she said he could not understand.

Johannes burst out laughing and said,

"Perhaps some silly husband has kindly locked up his better-half to teach her manners. The custom of the country, my man!"

"Rather harsh measures to cage a member of the gentle sex like a wild animal," Schlickeisen remarked.

"Sometimes members of the fair sex do not deserve a better fate," replied the other, laughing. "But let us see, I dare say I shall be able to understand her."

But before he had concluded Dalim appeared on the scene.

His explanation of the sobbing sounds they had heard completely unnerved our travellers. He reminded them of the lake Ampang, when Harimaoung Boekit had besmeared his victor with his own, and himself with his victor's blood.

"That was only a preliminary ceremony," the Dayak continued, "and a very short one for the occasion. Both of you became from that time converted from two deadly enemies into brothers. But Dayak custom demands a more elaborate rite to cement that bond of brotherhood. This rite, called the oath of atonement, will take place to-morrow and will be combined with the bond of blood. Yesterday, directly after our arrival, Harimaoung Boekit informed his uncle of your peculiar relationship to him, and they together have chosen a hireling, who will be sacrificed to-morrow."

"Sacrificed!" the Europeans cried with astonishment.

"Yes, sacrificed," was the calm reply. "Harimaoung attacked us, as you will remember, and men were killed and wounded during that attack. This constitutes a capital crime according to Dayak law, only to be expiated by the immolation of a hireling, who will hereafter in the Dayak heaven become the slave of Wienersdorf."

"I will never allow this hireling to be sacrificed," the Swiss cried, full of emotion. "I will prevent it at any cost."

"You can do nothing of the sort," Dalim interrupted. "Whatever you attempt will only damage our cause. It will seem as if you repent having spared the life of the Poenan. The victim has already been chosen, has already lost the name of human being and is now called kabalik, the lifeless."

"Horrible!" Wienersdorf despairingly cried. "By Heavens!

can nothing prevent such a crime? But," he wildly continued, "the Poenan may think what he likes. I am sorry now that I spared him. I will seek the wretch and beg for the life of the woman. If he refuses my request may God have mercy upon him, for only my death will save his life."

"Calm yourself and reflect that all our lives are at stake," Johannes observed. "You nobly wish to save this woman, but I repeat by so doing you will endanger our lives as well as your own. Now of your own life you are master, but do you think that we intend to sacrifice ours in defence of your own fancies? No, I say. Ask your own conscience whether a woman like that, a woman who is already looked upon as dead, is really worth such a wholesale slaughter as your interference will certainly provoke. Besides if you deliver her to-day at the cost I have just figured, she will be chosen again in another week and the bloodshed caused by your intercession will have been practically useless."

"Horrible, horrible!" the Swiss cried, wringing his hands in despair.

"Listen!" Johannes solemnly continued. "You voluntarily chose me as your leader in our escape; you have all promised to obey me when we should find ourselves among the natives of the interior. I now demand prompt obedience as a guaranty for the safety of all of us. This obedience will first of all consist in offering no resistance to what cannot be prevented. I am not speaking from any intolerance or want of compassion, but solely in the interests of self-preservation. If we cannot prevent cruelties from being perpetrated under our own eyes let us blame the civilized nation which rules the greater part of this immense island, and yet does not possess the power to grapple with horrors such as we shall witness to-morrow."

He was glowing with earnestness. His head was thrown back and his chest heaved violently. His handsome face clearly expressed the indignation of his soul.

"To-morrow," he continued, "I will attach the Dutch colors to the stake when the sacrifice is being consummated. The crime will thus be presided over by the banner of Holland; and I shall take care that the blood of the poor woman writhing under her tortures shall bespatter its pure breadths and cover it with pollution."

After a few moments he calmed down and continued:

"But let us go to our posts; Wienersdorf and I will rest while the others keep watch." Then addressing Schlickeisen and La Cueille, he said, "Call us at midnight, when we will relieve you. And now good-night!"

"Good-night! Oh heavens, what a night!" Wienersdorf muttered, impatiently following.

At about five in the morning, after the moon had gone down and everything around was dark, Wienersdorf, seizing the opportunity while Johannes was talking to one of the sentries, crept to the cage in which the poor woman was confined and found her sleeping soundly. He quietly awoke her and after a great deal of trouble broke some of the bars of her prison. He then urged her by signs to leave it and escape to the wilderness. Alas! the poor woman, frightened at seeing a perfect stranger in the darkness of night, refused to move. The Swiss entreated her to go; he wrung his hands and grasped the trellis-work of her cage. But all in vain.

Thus Johannes found him lost in despair. While leading him away he tried to convince him of the absurdity of the escape of the woman. The expiation ceremony would not even be postponed by her flight, for another victim would soon be chosen in her place, while a hot pursuit would be made after the fugitive, eventually to end in capture and a terrible death.

The night passed quietly. Not a sign of the enemy was seen. As soon as day began to break Amai Kotong despatched a few of his Dayaks in a djoekoeng down the stream to take their post at the nearest angle formed by the river. They would serve as an advance guard, for from that point they had an extensive view over the stream and could signal to the kotta the approach of any canoes.

CHAPTER XI.

FURTHER MEANS OF DEFENCE—THE OATH OF ATONEMENT—JOHANNES AN ORATOR—TWO GUN SHOTS—THE ATTACK—WIENERSDORF IN A FAINT—A GRATEFUL POENAN—A DAYAK BEAUTY—AN OFFER OF MARRIAGE—WIENERSDORF IS ENGAGED TO HAMADOE—AN AMBASSADOR FROM THE COLONEL—HE CARRIES BACK HIS MESSAGE.

AT daybreak every man in the fortification again set to work to complete arrangements for defence. Johannes and Wienersdorf were among the earliest and most active workers. They hauled up all the canoes and placed them in security, and then levelled the banks of the river in order to render a surprise by water impracticable. These tasks finished they dug a quadruple circle of pits around the fortress, and after driving a couple of pointed stakes in each of them they covered them with a layer of long grass in order to conceal them from view. They also planted rows of spikes of hard wood in the vicinity of all the principal approaches.

The Poenans of Harimaoung Boekit were in the meantime occupied in preparing the stake at which their victim was to be immolated. This, when finished, was planted in the centre of the quadrangle, the area of which was swept and strewn with white sand in accordance with the custom observed on similar occasions. The women were busily engaged in cooking as the ceremony of the oath of atonement invariably concluded with a grand festive banquet. They killed two buffaloes and four large pigs, the flesh of which was made into numerous savory dishes, boiled, roasted and stewed. Instead of the usual pileworms they had slices of snakes and a bangamat, or flying dog, roasted whole and served like our sucking pigs. The principal side dish consisted of baloedoek, an amphibious animal about a foot long, white and covered with fine scales. Its body resembles a fish and it has the head of a frog. Besides these there were hambatar, or the larvæ of beetles. They also prepared cakes of rice meal, sago and pisang, while finally, in the way of confectionery, they had shells filled with tangoeli, the larvæ of bees stewed in honey, a highly prized delicacy. Every one being thus busily occupied, the hours of the morning soon passed.

It was close upon noon when all was ready for the ceremony. Amai Kotong then called the inhabitants of kotta Djangkan together and Harimaoung Boekit formally invited the Europeans to be present at the ceremony of the oath of atonement. All of them however could not attend, as they had undertaken to keep the lookout in turns while the festivities were in progress. La Cueille was first detached for this important duty. Wienersdorf and Harimaoung Boekit took their places in the midst of six young men who, with palm branches in their hands, formed a guard of honor for the two heroes of the festival.

Arrived at the quadrangle, they found all the men dressed in full war costume and their faces covered by a taboekah or wooden mask. They all carried their mandauws and lances and now formed around the stake. When everything was arranged the priestesses commenced their chants accompanied by the sound of their katambongs.

The singing lasted until past midday when the signal for producing the victim was given. While she was fetched from her cage one of the priestesses mounted an especially prepared ladder and sung an invocation, beseeching that a favorable omen might be vouchsafed the impending ceremony.

A falcon, as if it had understood the invocation, immediately appeared above the border of the forest. Rising to the left of the fort it soared higher and higher in the air, describing large circles until it had mounted midway in the zenith, when it stopped for a few minutes. After remaining thus motionless for a short time it suddenly uttered a piercing cry and flew away in the direction whence it had come. Every Dayak present was affected. The cry uttered by the bird was construed into a warning and regarded as a most unfavorable omen.

In the meantime the poor woman had entered the circle and two men began to tie her. She had scarcely strength enough to stand and kept her head gently hanging sideways. For the rest, she appeared to be calm and freely viewed the environing circle.

After having been securely tied Harimaoung Boekit approached Wienersdorf, made a slight incision with his knife on his naked chest and collected the blood in a vessel. He then made a similar incision on his own body, caught the blood in the same vessel and filled it with toeak. He thereupon raised the bloody mixture and pronounced a fearful curse upon himself in case he should ever break the tie of brotherhood which he was now on the point of cementing. He called upon every deity and demon to witness his brotherly affection for the saviour of his life. He invoked their most fearful punishment if he should ever prove false to him and finished by half emptying the vessel held in his hand. This he next offered to Wienersdorf who swallowed the contents although his stomach rebelled against the mixture. After this ceremony the Poenan chief again spoke, addressing the Swiss:

"We are brothers now and I will always treat you as such. But another debt of blood still exists between us. When I attacked your party I tried to get your heads. During this struggle one of your companions was killed, several of my own followers perished, and—blood requires blood. See! in order to satisfy this demand we sacrifice one of our hirelings. We will besmear her with our own blood which will cancel this debt and render us free of each other."

Johannes now took Wienersdorf by the hand and mounted with him the steps recently vacated by the priestess.

"My brethren," he addressed the congregation, "my friend Dohong (War Sword), who from his infancy has lived in Bandjermasin where the great lord of the Dutch reigns, cannot sufficiently express himself in Dayak and has begged my assistance to speak to you. He gratefully accepts the bond of Harimaoung Boekit and, happen what may, will always be a good brother to him. Like the water which, cleft by a mandauw reunites again, their friendship will remain undisturbed, so that in life and death they may count upon each other. But our Dohong has been brought up amongst the whites. They have taught him that no one is allowed to kill a human being. Even in Kwala Kapoeas such an act is strictly forbidden. Dohong follows their customs and abhors the killing of men, unless it is on the battlefield. He therefore proposes to his brother to spare the life of this woman, and in order to wash away the debt of blood he suggests that a buffalo shall be sacrificed. You have noticed the evil omen of the falcon. This only happens because we inhabitants of Kwala Kapoeas were going to commit a sin by violating the obligation solemnly undertaken by us not to kill any human beings. Let us then kill a buffalo instead of this woman and you will see that the omens will change and become favorable."

Dead silence reigned within the square of kotta Djangkan. At the end of the speech every face had become darkened and exhibited the greatest dissatisfaction. The Poenans especially showed their feelings by grasping their mandauws. They considered the words just uttered as a grave offence against their chief. Harimaoung Boekit now mounted the steps and addressed the assembly:

"Here in the upper country," he commenced, "the whites have nothing to say; whenever they wish to command here, let them come! Are they so careful themselves of human life? How many thousands of lives have been sacrificed during the war in this beautiful island? And who caused that war? Did not their avarice? Who will tell of the numerous Javanese starved to death, because they had to plant coffee or to build kottas for the palefaces, so that they had no time left them for the cultivation of their own fields? Do you think we are ignorant of all this? They forbid us to kill our hirelings and pretend to have veneration for slaves. Do not trust white men; their lips are oily but they are hypocrites." With increased passion, he continued, "Touch their purse and they will kill hundreds of free men as well as slaves. They do worse than killing men in order to make money."

The Poenan paused awhile as if waiting to take breath, when he thus resumed: "But who cares for the orders of these whites? It behooves every man to follow the institutions of his country. The ceremony must proceed——unless my brother Dohong refuses to accept my friendship."

These last words were uttered in a subdued tone accompanied by a sob. The thought that his saviour would refuse his friendship visibly affected the child of Nature. For the rest, the Poenan stood there proud and gallant, his nostrils dilated and his head thrown back, while his mandauw was already half unsheathed.

Wienersdorf anxiously scanned the surrounding men. La Cueille was absent; Johannes stood with his head bent upon his chest; the Dayaks of kotta Djangkan uttered a murmur of approbation and joined the side of their relatives, the Poenans. Even Dalim and his companions stood motionless. They could not count upon any assistance. A second's hesitation would suffice to cause a quarrel which could only terminate in the death of the Europeans. Wienersdorf foresaw all this and suddenly seizing the hand of Harimaoung Boekit he raised it to his lips and bowed his head.

Johannes now came forward to the flag-staff, produced a small bundle, tied it to a line and hoisted it to the top. The boys ranged themselves in file; the eldest of them stepped forward and uttering a fiendish laugh stabbed the victim under the left breast. All single men would have followed his example by piercing the flesh of the victim with the point of their lances to the depth of about half an inch but for the events which now occurred and which served to divert all attention from the victim.

First, she uttered a piercing yell. She had remained calm up to the present, but now her shrieks were heart-rending.

While all this was taking place Johannes shook the flag line and disentangled the parcel just hoisted, when the Dutch ensign proudly unfurled itself above the head of the poor woman.

It seemed as if this tricolor was her salvation, for suddenly two guns were fired in rapid succession summoning the garrison to the ramparts. Johannes, taking advantage of the general confusion, rushed forwards, severed the cords by which the victim was bound and thus liberated her. He then joined his confederates to see what had occurred.

La Cueille, seated in his elevated box, which overlooked the river for a considerable distance, placed the two loaded guns in position, possessed himself of a lighted torch and waited his opportunity with a vigilant eye on the river. At last he saw a fleet of canoes appear from behind an angle of the soengei. He remained quiet, however, and allowed them to approach nearer still.

The time for action at length arrived. Adjusting the elevation of his guns he applied the torch to the touchhole, and sent a couple of balls in the midst of the fleet, sinking one of the canoes and causing no little confusion amongst the rest.

The Colonel hereupon ordered his men to land so as provisionally to place them out of danger, and accordingly the whole of the attacking force was soon hidden among the shrubs and trees of the bank. He knew, however, the danger of leaving his troops under the influence of this first repulse, and therefore, although the mystery of the Dutch flag waving from the fortress still puzzled him, he determined not to hesitate, but collected his forces and advanced to storm the fortification. He remembered the experience of former contests, that in Indian warfare boldness secures success.

He would undoubtedly have been successful now but for the Europeans within the fortification. These, as soon as they perceived the enemy to be within range, discharged their guns loaded with grape, which made the assailants waver. A lively rifle fire terminated the hesitation of the heroes and drove them to flight before they had had an opportunity of discharging a single shot. When Harimaoung Boekit witnessed their retreat he could hardly control himself. He darted out of the fortification to hunt for heads. But while hacking about among the struggling fugitives a troop of armed warriors suddenly appeared from behind some ambush and surrounded him. They threw a lasso round his neck and dragged him away half strangled. Wienersdorf and Schlickeisen, on seeing this, collected some of their men and hurried to the spot with all speed.

Arriving at the slope of the hill they saw the body of the Poenan being carried off by a few men. Taking careful aim they discharged their rifles and laid four of the enemy lifeless. The others hesitated, but knowing their prey to be a chief and therefore too valuable to be left behind, they persevered in the attempt although two more of them were struck down. Suddenly from the fort there issued a reinforcement. Several natives appeared upon the scene, who rushed forward with their naked mandauws and after a brief struggle Wienersdorf had the satisfaction of freeing the Poenan from the rope which had almost strangled him. He offered him his hand, assisted him in getting up and whispered a salamat, congratulation, in his ear, as he rose to his feet.

The Poenan took the two Swiss by their hands, which he placed on his own head, saying, "Paharingkoe, my brethren."

After a few more shots from both sides everything became quiet.

The assailants effected their retreat and proceeded to count their loss. Five of their dead they hurriedly buried, but they left more than treble that number of wounded behind them groaning amongst the shrubs. The garrison of the kotta had lost only one man, a hireling who had been killed by a rifle shot.

The festivities thus interrupted, were not, however, abandoned. The besieged partook of the banquet in divisions, one part feasting while the other stood ready to defend the fort against a renewed attack. All, however, celebrated their victory by partaking of a bowl of toeak, though they carefully kept within the bounds of sobriety.

Faithful to his reverend character the Walloon abstained from all such food and drinks as are prohibited by the Prophet. With holy indifference he saw the tidbits disappear down almost insatiable throats, and he remained perfectly calm when Johannes held a delicious pork chop under his nose. As for the toeak, he could only sigh deeply at the smell of it. He was, however, comforted by a promise conveyed by Johannes to reserve for him his fair share to be enjoyed after leaving the circle of these profane ones.

While our Europeans were partaking of the numerous delicacies a Poenan entered and threw a couple of skulls in the midst of the company. A deafening applause greeted this action. Two of them grasped the skulls, severed the remaining cervical vertebræ and with a bamboo knife began to empty the substance of the brain into a dish through the spinal opening. Another Poenan severed large locks from the heads, cut the hair into pieces of about one and a half inches and added them with some powdered Spanish pepper to this bloody mass of brain. The deserters viewed all this in silent horror. When every particle of brain had been removed from the skulls and the dish was properly prepared, a Poenan took it up, placed an earthenware spoon in the mixture and offered it to Johannes who refused it politely. When it was presented to Wienersdorf he glanced at it, became suddenly overpowered by a feeling of nausea and fell down senseless.

The other Europeans in their consternation took no notice of Wienersdorf's faint, and the Dayaks, though a little surprised at the refusal of the foreigners to taste of this delicacy, were but too delighted to see it all left to themselves. The one who carried the dish grasped the spoon, filled it, threw his head back and closing his eyes allowed a fair quantity to glide down his throat, his features all the while beaming with the utmost delight. He then handed the dish to one of his companions who went through the same manœuvre and then passed the delicacy further. Slowly and with ecstatic happiness they sucked at the hairs which are included in the mixture for the express purpose of compelling them to enjoy it deliberately.

This loathsome feast was too much for the Europeans. The scene turned their very souls, and jumping up to fly from this terrible drama, they noticed for the first time that Wienersdorf had fainted and was lying senseless.

They carried him away with them to the open air where, assisted by draughts of cold water, they all soon regained their composure.

Harimaoung Boekit now for the second time owed his life to Wienersdorf. He had learned from his followers with what courage his new brother had come to his assistance. He approached his rescuer and putting his hand on his shoulder asked whether he could do anything for him. All he possessed he placed at the disposal of his deliverer and even offered to become his hireling at the sacrifice of his personal freedom.

Wienersdorf, though still under the influence of the scene recently witnessed, did not long hesitate. He took the hand of the Poenan, shook it passionately, and begged for the life of the poor woman who had been temporarily saved from a miserable end by the unforeseen arrival of the hostile fleet. This request was granted after some hesitation, the Poenan averring that he could not comprehend why he thus insisted upon sparing the life of this woman, who besides being the mother of two children was middle-aged and ill-looking. He felt greatly astonished at the perverted taste of the Swiss. Anxious, however, to render his deliverer happy by the possession of a comely wife he now offered him his own sister, a young and comely maiden, the pride of her tribe. Thus by a suitable marriage they would strengthen the tie of brotherhood.

Hamadoe, as the young lady was called, was a splendid creature with a fine complexion delicately tinted. Her mouth was exquisitely chiselled, her eyes large and dark beamed with a soft languishing expression, but were also capable of that fiery brilliancy so often met with in eastern races. Her figure was magnificent, tall, lithe and graceful; she possessed the carriage which peculiarly distinguishes the child of nature and which is so rarely encountered in the lands of a civilized society.

Our Europeans had often admired the beautiful Hamadoe and thought her worthy of the name she bore, sweet honey. Now, however, that this pearl of female beauty was offered to him, Wienersdorf hesitated and was on the point of refusing. Luckily Johannes interfered and adroitly answered the Poenan that his friend would gratefully accept his offer to become the husband of the fair Hamadoe.

Astonished at this unexpected intervention the Swiss looked up and wished to speak; but Johannes politely begged him to retire; Wienersdorf withdrew accordingly, not the less determined that however captivating the beautiful Hamadoe might be, he would not be forced to commit any act of folly.

Harimaoung Boekit led Johannes to his dwelling, the maiden was called, and Johannes formally proposed for his friend according to the existing Dayak custom. At first she seemed favorably inclined, but seeing that the agent had not one single skull to offer as a marriage gift she hesitated. At last she took a female dress which was hanging up to dry and offered it to Johannes, saying, " Your friend is no man, he is only a shy woman and unworthy of male attire ; tell him to wear this petticoat."

Johannes only smiled without accepting the dress. Harimaoung Boekit here told her how this stranger had twice saved his life and explained to her that as in the lower country the Dutch had prohibited head-hunting, his deliverer had to submit to command, but that he was nevertheless one of the bravest of the brave, a true Dohong.

After this explanation the girl did not further hesitate, but frankly declared that she would retract her words. She added that she would be proud to please her brother, and was ready to become Dohong's partner for life and to share his weal and woe. She begged her brother to prepare everything for the speedy celebration of the blako ontong, when they would implore blessings on her marriage from the Radja balawang boelau, the King of the Golden Gate of Heaven.

All this was said with such charming modesty that Johannes became enchanted with the maiden and almost envied the goodfortune of his companion. When Hamadoe had retired, the real marriage treaty was proceeded with. Johannes began with the explanation that Dohong, being a liberated hireling, was not blessed with any earthly treasure, and was consequently unable to produce either a high palakko or the usual sums of money required for the celebration of the marriage. The palakko is a settlement deposited by the bridegroom with the parents of the bride, amounting, according to the wealth of the bridegroom, to a sum ranging from fifty to eight hundred guilders.

This money serves to keep the lover constant; for at the slightest proof of unfaithfulness, it becomes the property of the wife. Harimaoung Boekit smiled at this communication, took a few bamboo boxes from the wall and presented them to Johannes, with the information that they contained about twenty thaels of gold dust, sufficient to provide for all emergencies.

"Could I refuse to part with this gold, and in order to make my brother Dohong happy?" the generous Poenan chief asked. "I have offered him my body and after that he may consider everything belonging to me as his own."

All being thus far settled the wedding-day was next fixed. It was proposed that the ceremony should be solemnized two months thence, in Harimaoung Boekit's home, situated on the soengei Miri, and that in honor of Kadjanka, the ruler of the moon and the protector of newly married women, it should take place on the day of the full moon.

"And let us hope," Harimaoung Boekit added, "that our besiegers may have departed long before that time."

When Johannes rejoined his comrades a dispute immediately arose between him and Wienersdorf, who refused to entertain the project of a Dayak marriage.

"I believe you are temporarily insane," Johannes answered, "however, you speak as if a separation is so very difficult among the Dayaks. Why, it is even easier to divorce than to marry here. Each goes his own way and all is over."

"And all is over, ha! ha!" the Swiss laughed bitterly. "It is very easy indeed to abandon your unfortunate wife, is it not? I never thought you were such an unscrupulous scoundrel."

"Well, I like that," Johannes vehemently interrupted. "Here am I, doing my best to counteract the fatal consequences of your absurd and infirm philanthropy. An angel of a girl is thrown across the path of your lordship, and because I have accepted her for you, in the hope of removing the traces of former follies, you coolly reward my services by calling me an unscrupulous scoundrel. Let me tell you then," he continued with increased passion, "you Europeans are not only the most ungrateful, but also the most impractical beings in creation, thanks to your inflated principles. I am sure the Creator must now and then feel utterly ashamed of the stupidity of the white race."

Johannes appeared supremely handsome in his disdain; his eyes flashed, his nostrils quivered and the veins of his forehead were visible like swollen cords.

Schlickeisen now appeared as pacificator, saying,

"Don't feel hurt at an unguarded expression of your companion, which I am positive he did not mean—did you?"

"The words were certainly spoken without reflection," Wienersdorf answered solemnly, "and I will willingly retract them. I was angry at hearing my friend speak so coolly about marriage and divorce in the same breath."

"I only made the remark to remove your impression that marriage meant a compulsory residence in this island. I would feel loath to make a jest of serious subjects, but I sought to convince you how necessary it is for us to yield to unavoidable circumstances. As soon as I find myself among whitefaces I will respect their ideas of marriage and divorce, but while I am among Borneans I accept their customs and institutions."

"But permit me to say that I do exactly the same. I fully respect Dayak customs and nobody will ever reproach me with this want of toleration which you condemn. The people here and everywhere are at liberty to intermarry and separate as much as they choose, provided you leave me out of the question."

"And yet you will have to get reconciled to this marriage," Johannes answered.

"Never!" exclaimed Wienersdorf.

"But for once, reason sensibly."

"Reason is out of the question. I will never marry a woman with the knowledge that in a little while I must put her away from me."

"But listen; as matters stand just now, the marriage is unavoidable. You have already seriously offended the Poenan chief during the expiation festival and the mandauws were half unsheathed. Beware of refusing the hand of his sister for he will take terrible vengeance. And I repeat what I observed on a former occasion that if you do not yourself value life you will have to consider us."

"But," said Wienersdorf, "is not yours an exaggerated supposition. Will the Poenan really take the refusal so seriously?"

"Can you doubt it? Have you already forgotten how your behavior during the execution of that slave made him fear that you did not value his friendship? What will be the effect of your refusing the hand of his sister so cordially offered to you? It will most certainly cause a coolness not far removed from animosity. The Poenan will then withdraw with all his followers and leave us to our fate."

"And what if he did?" Wienersdorf said defiantly.

"It would simply deprive us of all assistance from kotta Djangkan. You seem to forget that we have to thank Harimaoung Boekit for this timely refuge. As soon as the Poenan leaves us a reconciliation between the kotta and our besiegers will follow, and the first condition of this reconciliation will be to deliver up the deserters. Such will be our fate if you persist in refusing to marry."

"Stop!" Wienersdorf cried, "you drive me mad. To what an extremity have you brought me?"

"Only to the extremity of marrying a handsome girl, you lucky dog!" the Walloon said smilingly.

"Listen again," Johannes continued, firm as fate, "and consider on the other hand the consequences of this marriage if duly carried out. Harimaoung Boekit's affection towards his deliverer will undoubtedly increase, you will belong to his relations and we will have gained faithful allies. The Colonel will raise the siege of kotta Djangkan, being unable to capture it with the slender means at his disposal. We will then travel in company with the Poenan chief to the Miri country where we shall be in perfect security until we find means to escape."

Wienersdorf sighed heavily; then offering his hand to his companions he said, with tears in his eyes:

"Friends, I accede and agree to the marriage."

"He gives way," La Cueille cried. "Allah be praised, he consents to marry a most charming young girl."

While the deserters were thus busy arriving at a decision, Amai Kotong and Harimaoung Boekit approached with the intelligence that a Dayak of Kwala Kapoeas had appeared at the gate of the kotta bearing a letter from the Commander. The two chiefs wished to have the opinions of their friends. They themselves proposed to refuse admittance to the messenger, as neither of them could read the letter and feared he might be a spy. Johannes asked Dalim to follow him and they both went outside the gate to learn the errand of the ambassador. He was a simple Dayak, a follower of Tomonggong Nikodemus, who was commissioned to deliver the letter into the hands of Amai Kotong himself. At first he refused to part with the missive, but after Dalim had informed him that he might return whence he came, but that he could not see the chief of the kotta, he altered his tone and gave the letter to Johannes. After having perused its contents, the messenger was bidden to wait outside where the answer would be brought to him.

The letter contained the request of the Colonel to be allowed to enter the kotta unarmed, accompanied by Tomonggong Djaja Nagara and one other, in order to have an interview with Amai Kotong. Johannes smiled on reading this. But once inside the fort again, he called the garrison together in the square, mounted the steps and read with a loud and penetrating voice, looking solemnly at the paper, how the Commander of Kwala Kapoeas, in the name of the Resident of Bandjermasin, ordered Harimaoung Boekit with his Poenans to be delivered up to the gallows as murderers. On hearing the pretended contents of the letter, a cry of rage arose from all the assembled natives. The Poenan chief mounted the steps to satisfy himself by looking at the horrible words which pronounced his sentence. Johannes, after having allowed them for a few moments to give vent to their

AN AMBASSADOR FROM THE COLONEL.

feelings, commanded silence as he had some further communications to make.

"I have not read all," he said in a loud voice. "Listen, brothers, to what follows: If these Poenans, those horrible murderers, are not delivered up before sunset the inhabitants of kotta Djangkan will feel the avenging arm of the Dutch Government. The kotta will be taken and levelled to the ground. The soil on which it now stands will be dug up and the priestesses will sow salt in the furrows as a token that the spot will be accursed forever and ever by Mahatara."

The cries of the multitude now became deafening.

As soon as Johannes saw another opportunity of being listened to, he continued: "Attend! All the men will be killed and strung up like animals; the old women and children will be sold as slaves, and the maidens and young married women will be divided amongst the assailants!"

Their rage became unbounded, and the wild band would have sped outside and put the bearer of this fatal letter to the most horrible martyrdom, but for the timely intervention of Johannes and his companions. They placed themselves at the gate of the kotta and after much trouble succeeded in convincing the enraged people of the innocence of the messenger who was wholly ignorant of the contents of the document.

"No, friends!" Johannes exclaimed, "we must not answer this threat with a murder. But it will be wise to show that we are no cowards."

"I will go to the Commander myself!" Amai Kotong cried, "and explain that I cannot possibly give up a member of my family; such a course being quite against our moral teachings."

"No," Johannes said. "You would not be proof against the honeyed language of a paleface. Besides, they will keep you a prisoner if you don't submit."

"But what am I to do?"

"See here?"

And at the same time he tore the letter into a thousand pieces, collected them in a pisang leaf and tied them up into a parcel.

"That is the way to return the letter to the Commander!" he exclaimed victoriously.

A loud cry of satisfaction was the answer, proving again that whoever has tact, may lead any assemblage as he wishes.

A few moments afterwards he placed the parcel into the messenger's hand, with command to deliver it to the Commander, at the same time advising him never to return to the kotta with similar messages unless he wished to be cut to pieces. The frightened native accepted the parcel and hurried away from such dangerous quarters as fast as his feet would carry him.

In the meantime the two Dayak chiefs were seated with the Colonel on the trunk of a tree under a shed made of branches and leaves, and were waiting for the return of their messenger. The Colonel seemed very impatient; he stamped with his feet, drummed with his fingers on the sheath of his sword, and distinctly showed that he had not yet acquired the Eastern reserve so natural to his companions. At last he said:

"He is a long while coming, is he not?"

"It certainly is not far from here," Tomonggong Nikodemus

answered, "but your honor must not forget how cautious our messengers have to be."

"But do you really fancy this letter will lead to the result you expected?"

"Yes, sir! The inhabitants of the kotta will see no danger in admitting the three of us unarmed inside their walls, and once there, we will find no difficulty in persuading Amai Kotong to deliver up the Europeans. The Chief will never risk the lives and property of the whole of his tribe, in order to protect four deserters."

"And yet their influence seems considerable, judging by our reception," was the bitter reply of the officer.

"I must own that it looks very suspicious; but who knows what tale they have told those ignorant upper countrymen?"

"But will Amai Kotong be able to read the letter?"

"No, sir, he cannot read himself; but undoubtedly some one will be found inside the kotta capable of deciphering it."

"Did you know that the kotta was so heavily armed?"

"So heavily armed?" the Tomonggong asked in surprise.

"Certainly; I have just now observed through my glasses that the battery carries six pieces of cannon, while, when I was here last year, as you must remember, no sign of a gun could be discerned."

"I certainly do remember it; but you seem to forget the guns of Kwala Hiang, which the deserters must have carried away with them."

"But at Kwala Hiang there were only two guns, while here I can count at least six."

"If such is the case, I am at a loss to find an explanation," Nikodemus answered with a sigh. "And yet I do not believe that the intentions of kotta Djangkan, armed as it appears to be, are hostile towards the Dutch Government, or we should have heard of it before now. Such proceedings do not remain a secret in the Dayak country. These pieces must have been conjured hither, unless the Commander is mistaken."

"You doubt whether I have seen rightly," was the passionate reply of the Colonel. "I have even seen more than these guns. The principal passages leading to the kotta are planted with spikes and rendered impassable by pits, so that an assault is most difficult. All this has taken time to accomplish and I very much fear that I have no reason to be satisfied with some of my younger brothers. Speaking in the mildest terms, they have been opposing their elder brother."

Both Tomonggongs remained speechless for a few minutes, their emotion being distinctly visible. The face of old Nikodemus displayed a feeling of grief and pain, while that of the other was drawn into angry wrinkles, his eyes rolling wildly and betraying the fearful passion raging in his bosom.

"It is a great untruth!" he screamed, jumping up as if electrified. Nikodemus, however, took him by the hand, compelling him to resume his seat.

The Colonel witnessed this scene, which lasted for a few seconds only, with some surprise. He felt that he had gone too far in his remarks. Then ensued a painful silence—that silence which is more eloquent among Eastern tribes than the most violent utterance. At last Nikodemus spoke:

"The words spoken just now," he said, with a deeply affected voice, " were painful, but I am convinced they did not come from the heart. But the Colonel forgets the deserters. I have not the least doubt but that they have found a refuge at kotta Djangkan. How they have succeeded in gaining the confidence of the people is a mystery to me. But everything has taken place through their influence and it is they who have supervised these operations."

The Colonel reflected for a few minutes.

"Yes, they are brave boys," he muttered inaudibly, "capable of anything. Ah! I have not caught them yet."

And turning to both chiefs he said, cordially offering them his hand, " My younger brothers, you may be right. Pardon the anger I just now displayed; but my heart was bitter. At that moment I thought of the blood already spilled and yet to be spilled in consequence of this dispute with kotta Djangkar."

Both Tomonggongs bowed their heads and cordially pressed the offered hand. The Dayak is never vindictive, and soon forgets and forgives if only met half way."

They were still consulting together when the return of the messenger was reported. They all arose, showing the greatest excitement. The messenger respectfully handed his message to the Colonel, saying:

"This is for you, sir."

The Colonel took the parcel, anxiously undid the string, opened the pisang leaf and turned deathly pale when he saw the torn pieces of paper which he recognized but too well.

" And what message did you bring with you?" he asked.

"Nothing but this: that whenever I dared to bring similar letters they would cut me to pieces. On hearing that I ran away as fast as I could."

"Who spoke to you?"

"A tall Dayak whom I did not recognize."

"Have you seen any palefaces?"

"Not one, sir!"

"Did you speak to Amai Kotong?" Tomonggong Nikodemus asked.

"No, I was not admitted inside the kotta."

"And to whom did you deliver the letter?"

"To Dalim, who accompanied by the Dayak came outside to hear what I wanted."

The Tomonggongs and the Colonel hereupon exchanged a glance.

"Then you did see Dalim?"

"Yes, sir!"

"And you spoke to him?"

"Yes, sir!"

"Why did you give the letter to him?" Nikodemus asked, "after I had instructed you to give it to nobody else but Amai Kotong?"

"I did not wish to act in opposition to your orders, but Dalim told me that I might return whence I came, that I would not be admitted inside the kotta, nor could I see Amai Kotong. I thereupon handed him the letter, hoping that the kotta Chief might come to me after reading it, instead of which that tall blackguard reappeared and frightened me terribly."

"So you did not see anything?"

"No, sir! nothing; but after I had given your letter I heard somebody reading out aloud. Then came loud and horrible cries from inside the kotta. I also heard threats against you, against the Resident, against the Government, as well as against myself and was on the point of running away. After the cries had somewhat subsided, however, the tall one handed me this parcel with instructions to give it to you."

The Colonel exchanged looks of disappointment with the Tomonggongs. The messenger at a given signal withdrew.

"The affair has not improved," the Colonel said. "Are not you of the same opinion?"

Both Tomonggongs nodded affirmatively.

"Can Dalim read?"

"No, sir!" was the answer of Nikodemus.

"It is quite clear that Amai Kotong has not been informed of the contents of the letter, and that they have read something else to him and the inhabitants of the kotta. Nevertheless we dare not hesitate. The situation becomes more grave with each moment. Is such your opinion also?"

"Yes, sir!" both Tomonggongs replied.

"I then propose to surprise the kotta to-night."

"Only listen to me once more, sir!" Tomonggong Nikodemus said quietly. "After the fight of this afternoon we must not dream of leading our Dayaks against the kotta. It will take several days to remove the impression of defeat, and I therefore earnestly implore you to postpone the attack. Besides, its chances of success will be very poor indeed with this clear moonlight, and it will certainly entail considerable loss of life."

"But what then, Tomonggong?" asked the Colonel.

The old Chief did not reply at once. He reflected, sighed, and placing his hand on the shoulder of the Colonel, said:

"Listen! I will go!"

CHAPTER XII.

CONSULTATION—THE "BLAKO ONTONG"—A SALVO OF GUNS—THE OFFERING—A NATIONAL DANCE—DOWN WITH THE TURBAN—A CONFERENCE DISTURBED BY TWO RIFLE SHOTS—A FLOATING ISLAND—AN ATTEMPT AT SURPRISE—A FATAL SHOT—THE SIEGE RAISED—THE EPISODE OF THE CROCODILE—JOHANNES SPEAKS—A NEW CHIEF

"BUT, Tomonggong!" the Colonel interrupted, "after what has taken place, any approach from our side will be impossible. Besides, your life will not be safe."

"You will not be offended with an ignorant race for having sinned against the customs of the whitefaces. I know you too well to believe that. As for my own person, not a hair of my head will be hurt. I am Amai Kotong's brother in the blood; we have often drunk each other's life stream and sworn to assist each other. I am known to every member of the kotta, even to the children; I am the friend of all. Who would molest an old man like me?"

"All this may be perfectly true, Tomonggong, but what and how, if one of these deserters on sentry-duty should see you first? A bullet will be your greeting."

"I will run that risk; I am not so fully convinced that these whitefaces, whom I have never harmed, will aim directly at my life. But I intend to bend my steps towards the kotta before daybreak, when the Europeans will be still asleep. Your countrymen, sir, as a rule are not such early risers."

"May Hatallah guide and protect you, Tomonggong!" the Colonel said, after a few moments of reflection. "I believe your proposal to be the best under present circumstances."

The night passed by undisturbed, no act of hostility being attempted on either side.

In the fortification, however, after the sentries had been placed, a true Dayak festivity was held. It was the blako ontong which they were about to celebrate, to invoke a blessing on the approaching nuptials of the beautiful Hamadoe with Dohong, alias Wienersdorf. Harimaoung Boekit, who loved his younger sister devotedly, was determined that the festivities in honor of the occasion should be long remembered among the inhabitants of kotta Djangkan.

As soon as the moon bathed the earth in her soft silvery rays, the bride was conveyed from her residence by a guard of honor consisting of seven young ladies who, like herself, were only attired in their saloi or short sarong. Seven Poenans in full war dress also went to escort Wienersdorf from his apartment. The betrothed pair were then led into a large shed which they were made to enter simultaneously, though from opposite directions. As soon as they appeared under the roof of the shed, the priestesses began to beat their drums and to chant a hymn in honor of bride and bridegroom, who in the meantime were conducted to the centre of the apartment. Hamadoe now presented her intended with a mandauw in token of claiming the protection of his valor. They then sat down together, each on a handsomely ornamented rattan mat. Their seats were so disposed as to leave a large space in the centre of the shed in which the priestesses took their places and commenced the rites.

Two hymns were chanted, the object of which was to drive away all misfortunes. These finished, each of the company present, including the bride, took a large stick and, led by the priestesses, proceeded to beat with all possible force against the posts, pillars, walls and roof of the shed. All the other houses and buildings of the kotta were next visited in turn and the same ceremony repeated in order to disperse ghosts and spirits. The noise, as may be imagined, was deafening.

The part taken by our Walloon, La Cueille, the pseudo Sheik, was truly comical. He had seized the branch of a tree and was beating about with it like a madman, making more noise than any twenty-five of the others. It amused the Dayaks to see the holy man so busily occupied, but an attentive observer might have remarked how carefully La Cueille managed to remain in the vicinity of one particular maid of honor, and how, while beating with his branch, he was steadily playing the gallant and trying to attract her notice. He was thus busily engaged when suddenly from every gun of the kotta there burst forth a terrific discharge. Our Sheik, almost dead with fright, turned a summersault, jumped up again, and followed by the laughter of the Dayaks fled toward the bastions where, as first artillerist of the fortification, he thought his presence might be needed. He there learned what had taken place. It was only Dalim firing blank cartridges in order to co-operate in the dispersion of malignant spirits. The pervading superstition is that evil spirits cannot endure noise and especially abominate the fumes of gunpowder, seeking a safe retreat as soon as they smell it.

The mirth had not abated when the Sheik reappeared inside the shed, where the betrothed had resumed their original places, surrounded by their respective guards of honor.

The priestesses now spread upon a mat in the centre of the shed all the offerings brought for presentation to the deities, which comprised seven full-grown hens, one egg, seven parcels made of pisang leaves and filled with boiled rice, seven joints of bamboo filled with raw rice, seven pieces of sugar-cane each a fathom long, besides pastry, confectionery, and fruits. The priestesses kindled two fires of green wood which emitted dense columns of smoke. Having finished all these preparations, they pronounced their incantations, the purport of which was to compel the King of the Antangs to convey the souls of these offerings, for the Dayaks believe that inanimate objects have souls, to the Radja ontong.

During these incantations the young men gathered round the fires, where they occupied themselves in blowing little poisoned arrows through their blow-pipes into the midst of the rising smoke in order to prevent the return of the unclean and evil spirits. The other guests, men as well as women, formed a large circle around a post planted in the northern half of the shed, to which a buffalo had been tied. Here, holding each other by the tips of their fingers, they moved a few steps backward and forward alternately, then bowed down as low as their knees, to leap up again uttering fearful yells.

This was the national dance called bigal. When it had lasted for about an hour the buffalo was gradually tortured to death by lance stabs. The quivering flesh was then torn away by some old women, hurriedly roasted and offered to the surrounding guests, who devoured it from their fists.

Some of the blood of the buffalo was smeared upon the foreheads, chests and hands of the bride and bridegroom. The priestesses next placed in front of each of the candidates for wedlock a piece of rattan about eight inches long, covered with a layer of dough made of rice meal mixed with gold dust. They then took a cocoanut shell full of toeak, drank a deep draught themselves, passed it over to the betrothed, both of whom partook of it, when it was handed around amongst the company for general delectation.

The Dayaks, men as well as women, are, as a rule, confirmed drinkers, and as many a hearty cup was emptied and the delicious liquor was liberally supplied, their revelry soon reached its climax. Johannes, however, with Schlickeisen, Amai Kotong and Dalim, took good care to restrain themselves within a certain limit of conviviality. Thus after drinking to the health of the young couple they refrained from taking any more of the alluring liquid.

Sheik Mohammed Al Mansoer was seated cross-legged on his little mat looking on the gay proceedings with a mournful face. The smell of the toeak irritated his olfactory nerves and with a disdainful look he surveyed the tumultuous scene. He maintained his priestly character, although it revolted against his Walloon nature; he had promised not to soil the garb of the descendant of the Prophet and he would keep his promise. He would show his companions that he also could sacrifice himself if needed, for the common weal. He was sitting thus disconsolate when suddenly a charming little face bent over his shoulders and passed a bowl of toeak under his nose.

He jumped up and tried to catch the enchantress, but quick as lightning she had outdistanced him in a moment.

"Mohammedans must not drink toeak," she slily cried out from afar.

"Confound the consequences," the Walloon cried, tearing his turban from his head and throwing it across the shed.

He then rushed towards the girl and in another moment was tenderly embracing her. He took the bowl from her hand and emptied it at a single draught.

A loud hurrah followed and when the turbanless Arab looked around he found himself surrounded by the guests, who with jovial and smiling faces felicitated him upon his choice.

Midnight had now arrived and as soon as the moon reached the zenith, the priestesses took the pieces of rattan put aside for Dohong and Hamadoe, removed the dough, measured the sticks and declared them to have grown longer, a favorable omen. The dough itself was now inspected. The gold dust was separated from it by washing, and carefully weighed, when it was found to be heavier than before. Thereupon the general joy became boundless, for it was thus proven that the invocation of the priestesses had been favorably received. The omnipotent Radja balawang boelau had promised his assistance, and the betrothed might rest assured that their impending marriage would be lucky and prosperous. Both of them were charged to preserve their piece of rattan by which their earthly fate had been revealed. Harimaoung Boekit undertook to have the gold dust converted into two wedding-rings, which both could wear forever. The Poenan chief also paid the priestesses a princely sum for their priestly services and the ceremony of the blako ontong was ended.

The festivities however were continued; toeak and confectionery were abundantly handed around after the religious ceremonies, and the most liberal hospitality prevailed during the night.

The day was just breaking when Johannes and Schlickeisen from their post of observation noticed a suspicious movement on the border of the forest. They saw two men, one of whom they thought by his uniform to be the Colonel, shake hands and separate, one making straight for the kotta while the other retired within the forest. In order to prevent a panic Johannes went down for Amai Kotong, who at once recognized the Tomonggong of Kwala Kapoeas.

"It is one of my oldest friends," he said, "and you must not harm him."

"Certainly not," Johannes replied. "He is too honest an old man. But I refuse to admit him inside the kotta. You go and speak to him, Harimaoung, and think of the gibbet which the whitefaces have promised you."

The Poenan smiled disdainfully.

Old Nikodemus in the meantime came nearer, carrying in his right hand a small Dutch flag tied to a short stick, while in his left he bore a handsome rattan walking-stick with a heavy golden knob, engraved with the Dutch coat-of-arms. When arrived at the distance of about one hundred steps from the fortification, he suddenly saw a head appear above the ramparts and heard a voice addressing him:

"Be saluted, Father Tomonggong! what may you want here?"

Frightened at the voice, which seemed familiar to him, he looked attentively and became alarmed on recognizing the well-known, smiling face of Harimaoung Boekit, the Poenan chief, the tiger of the mountains. What was *he* doing there? Was the Colonel right after all in supposing an insurrection to be on foot in' the upper country? The Tomonggong was so terribly frightened that he quite forgot to answer the question and remained fixed like a statue. Suddenly two rifle shots aimed with remarkable precision carried away the flag from one, and the walking-stick from the other hand. Johannes and Schlickeisen had given a sample of their marksmanship, with the sole intention of frightening and not harming the old man. They succeeded admirably, for he stood still looking down at the pieces of his shattered cane which, being a present of the Dutch Government, he valued more than all his other possessions. But when he heard the voice of Harimaoung Boekit again saying:

"Father, get away quickly," he took to his heels, his flight being accelerated by a few blank discharges from the Europeans.

"That has set the puppets going!" the Colonel said, on hearing the shots.

He had scarcely uttered these words when the Tomonggong himself appeared, terribly frightened and out of breath from running so fast. The old Chief sank upon the trunk of a tree, and was for some moments quite unable to utter a single word. At last, after having taken a draught of brandy from the flask offered to him by the Colonel,

"The Poenan chief is there."

Fear and horror were visible on the face of the Tomonggong of Kwala Hiang on hearing these words, though the Colonel was at a loss to account for his perturbation. Presently Nikodemus calmed down a little and related his experience, concluding with the opinion that their position had now become very alarming indeed.

"In what way, Tomonggong?"

"The Poenans are daring men, and I can only express my surprise that the night has passed so quietly. They are unequalled in the execution of night attacks."

"Oh, Tomonggong! It won't be so bad as all that," the Colonel remarked. "I am not at all alarmed."

"But I am, sir!" was the solemn reply. "I attribute our escape from some great calamity partly to the clear moonlight and partly to some festivities celebrated last night inside the kotta. Did we not hear the boom of their guns at nine, and the yells of the priestesses all night long?"

"It is true, Tomonggong, that your countrymen are unequalled in keeping up festivities. Being once together they will undoubtedly make a second night of it. I therefore believe that we have an admirable opportunity now to risk a well-directed assault on the kotta."

The old Tomonggong shook his head sadly.

"Impossible, sir; to-morrow will be full moon, the night will be like day; we should only cause unnecessary bloodshed."

"We won't act rashly, Tomonggong. We will only keep our men ready for any emergency."

"If once our men know that Harimaoung Boekit and his Poenans are inside the kotta, nothing will make them attack it; and more, I sincerely believe that they will even run away."

"So do I," said the Tomonggong of Kwala Hiang.

"But what business has this Poenan chief at kotta Djangkan?" the Colonel asked.

"I do not know, sir; it is above my conception. If I could only speak with Amai Kotong."

"But did you not see any Europeans during your visit to the kotta?"

"Not one, sir. I only noticed the smiling face of Harimaoung Boekit."

"Who fired at you?"

"I do not know; for the shots were fired from behind the palisades and through loopholes. Their shots were badly aimed or they would have killed me at such short range."

The Colonel smiled.

"Believe me, Tomonggong, they aimed admirably. It must have been the two Swiss who fired with the intention of not killing you."

"May Hatallah bless them!"

"Amen," the Colonel said smilingly.

They now decided to keep the presence of the head-hunters in the kotta a profound secret and to invest the fortification as closely as possible. Perhaps the stock of provisions in the kotta might not be large and famine would compel the garrison to capitulate.

Two days and two nights passed by undisturbed after this attempt of Tomonggong Nikodemus to interview Amai Kotong. Each night the moon rose brilliantly above the edge of the forest and brightened everything with her soft, clear white light, so that nothing could happen within a radius of two hundred yards without being observed by the besiegers. To attempt an assault under such circumstances would have been sheer madness. But in the same manner the moonlight protected the besiegers from the attacks of the Poenans, for Harimaoung Boekit did not hesitate to express his longing for a stormy night in order to wipe out his debts to those whom he thought were bent upon his capture.

Shortly after nightfall of the third day it became quite dark, as the moon would not appear above the horizon until about half-past eight. Johannes was sitting in conversation with Amai Kotong, Dalim and Harimaoung Boekit, when one of the sentries reported that a huge, shapeless object was visible abovestream quietly coming down with the current. They all started up in great haste, took their arms and hastened towards the side of the river to see what was in progress there. And truly at a distance of about 300 yards they observed slowly advancing toward them an object much too ponderous for a canoe and too irregular for a raft. It resembled more a floating island. The men were called to arms and held prepared for any emergency.

While they were all busy looking at the advancing object and speculating upon its nature, there suddenly arose from behind the kotta a cry of alarm, immediately followed by several rifle shots. Profiting by the general darkness the Colonel had succeeded in advancing with his Dayaks close to the palisades, and while the whole attention of the garrison was directed to the river an escalade was attempted and nearly met with success. One of the women, however, saw a figure leap from the ramparts into the darkness below. She had a hatchet in her hand and was busily cutting wood. Before the intruder could recover from the effects of his leap, she dealt him some violent blows on his head and arms, which soon laid him defenceless and weltering in his blood. Some of the garrison approached on hearing the cries of the woman just in time to receive the assailants who now appeared above the palisades. They were soon made acquainted with the Poenan mandauws and fell heavily wounded on the sharp landjoes planted at the foot of the parapet. The two Swiss and La Cueille, accompanied by the Poenans, now appeared on the ramparts and at once opened a heavy fire, although they could discover nothing in the darkness which reigned around.

They kept up their fire for some time, until the yells and cries becoming lost in the distance led them to conclude that all immediate danger was past. Proceeding to the spot where the escalade had been attempted they found one dead body inside and four severely wounded outside the fortification. It was impossible to prevent the Poenans from beheading these unfortunates. In fact, during the prevailing darkness and general confusion the Europeans gave no thought to Poenan barbarities. When, however, in the succeeding calm they saw a fire lighted in the square of the kotta, they knew what it portended, and as soon as the flames shot up, they observed these wild men dancing with the captured heads in their hands and besplashing everything round them with the still oozing blood. Harimaoung Boekit in particular seemed delighted; he had been amongst the first to sally from the fort in order to dispatch the wounded. He now skipped about like a madman, crying his "lēēēēh, lèlèlèlè ouiiit," and held a captured head to his mouth again and again, that the warm blood might run down his throat.

"They have not got the head-hunter yet!" he cried victoriously.

In a very short time the whole garrison of kotta Djangkan joined in the really diabolical dance, and the heads were passed from hand to hand in order to afford them all an opportunity of swallowing a few drops of the delicious red fluid. After the blood had ceased to flow they applied their lips to the bleeding necks and sucked them.

Disgusted at this scene the two Europeans sped away from the horrible tragedy and looked for Johannes. He too, upon hearing the firing, had gone to that part of the fort whence it had proceeded; but seeing that everybody was at his post, that the whole male population was under arms, he and Dalim had returned to the riverside.

The shapeless object came nearer and nearer, until they could distinctly discern that it was constructed of recently cut branches interwoven with long grass. Although the tide made for the opposite bank, the island seemed as if steered by a human hand. When it entered the circle which had been laid bare around the fortification it became distinctly visible in the moonlight. Johannes now fancied that he could discern something moving behind that floating mass and had already shouldered his gun when a voice was heard coming from the surface of the water.

"Ohoi! Amai Kotong."

"Who are you?" cried Dalim loudly.

"Somebody from soengei Mawat. I bear a message from the people over there."

The island in the meantime had floated to the front of the kotta, a narrow piece of water only separating it from the shore. Johannes and his men were lying stretched out on the bank, guns in hand, prepared for all emergencies. A native now appeared above the island, jumped into the water, and was proceeding to swim ashore when suddenly a shot sounded, followed by a loud shriek from the swimmer. The Colonel had also been watching the floating island, and upon seeing the native take to the water fired this shot after him. Before he could reload Dalim sprang into the river and seized the native, who but for his assistance would have sunk. He struck out for the shore supporting the wounded man and succeeded in bringing him inside the fort.

Alas! the poor messenger had received a fatal wound in his chest. He gave his message that the warriors of soengei Mawat, numbering about fifty men, had arrived and were posted in the forest to the north of the kotta, with the intention of attacking the besiegers that night.

This information given, the poor fellow expired.

The first act of the Dayaks of kotta Djangkan was to discharge their duty to their deceased brother. The body was dressed in a new suit of clothes and laid out on the floor of one of the dwellings of the kotta, on a handsomely flowered mat. A burning lamp was placed at his head, and the corpses of the four fallen enemies were ranged round him, their dissevered heads being placed upon the chests of the bodies to which they respectively belonged. Each had his talawang or shield in one hand and his mandauw in the other. The Dayaks believed that by this arrangement the souls of the beheaded enemies would be compelled to recognize the deceased Mawat as their lord in the Dayak heaven and there become his slaves. The titih now sounded the funeral knell, to be kept up during the whole of that night.

When daylight began to appear the toending was commenced. This consisted in gilding the nails of the hands and feet of the defunct and in painting seven red spots on his forehead. He was then placed in the coffin, and as he was known to have been a man of undaunted courage and had fallen like a warrior, they also placed his weapons beside him.

In the meantime the besieged had observed some signs on the part of the besiegers which clearly indicated their approaching departure. They had also heard the sound of oars and were eager to learn what had taken place.

At daybreak the sentries looked around, but could not find any trace of the enemy; not even a cloud of smoke arose to indicate that they were preparing their breakfast. A few men of the garrison crept outside, scoured the neighborhood and returned with the report that the enemy had departed. A loud hurrah greeted this piece of good news, the Europeans congratulating each other warmly. A messenger was despatched to the warriors of soengei Mawat to inform them of the departure of the besiegers. As, however, that unaccountable retreat might be only a ruse, due caution was not neglected and a lookout was again posted at the angle of the river below the kotta. The stirring question now was: What had driven the besiegers to quit the scene of battle so suddenly?

The solution of the mystery is as follows:

After the last skirmish the whole camp seemed downcast. The Colonel had been amongst the assailants who had scaled the palisades, but fortunately for him he had not yet acquired the art of climbing like a monkey. He had, therefore, been outstripped in the escalade by the more agile natives. While endeavoring to mount the barrier one of his men was wounded and fell back against him, bearing him down to the earth. His dress, but especially his boots, protected him from the sharp points of the randjoes, so that he only received a trifling scratch in the arm. The accident was witnessed by the two Tomonggongs, who immediately raised him and bore him away in safety. A few seconds more and nothing would have saved his head from the mandauw of Harimaoung Boekit.

It was immediately after this repulse that the arrival of this floating island was noticed by the Colonel and his coadjutors, who regarded it with the utmost suspicion and alarm. They were seated together on the trunk of a tree, watching its advance. Deep gloom was depicted on their countenances. They were conversing, but the subject of their conversation was far from enlivening. Both Tomonggongs urged a retreat on the plea that their condition had become alarming, especially now that some messenger had reached the kotta on this floating island. Who he was and whence he came they could scarcely guess, but certainly his visit boded no good to them.

The Colonel thought that the kotta ought to be more closely invested. Meanwhile he proposed to hasten to Bandjermasin, report the events and return in a steamer with a reinforcement of soldiers to punish this obstinate kotta.

Both Dayak chiefs listened to him with much consternation. That the Colonel could leave them behind was beyond their conception and they could scarcely find words to remonstrate. Tomonggong Nikodemus asked, with a faltering voice: "And how long will you be away?"

"You may expect me back again in nine, or at most, in ten days."

"It is not to be thought of, sir!" was the solemn reply of Nikodemus. "When you return you will find us all killed."

"But, Tomonggong!"

"I am in earnest, sir! Not a night will pass without our being attacked, and in those constant raids we shall be exposed to terrible losses. And when finally we are exhausted by these daily skirmishes and by nightly watchings, the great battle will be fought which will annihilate us altogether."

"But are you not three to one, Tomonggong?" was the bitter reproach of the Colonel.

"That means nothing against a well-entrenched army. And how long will our superiority in number continue after the tribes of the upper country shall have joined them?"

"But you forget that in ten days I will be here with a force sufficiently large to deal with all the tribes of Borneo."

"It will be too late then, sir!"

"Then what are we to do, Tomonggong?" the Colonel said, impatiently.

"Nothing but to let us go with you and return with you if necessary."

"And in the meantime we allow the deserters to escape," was the bitter reply.

"Very possible, sir! but rest assured they will escape just the same when you go away and leave us here."

"But they are caged like mice."

"Quite so, sir! But we are unable to keep the mice in their trap; they can leave it whenever they choose."

Although convinced of the correctness of Tomonggong's argument, the Colonel would not yield. For a moment he thought of remaining himself and of sending one of the chiefs to Bandjermasin. But knowing that the wavering character of the native would certainly involve a considerable loss of time, and that at headquarters the authorities would demand and expect the fullest information, he abandoned the idea. He was about to try once more to persuade the Tomonggongs to remain when one of the followers of the Chief of Kwala Kapoeas approached hurriedly and whispered something into the ear of the old gentleman.

"As I thought," the latter exclaimed, "the men of Kwala Kapoeas recognized Harimaoung Boekit and his Poenans during the last fight. They are terribly frightened and wish to leave. Most of them are already preparing their canoes. I must go and see what it all means."

"We will join you," said the Colonel and Tomonggong Patti Singa Djaja.

On arriving at the encampment they found their men in the greatest excitement. Terrible accounts were current of the ferocity and cruelty of the Poenans. Most of the inhabitants of kotta Baroe had already gone away and the others were on the point of taking to their canoes. The Colonel begged, nay commanded them to stay; but the little troop was panic-stricken. In a few moments he was left with only the two Tomonggongs, the canoes having disappeared one after another behind the first bend. The two Dayak chiefs exchanged looks and muttered a few words, after which they deliberately seized the struggling Colonel by his arms, forcibly carried him to his canoe and as soon as they had entered it, it shot away. It was truly an ignominious flight, but necessity compelled and they were forced to go.

As the canoe shot round the angle of the river the Colonel cast a parting look in the direction of the fortification, and shaking his fist exclaimed:

"I will return and be avenged!"

The siege had lasted only four days.

The joy of the inhabitants of the kotta was boundless. They all hurried outside to enjoy their regained liberty, and the first want which each of the inhabitants hastened to supply was a bath. It seemed as if suddenly the people were metamorphosed into amphibious animals. The whole population, men, women and children, splashed about in the clear river, performing rare feats of swimming with evident enjoyment. Their pleasure however was interrupted by a sudden cry of alarm, "Badjai! Badjai hai!" a crocodile, a large crocodile. The bathers thereupon sped away from the water as fast as possible, but the monster had already singled out its prey. It shot forward like lightning until it arrived near the bank, where it seized one of the women by the leg and tried to drag her under water. The poor victim's shrieks were heart-rending. Grasping the branch of an adjacent tree she clung to it desperately. A horrible and fearful struggle now ensued. The crocodile had seized her by the muscles of the thigh and it pulled and tugged away, determined to tear its victim from her hold. The woman yelled fearfully, her body describing the most awful contortions as her flesh was torn into shreds. Still she clung desperately to the saving branch which, though bent double, still resisted the vigor of the saurian.

But the poor woman, though struggling bravely, was fast becoming exhausted by the loss of blood and the intense agony of her sufferings. She must soon have succumbed but for the timely assistance which now arrived.

Dalim had left the river before the appearance of the crocodile, but when the fearful cry of Badjai reached his ears, he hastened back and from among the randjoes planted at the foot of the ramparts he selected a strong, sharp-pointed one, about two feet in length. This he firmly grasped in his left hand and then enveloped the entire arm in his wet saloi. His right hand he kept free for the use of the dagger which he put in his belt. Thus armed the Dayak approached the crocodile, which opened its mighty jaws to snap at the courageous opponent. Dalim instantly pushed his protected arm within its mouth, keeping it in such a position that when the animal sought to close its jaws, the points of the randjoe became fixed in the soft parts of the palate and effectually prevented their coming together.

An exciting struggle now followed which brought Dalim to the verge of exhaustion, when La Cueille, armed with his gun, broke through the circle of panic-stricken spectators. Availing himself of a favorable opportunity he took aim and fired. The crocodile, hit in a vulnerable part, gave a desperate leap, displaying his body five or six feet above the water. This movement also compelled Dalim to let go. He disappeared in the depths of the river, and almost at the same moment the monster was seen floating on the surface.

Dalim soon reappeared, floating at the side of his late enemy, motionless and insensible, but still grasping the randjoe. A djoekoeng was hurriedly procured, the crocodile was attached to the stern and both were thus conveyed ashore.

Wienersdorf vigorously rubbed Dalim with gin and soon succeeded in restoring him. His fainting had only been the result of his prolonged exertions and except a few slight scratches he had not received any injury.

The head of the crocodile was carefully bared of all skin and flesh. In the event of the death of the poor woman, it would serve as a fitting monument to surmount her grave. Alas, that same evening she succumbed to loss of blood. They tried to stop the bleeding but without success. The titih for the fallen Mawat had scarcely ceased when it had to be sounded again for this new victim.

As soon as the river drama was concluded the principal inhabitants of the kotta assembled to consider what further action was now to be taken. They had undeniably defied the authority of the Dutch; they had defended themselves arms in hand, and during the encounter several Dutch subjects had perished. How would all this be taken? That summary punishment would be dealt out to them was only too probable. The only way of preventing reprisals would be by the dispersion of the whole of the inhabitants of kotta Djangkan and their retirement to the inner country far above the falls, where whitefaces could not easily reach them. This course was now suggested; but although the proposition was applauded by the majority, it did not meet with undivided approbation. It was true they were descendants of the Badjankans; but they had intermarried with the neighboring tribes and had gradually become identified with them. The graves of their parents were here, here they had seen their first days and had had children born unto them; their fields and homesteads were here; therefore, to emigrate would be painful to all.

When the discussion had taken this shape and threatened to end in discord Johannes rose. He had previously spoken to Amai Kotong, the kotta chief, and to Harimaoung Boekit, the Poenan. He thus addressed the multitude:

"It would be folly to quarrel about a point which can be satisfactorily settled. One party desires to go away, the other insists upon remaining. Believe me, those who wish to remain are right. What is the origin of the quarrel with the Dutch? Your chief Amai Kotong has refused to deliver up Harimaoung Boekit, his guest and the son of his elder brother. At his command you have defended your kotta and have kept the laws of hospitality intact. He, and he alone, is the culprit, and he alone can be held responsible. The Dutch will never trouble any one but him who gave orders for opposition. On their return they will insist on the surrender of Harimaoung Boekit and of your chief, who has dared to oppose them."

A howl bursting forth like a thunderstorm was the immediate response to these words.

"Do you think we are mad? Never! Never!"

"Silence! Allow me to finish. The Dutch, I repeat, will only demand the extradition of Harimaoung Boekit and Amai Kotong, and—"

"But that is just what we will not consent to," cried the whole host.

"I know it; I know that a Dayak is incapable of delivering up his chief. Although high premiums are daily offered by the Dutch for the apprehension of offenders, not a single Dayak has ever sought to earn them, because there is not one among you who would buy his life with such money."

"No! No!!" was the enthusiastic cry.

"Good, that is how I like to hear you. Besides, such surrender will not be necessary. Harimaoung Boekit will take care to get away with his Poenans before the Dutch come back. Amai Kotong will accompany him; for he has assured me of his intention to return to Miri, his native country."

Perfect silence reigned amongst the multitude. They all looked towards the kotta chief as if eager to hear him avow his intentions. He simply nodded and said:

"I go away with the whole of my family."

"After this decision," Johannes continued, "the solution of the difficulty becomes more simple. You choose a new chief who sends a deputation to Bandjermasin to convey to the Dutch his regrets for the past, to explain all the circumstances, and to offer his submission and that of the whole kotta Djangkan. The deputies will relate how after the departure of the Kwala Kapoeëse, the population of kotta Djangkan, assisted by the men of soengei Mawat, deposed their chief Amai Kotong, and how he, in fear of being punished, saved himself by flight."

"But that would be a falsehood," cried the same voice as before.

"And would you tell the truth? Will you inform the Dutch that you have deliberately fired at their soldiers, and that you are sorry you did not continue to do so? As you like," Johannes smiled defiantly, "but," he solemnly continued, "remember that if you do not act as I advise you, you will in a couple of weeks have a whole fleet of steamers here, which in half an hour will level your kotta to the ground. No, believe me, and do as you are told. The advice I give you is good. An innocent fib like this will not anger Mahatara. It will harm nobody and prevent much mischief. Your souls, when led by Tempon Telon through the fire-fall into the land of souls, will consider themselves happy; for the roasting they will suffer will be too insignificant to complain of."

Johannes spoke mockingly and incisively, and he might have continued his oration indefinitely without meeting further interruption. They all gathered round Amai Kotong, who declared that he had long ago wished to end his days in the home of his ancestors, and that he now rejoiced in the opportunity of utilizing his departure for the welfare of the inhabitants of kotta Djangkan.

All gave their sanction without further murmur.

A few hours afterwards, when the Mawattese entered the fortification, they were informed of the proposed arrangement and the election of a new chief was immediately proceeded with. The greatest number of votes was given to a youth named Njawong, who consented to accept the title and post of Amai. Under the guidance of Johannes, the new chief selected a deputation consisting of two Djangkanese and two Mawattese, all prominent men, to offer the submission of kotta Djangkan. Johannes and Amai Njawong insisted upon the immediate departure of the deputies in order to arrest the preparations for war by their appearance and submission. They had strict orders not to overtake the departed besiegers of kotta Djangkan, but to keep at a respectable distance in order to prevent the the Commander of Kwala Kapoeas from returning to kotta Djangkan under the impression that an easy victory was now possible.

Johannes, like a good general, had thought of everything.

The sun had not yet sunk beneath the western horizon before the deputies had started on their journey.

The inhabitants of kotta Djangkan, who during the last few days had been in a whirl of excitement, gradually returned to their normal mode of living. Nothing was left to remind them of the siege and its incidents save the body of the poor woman, the victim of the crocodile. While that remained in the kotta only the melancholy sound of the titih would be heard. The noise and revelry of yesterday had given place to silence and perfect calm, and the contrast seemed to spread an air of desolation over the place.

CHAPTER XIII.

PREPARATION FOR THE JOURNEY—AN EMIGRATION—THE FISHING—A DAYAK TRIBUNAL—THE FINGER TEST—THE PROOF WITH THE LANCE—WIENERSDORF FINDS HAMADOE A TREASURE—LA CUEILLE DISCOVERS A COAL BED—A MISUNDERSTANDING—THE GOLD FEVER.

FOLLOWING upon the excitement and activity of the last few days, a short period of repose was truly welcome to all the denizens of the kotta. The Europeans, especially, found it desirable to take a thorough rest after their recent exertions before commencing preparations for the resumption of their journey. They were now to be accompanied by a whole colony consisting of one hundred and fifty souls, women and children included.

The distance to be traversed was not very great, kotta Djangkan being separated from kotta Rangan Hanoengoh by about ninety-three miles, as the crow flies. In a territory, however, like the upper Dayak country, the windings of the main road are so numerous as almost to double the distance.

Johannes kept hurrying them on, impressing upon the minds of the simple Dayaks that time was worth more than gold, and explaining that if the members of the deputation should be unsuccessful and the Dutch determine to return to the upper Kapoeas they might be there sooner than expected.

Having at last convinced them of the necessity for despatch, the first thing he thought of was the means of transport. The Kapoeas, in the absence of great droughts, is easily navigable as far as Kiham Hoeras, situated at half a day's journey beyond kotta Sambong. But at the first ebb-tide, or rather first acceleration of the tide, the great difficulties of a journey into the upper country begin. Then only a small craft can be employed and the utmost care is necessary in its management.

There were plenty of rangkans and djoekoengs at kotta Djangkan. All provisions and portable goods were placed in baskets made of woven rattan, shaped like inverted cones, about seventy-five inches high, tapering from forty inches across the opening to twenty-five inches at the bottom. These baskets are lined with waterproof bark and are further provided with tight-fitting lids.

The guns were left in the battery in case of the return of the enemy; but they were provided with strong rattan loops and kept ready for removal at a moment's notice. They had plenty of provisions, especially rice, and a good supply of lombok and other delicacies. Meat was scarce, the last salt beef and pork brought by the deserters having greatly diminished during their journey under the attack of the Dayaks. Amai Kotong and Harimaoung Boekit declared, however, that there would be no lack of animal food during their journey, as they would find many opportunities of shooting deer.

But in order to ensure a sufficient supply they decided upon having a fishing expedition on a gigantic scale.

Amongst the preparations for this, an important one was the

gathering of a large quantity of the roots of the tobah shrub, abundantly found among the surrounding hills. These roots were placed in djoekoengs filled with water and left to soak thoroughly. They were then beaten with flat pieces of wood until the water in the djoekoengs became of a milky-white color. The soaked fibres were then thrown away, the liquor properly skimmed and mixed with a strong infusion of tobacco. Six djoekoengs were thus filled with tobah-water.

Next morning at daybreak a large number of light canoes, amongst which were those containing the mixture, sailed up soengei Mawat. Their crews were charged with the duty of closing the stream with a salambouw, a great square net with medium-sized meshes. One edge of the net was anchored in the bed of the soengei by means of large stones which kept it fixed, while the other edge protruded above the water for about six inches. Thus the escape of the fish was effectually prevented. Two djoekoengs, each manned by three natives, were posted at the net to prevent its being damaged by passing canoes or carried away by the stream.

Having set their nets, the male portion of the expedition divided itself into parties of three men to each djoekoeng. The women —for many had come to witness the fun—were seated in two large canoes, while a third boat contained the priestesses—those unavoidable accompaniments of every native festivity.

They now rowed up the soengei quickly but quietly for about four hours, carefully blocking the mouths of some unimportant rivulets which opened into the Mawat.

Arrived at the selected spot, the tobah-water was thrown into the river at various points. The canoe floated noiselessly with the tide while the poisoned water was getting intermixed with the stream.

The fishermen in the meantime prepared for the collection of their booty. Of the three men occupying each canoe, the one at the stern steered while the other two, net or harpoon in hand, placed themselves expectantly on the bow and in the centre of the boat, all ready for action.

In about half an hour the effect of the narcotic fluid became visible. First, the smaller fish appeared on the surface, elevated their heads, swam about in gradually diminishing circles and seemed anxious to leap out of the water. These were simply fished up with the nets or baskets and thrown into the canoes.

The fish now increased in size and number, bringing the harpoon into requisition, as it was perfectly impossible to capture with the net giants over a yard in length. The noise and mirth became general, our Europeans heartily participating. The fifty canoes were continually shooting past each other over this restricted surface, the men steering their boats at the mere nod of the harpooners in pursuit of the fish as they leaped around, to be finally pierced by the harpoons.

The Europeans, not wishing to be behind in the national sport, endeavored to strike some big fish; and after repeated submersions, La Cueille actually succeeded in landing a large trout, though he excited the mirth of the spectators by his awkwardness.

At last the number of victims gradually diminished and the sport was considered to have reached its close. All the boats were suffered to drift with the tide and, still harpooning, laughing, yelling and joking, the multitude reached the mouth of soengei Mawat and the salambouw was hauled in. They then travelled homeward up the Kapoeas and the fishing party was received with a festival salute from the guns of kotta Djangkan. Ten of the djoekoengs were brimful of fish.

The greater part of the booty was divided among the company. Fish killed by tobah poison are perfectly harmless and can be safely eaten, but cannot be dried or cured, as they soon begin to putrefy. Most of the trout were cut into slices and wrapped in leaves to be roasted with some salt and powdered lombok. As these, when thus prepared, may be kept for a considerable time, they proved a valuable addition to the general stock of animal food.

On the day following this fishing expedition, our deserters witnessed a ceremony of quite a different nature. It really seemed as if fate had destined them to experience the whole of the interior life of these tribes among whom they now found themselves transplanted.

In the Dayak country it is customary to hold a judicial enquiry once a week. The chief of the kotta, surrounded by from three to seven of the elders, sits in judgment to settle all the differences which may have occurred during the preceding week and which are sufficiently important to require his professional assistance.

The Dayaks are as a rule the most litigious people in creation and never feel happy unless they have some "basara" or action pending. They would prove an unexhaustible source of revenue to European lawyers, could they be transplanted into our Western hemisphere. Their basara day therefore simply means another holiday for the inhabitants of a kotta, attendance at a sitting of the judges being a treat almost irresistible. The one which was now to take place was invested with special importance, as the new chief Amai Njawong would preside for the first time.

First of all several trivial charges were disposed of, in the progress of which the Europeans did not fail to notice the shrewdness and sagacity of the solicitors. With the utmost interest they watched the peculiar practices of these men of the law. They were provided with a number of small rattan dolls as part of their professional paraphernalia. Whenever a point was gained by the production of irrefragable proof, the plaintiff's lawyer stuck one of these dolls in the ground before him, so that at the end of his pleadings a number of these figures were arrayed around him. When in the defence any of his arguments or facts were disproved and the defendant's solicitor scored a point by planting a doll before his own seat, one of the plaintiff's collection had to be removed. Thus these dolls represented so many items of established evidence. At the close of the pleadings the verdict was awarded to the one who had most dolls standing. In these peculiar proceedings, sleight of hand plays no unimportant part. Dolls are sometimes nefariously planted or abstracted, and the recriminations which ensue necessitate a new action on the following court day, with the resumption of proceedings "de novo."

Among the most important cases there was one in which three persons stood accused of the same offence. Two of them belonged to people of distinction, but the third was a hireling.

The accusation being formally made the court proceeded to the manjapa or administration of oaths. A black hen was produced and beheaded by the accuser—who then solemnly swore to the truth of the charge. The accused in their defence observed the same formality and swore solemnly to their innocence. In this dilemma the judges had recourse to the Dayak ordeal.

They ordered three basins to be brought, filled with melted rosin. A large fire was kindled, on which the hens decapitated during the taking of the oaths were burned. In the meantime the three accused had taken their places around the basin. At a sign by the president, each of them was made to dip his right fore-finger in the melted rosin and to stir it around twice or three times. The fingers duly descended into the basins at the given signal; a horrible shriek being uttered by the hireling who, notwithstanding his agony, had the courage to stir the burning contents the required number of times. The fingers of the accused were carefully bandaged until the following morning when they would be judicially inspected. He whose finger would be found flayed or otherwise damaged would be adjudged the culprit.

The last case to be decided was one which had been under investigation for a long time. Some years before, an old man had died, supposed to be poisoned. His son had brought an action against a man who had been heard to vow vengeance against the deceased for giving false evidence against him in a charge of fish stealing. Whenever the case had been called before, the same result had always followed. The number of dolls had always been equal for both parties, and it had therefore been impossible to determine who was right and who was wrong.

Thus stood the matter until to-day, when it was proposed to proceed to the hagalangang in order to arrive at the truth. In the great square of the kotta, both plaintiff and defendant were placed in narrow bamboo cages closed in at the bottom, which while protecting the lower part of their bodies left their heads, arms and chests fully exposed. The cages were designedly made narrow to defeat any attempt which their occupants might make to stoop or plunge. Being placed facing each other at a distance of about thirty paces, both men were supplied with pointed bamboos a yard long, which at a given signal they had to throw at each other. The one who should be first wounded, however slightly, would be considered guilty. If it should be the accuser, his action would be lost and he would be compelled to pay to the accused a penalty of 1,000 rcar as shame money. He would also have to present him with a mandauw as a token that he accepted the decision and that he continued to respect him as heretofore. If, however, the accused should be wounded, he would be made to confess his guilt, handed over to the accuser, who would therewith acquire the right of torturing him to death.

When the judges had taken their seats a couple of youths were told off to pick up the lances and restore them to the combatants. Amai Njawong then gave the signal to commence. The first throw effected nothing and being wide of the mark was received with a howl of disapprobation. The second and third were better aimed, but the fourth was fatally decisive. Struck full in the chest the accused instantly dropped dead, while the accuser at the same moment also received his death blow. The weapon of his opponent had struck him at the side of the neck and severed the carotid artery. He survived a few minutes only, dying from hæmorrhage.

The president hereupon declared that their deities had interposed to prevent a verdict in order that the matter might remain a secret forever. He ordered the bodies to be delivered to their relatives for the usual burial ceremonies and shortly afterwards the titih was heard from two sides of the kotta.

Deeply moved by these strange scenes the Europeans sought their room, where for some time they remained wrapt in deep silence. At last La Cueille, like one trying to escape from a nightmare, cried out:

"What a queer lot we have come among!"

It seemed to break the spell and lift the veil of gloom from all the others.

"So we have," Johannes answered, "and we are always booked for the best seats in order that we may thoroughly enjoy the performance. And yet we dare not interfere."

"I should think not," Schlickeisen added. "Suppose they should place us in similar cages?"

"Or make us dip our fingers in boiling rosin?" said Wienersdorf.

"Yes," Johannes added warningly. "Even Hamadoe would not hesitate to start an action for breach of promise."

"And then good-bye to your finger," Schlickeisen smiled at the Walloon, for he too, like Wienersdorf, had been obliged to be betrothed to a Dayak maiden.

The Walloon looked wistfully at his index as if he already felt the burning pain.

"That is awkward," he muttered. "A man may now and then change his mind."

"So you may, but mind your finger; a basin of that rosin is far from nice."

"I thank you for your advice," said La Cueille; "I will mind my finger. But there is much that I cannot understand and am anxious to know more about."

"What may that be?" Johannes asked.

"Three of them dipped their fingers in the rosin, didn't they? Now suppose to-morrow morning they find two, or even all of them with burnt fingers?"

"Oh, holy simplicity!" Johannes burst out. "Well this is rich! All three, ha, ha, ha! That would prove trying to the wisdom of King Solomon. Ha, ha, ha!" and Johannes laughed heartily.

"What are you laughing at?" the Walloon asked angrily. "I cannot make it out. Three men have dipped their fingers in that molten rosin; now what could be more natural than to find the whole three of them burnt? But at all events tell us the cause of your laughter; perhaps we may join you."

"You are a donkey."

"I have been told that before, I know, but is that what you are laughing at?"

"Oh, you stupid! Did you not hear the shrieks uttered by number three of the accused?"

"Yes, I did."

"Well, he alone burnt his finger and nobody else. But I had better explain it to you. The first two are well-to-do young men who only had to interchange a look with the judges in order to be taken for innocence personified. Possibly the judges had received their fee beforehand; if not they are quite certain to get it. The third was a poor lad from whom nothing was to be expected. He had no significant looks to interchange."

"I would understand all this were it not that with my own eyes I saw their three fingers move up and down in the molten rosin; I looked most attentively."

"Did you now; and what else did you see?"

"What more could I see?"

"That is what you call looking attentively?" Johannes said mockingly. "And did you not see that the color of the rosin was not the same in each basin?"

"And suppose it was not? Rosin is rosin."

"No, stupid! Rosin is not rosin, or rather one is and the other is not. I see I must explain this also. The finest sorts of rosin, being pure, melt at a very low temperature, while the less fine, being porous and sandy, require a much greater heat to melt them."

"Aha!"

"Do you see it now? When therefore the judges order you to dip your finger in a basin of the best rosin, which only requires very little heat to liquefy, you can keep it in there as long as you choose without more pain than that of a slight scald. But let them put your finger in the poorer kind and you would bellow as the hireling, and to-morrow morning you would have that finger beautifully flayed. Now, good-night."

Johannes was quite correct in his prediction. On the following morning when the wounded fingers were unbound for official inspection two appeared wholly unhurt. The finger of the hireling was, however, frightfully burned, the skin coming off with the bandage. The accused was duly condemned.

In the meantime preparation for the impending departure to soengei Miri had not been neglected. Provisions and ammunition were all packed, guns and rifles were ready for shipment, and as nothing remained to be done except the confection of some trifling domestic preparations, the Europeans had a few days to spend as they chose.

Wienersdorf at first thought of botanizing a little, but abandoned the intention in order to devote himself to his betrothed and to prepare her for the amenities of European life and society. Although customary among the Dayaks for lovers to remain separated until the day of their wedding, the preparations for the journey rendered it almost impossible now to adhere strictly to this rule. Besides would not Dohong have to watch over his intended during their travel? Had not Harimaoung Boekit almost intimated as much when he said that nobody could protect his sister better than the brave Dohong, the infallible marksman. All restraint between the two lovers was thus temporarily relaxed, and our Swiss lost not a single moment in making himself cognizant of the character of her whom he was about to marry. The result was highly satisfactory. Hamadoe, who externally was very beautiful, proved also to possess a heart and a character of the noblest mould. That she was clever Dohong at once perceived; now and then she seemed ignorant of the most trivial matters, but her quickness and docility in receiving impressions were truly remarkable. Her goodness and affability he had repeatedly observed. She detested cruelty and prevented all unnecessary suffering as much as lay in her power, while morbid cowardice was strange to her. She was the proud child of nature. Secluded from the impressions of the outer world she had never seen anything beyond the horizon of her native forests and for her human nature did not extend further than her tribe. Whenever cruelties and tortures were practiced by the members of that tribe she turned her face and revolted against the idea of being powerless to contend against the influence of native morals and laws. And yet she would never have given her hand and heart to a coward. The husband of her choice must be able to wield his sword with a strong manly hand, must know how to support and courageously defend his wife. She had never tasted human flesh, and once when she had been offered a dish of human brains had fainted and was heartily laughed at by the company. She felt ashamed of this weakness, but she so earnestly begged them not to repeat the jest that even the most ignorant amongst them promised obedience.

She was extremely modest. Moving in an atmosphere of impurity she had always tried to keep her character spotless. Whenever she heard expressions uttered in her presence whose meanings she could not ignore, she knew how to silence the realists by a stern look. Thus she had succeeded by the mere influence of her presence in commanding a propriety which was contrary to the general behavior of these forest people.

Like all Dayak young ladies she had gone unclad up to the age of maturity, simply wearing a "sapieng" in imitation of the fig-leaf of our primitive parents. Later on she had clothed herself in a saloi like other young girls of her tribe, and in her innocence had never seen aught of impropriety in that attire. She knew no better. But when at the blako ontong she had felt the piercing glance of her bridegroom there stole over her a sensation of shame hitherto unknown to her, and she seemed to wish that the earth would open beneath her to rescue her from the gaze of all these men collected around her. The sensation was intolerable, and therefore from that moment she always appeared dressed in a badjoe, although her companions reproached her for already assuming the exclusive garb of a married woman when in company. The same charming simplicity characterized all her intercourse with Wienersdorf. Though she was ignorance personified, she yet understood all that was told her and was especially attentive when he spoke of the outer world, that world which he so well pictured to her, but of which she could form no idea. Her brothers had been to Bandjermasin and had seen so much there as to render their narratives inexhaustible. But what was Bandjermasin at the side of Singapore? And what were those again compared to the cities of the land of the whitefaces? Had he ever been there? she asked.

For a moment he hesitated. He still wished to keep up his disguise of Kwala Kapoeas and was on the point of telling her that he had been to Java and that from there he had embarked on board a very large ship bound for Holland, but a look into her beautiful, innocent and truthful eyes modified his intention. He threw his arms round her, drew her towards him, and disclosing one of his shoulders from which the drug with

WIENERSDORF AND HAMADOE.

which he had been stained had been rubbed off, he exhibited his white skin.

"Olo bapoeti!" a white man, she uttered with a smothered voice. He kept her prisoner in his arms for a moment; her bosom heaved violently; she then threw her lovely arms around his neck and whispered:

"Be it as you will: you are the iron tree; I am the creeper; together we are strong."

Vehemently he pressed her to his heart.

He now told her how he had deserted from the Dutch to return to his country. She seemed not to understand him. All white people were Dutch, she had thought, and with the greatest difficulty he explained to her that the whitefaces had more varieties still than the dark race, of whom she had only seen her own tribe and none beyond. She soon felt sympathy with the man who for the sake of seeing his native country again had exposed himself to so many dangers. Nevertheless she could not understand his feelings in the matter, for she argued could one not be happy anywhere? He smiled at her remarks, and making use of the opportunity he pictured to her European society and described the invaluable privileges which are conferred by the protection of civilization and strengthened by ties of mutual love. He explained how in his country the spilling of blood was prohibited, and how a white man might live amongst his companions independent of the differences existing between their various tribes. He told her that the whitefaces were all free; that they had no slaves who lived in constant fear of their lives and were subject to be killed in the most horrible manner. He explained the status of woman amongst the white people, her share in the battle of life, the estimation in which she was held, reigning next to her husband as a true companion instead of being regarded as she was here, as a beast of burden, the slave of her spouse.

As she listened attentively a new world rose before her eyes. He went on telling her of the beautiful dwellings of the whitefaces, so different from the hovels she had hitherto seen. He described the European towns with their squares, streets, churches, palaces, theatres, promenades, and in his description employed such charming enthusiasm that he created a complete revolution in her primitive mind. Involuntarily she embraced him with tenderness and almost inaudibly she whispered into his ears that she was willing and ready to follow wherever Dohong would lead her. She only begged of him for the present to preserve the secret that he was no Dayak. She would undertake to inform her brother Harimaoung Boekit of the fact at a fitting opportunity. While the lovers were thus enjoying some of their most happy moments, each of the other two Europeans had tried to kill time in his own way. La Cueille being also in an amorous mood had wished to amuse himself by courting, but his Moendoet had been entrusted with the culinary preparations and he was manifestly quite superfluous. Besides she was highly perfumed by garlic which she was manipulating and these odors compelled her adorer to withdraw. He went away disconsolate intending to take a solitary walk in the neighborhood, when he met Schlickeisen, who also having nothing to do joined him. Both men stepped into a djoekoeng and were quietly paddling along when suddenly La Cueille observed a lump of coal lying on one of the banks.

"Quite true," he said. "Johannes some time ago told me that at half-tide a coal vein is visible in the banks of the river just beyond kotta Djangkan. It is low tide now; let us have a look."

"I am agreeable," the Swiss replied. "But had we not better get our guns? In a country like this it is always well to be armed."

"We have our mandauws," the Walloon answered, "but I will take the opportunity of bringing a crowbar and pickaxe."

A few minutes later the two men with their rifles and implements were seated in a boat and quietly rowed up the river. They had hardly travelled half an hour when they began to perceive a black streak upon the fine, gray, scaly clay which composed the steep banks of the stream.

The explorers rowed towards the widest part of the black streak in order to examine it more closely. La Cueille detached a couple of pieces and found that he had come upon a mine of coal.

In color it was of a dull grayish black and was so fragile that it easily crumbled between the strong fingers of the Walloon. On fracture it exhibited a fine leafy structure, taking the shape of a parallelopipedon. Armed with his pickaxe he broke through the upper layers, which had been exposed for ages to wind and weather, and soon he had the satisfaction of discovering coal of quite a different quality. Not yet satisfied the Walloon mounted the bank, proceeded a couple of hundred yards inland and commenced to dig at a certain depression of the soil. The earth was loosened with pickaxe and crowbar and removed with their hands. In a couple of hours they came upon a layer of soft, gray-brown clay which caused the Walloon to cry out with joy. He broke through this layer and found it to be about eight inches deep. He examined the debris and recognized fine scales of iron ore which made him certain of the value of his discovery. Shortly afterward and under the combined exertions of the two Europeans the iron teeth of the crowbar and pickaxe produced their first large lump of true coal.

"This is quite a different product from the one over there," the Walloon exclaimed.

Schlickeisen looked at it carefully, but could find no difference.

"It seems exactly like the coal found near the river," he said.

"Only with this difference," added La Cueille, "that these are jet-black—and see how resplendent on fracture. But what are these spots? They look like amber! Good heavens, they are resinous spots, the best proof that this is fat coal. What a treasure!"

The Swiss smilingly looked at his excited companion, and although he little understood mining he could appreciate the rapture of the Walloon and greatly enjoyed it.

"Let us break up a good stock," the latter exclaimed, "so that I may test the quality by and by."

They proceeded with their task and soon collected a sufficient stock for the experiment proposed to be made by La Cueille. Most of the lumps were so large as to require their united strength to carry them into the djoekoeng.

As soon as they had landed their treasure at the kotta the

Walloon kindled a couple of fires with which to make his observations. Schlickeisen however did not remain with him. He went his way, leaving his friend to pursue his experiments. Three hours afterwards when the other Europeans sought the Walloon they found him still busy with his coal.

"Look!" said he, "you could not find better coal than this in any of the mines of Liege or Hainault."

The Walloon seemed mad with delight and his companions stared at him in utter astonishment.

"But of what practical use is your great discovery?" asks Johannes.

"Do not the Dayaks use coal?" observed Wienersdorf.

"No! the use of batoe kasientoe, as they call coals, is considered unclean. In some places it is forbidden to touch coal or to approach a coal fire. Whence this superstition springs I don't know; but the Dayaks have a legend which relates how Mahatara in a moment of wrath buried whole forests in the earth and turned them into stone. This may account for their horror of coal."

Is coal distributed all over Borneo?

In our present ignorance of the resources of the island such a question is difficult to answer. But as far as we know, we may safely say, yes; for wherever the Dutch are established numerous and valuable coal veins have been developed.

The coal debate might have lasted all night but for Harimaoung Boekit who now approached to join his friends. He held in his hands a tarodjok—a small pair of scales to which he drew Johannes' attention.

"Well, Amai, did you weigh it?"

"Yes," responded the Poenan grinning,—"it weighs just one 'boea kajoe.'"

"And what may that be worth?"

This question was too difficult for the Poenan to answer. He scratched his head and looked at the company one by one. At last, addressing his future brother-in-law, he asked him:

"If one thaël costs thirty reals, what is the value of a boea kajoe?"

Wienersdorf stared, his face looking so blank that his companions could not refrain from bursting out into laughter. He had not the remotest idea of what his interrogator wished to know. Harimaoung pointed to the scales, in one of which there was a fine metallic powder of a dark yellow hue, greatly resembling dirty copper filings, while the opposite scale contained a small brass plate representing a weight. Even now Wienersdorf did not know what was required of him and he consequently shrugged his shoulders.

"People coming from Bandjermasin always boast of knowing more than others," said the Poenan, "and now this blockhead cannot tell the value of one boea kadjoe when a thaël costs thirty reals."

"But what costs thirty reals? What? Which?" asked the Swiss, somewhat offended.

"What! This boelau oerei (gold dust)."

"Aha! this is gold dust, is it? and you wish me to tell its value. Well, I don't know."

"You don't know! Oh, my poor sister, what an idiot of a

husband she will have." Johannes burst out laughing and was joined by La Cueille and Schlickeisen.

"But, Amai," Johannes said, "Dohong does not understand your weights. They use quite different ones at Bandjermasin and Kwala Kapoeas. Listen," continued he, addressing Wienersdorf, "one thaël weighs two ringgits; one ringgit, two sadjampols; one sadjampol, two and a half sakobangs, and one sakobang, two boea kadjoes. Do you see it now?"

"Yes, I see, Amai, there is three guilders of gold dust there. But what is the meaning of all this? I don't quite understand yet."

"Oh," said Johannes, "I intended to surprise you all by turning you into gold seekers—in fact, make your fortunes without your knowledge. The fun is spoilt now. The Poenan and I have been washing gold to-day. I took my first lesson and this is the result of two hours' labor. I found all this myself. My teacher's share is much larger."

"Three guilders in two hours!" exclaimed Wienersdorf, "that is not bad pay. I am sorry we cannot stay here longer; we might make a purse worth carrying home."

"And yet we have been rather unlucky, have we not, Amai?"

The Poenan smiled and answered, "That was your fault. You did many forbidden things and made the sarok boelau fly away. It is a wonder you found any gold at all. But the sarok boelau will avenge himself, you may be sure you will be taken with the fever."

The Dayaks believe that all bodies animate and inanimate

have souls ; that of gold until it is conquered by man is called sarok boelau.

"Oh, Amai," said Johannes, smiling, "fever has no hold on me. When it comes I will pass it on to you."

The Poenan was by no means pleased at this joke, the intention of passing on the fever to him was just a little too much. He however proceeded to tell his friends that in his country, the soengei Miri, gold was much more common than here. He promised to assist them in seeking it, provided they would agree to conform strictly to the usages of the craft.

This promise set them all talking about gold ; they were already attacked by the fever—gold fever.

CHAPTER XIV.

A DAYAK IRON-FOUNDRY—A PAIR OF NATIVE BELLOWS—HARIMAOUNG BOEKIT DOWN WITH FEVER—WIENERSDORF BECOMES A PHYSICIAN—JOHANNES A MAGICIAN—NEWS FROM KWALA KAPOEAS—ONCE MORE EN ROUTE—THE WIDOW'S STONE—KIHAM HOERAS AND ITS PASSAGE—HALAMANTEK.

THE four friends continued sitting together till a late hour, their discourse dwelling upon the subject of gold seeking. La Cueille not feeling particularly sleepy reminded Johannes of a promise to narrate his experience of a Dayak iron-foundry.

"I am quite willing to kill another hour or so and shall be glad of the opportunity to interrupt our conversation about gold seeking, as that is a subject which only causes unnecessary excitement.

"But don't expect to hear of processes and machinery as found in the West. A Dayak foundry is of a very primitive nature, as you will soon understand. This is what I personally saw in one of my expeditions:

"Near the spot where the ore had been originally dug and under cover of a lofty roof, the Dayak iron-founders constructed on some small natural or artificial mound a trough of plastic clay measuring about a yard in diameter. The walls of this trough——"

"Had you not better first inform us of the spot where the ore was found?" La Cueille asked.

"As you please. The iron ore is generally found near the coal formation, both mineral products being met with together, and one layer generally covering the other. Seldom is the one absent where the other is found."

"Parbleu!" the Walloon exclaimed, "that is extremely fortunate."

"The layers containing the iron ore are generally visible at low tide in the lower banks of the river. The Dayaks choose their opportunity during the dry season and collect the necessary quantity of ore which, as it is generally saturated, is somewhat of a doughy nature. They first dry it in the sun, then cut it into lumps of the size of a walnut and store it away for further use. The ore does not always present the same appearance. It sometimes consists of a mixture of larger or smaller pieces of dull or occasionally shiny brown iron, and is a kind of iron oxy-hydrate of a yellowish-brown crystalline texture. Sometimes it is in the form of brown ochre, caused by the partial decomposition of the iron, and at other times in the shape of very hard sandstone in which the ore seems to be deposited. Each pound of ore yields five and a half ounces of pure iron. That is all I know about it, and that much I have been able to gather from the reports.

"The walls of the trough," Johannes continued, "were about four inches thick at their edges, but increasing downwards and leaving not more than thirty-five square inches inside for the diameter of the bottom. This trough, called laboerang, formed their real melting furnace, and as I was informed was dried in the sun for a fortnight, after which a hole for the reception of the nose of the bellows was made about seven inches above the bottom, while another hole, alier, was made in the opposite wall for the removal of cinders and for drawing off the melted iron. Our party just arrived when they were beginning to charge the furnace, which had previously been bound around with hoops of rattan and bamboo to prevent its splitting open. On the floor of the laboerang they strewed a thick layer of very finely-powdered charcoal, leaving free a square space, kakat, for the collection of the melted iron.

"Above the square space and in the hole arranged for it they placed the nozle of the bellows. This nozle, called boetoeng, was made of baked clay and reached half over the centre of the kakat. They then filled the oven about three-quarters full of charcoal, over which they spread the ore, previously roasted over large wood fires until it had acquired a red color. The charcoal above the kakat was now ignited and the alier closed with a layer of wet clay. The bamboo tube of the bellows was next introduced and the fire kindled by first blowing it gently and gradually increasing till the highest possible temperature was attained."

"You mentioned a bamboo tube just now; surely those bellows were of European make," La Cueille asked. "No native could manufacture such an article?"

"Spoken like a European," Johannes said somewhat bitterly "These bellows were decidedly not of European make. Listen and I will try to explain their construction: In a straight wooden cylinder, usually made of a hollowed-out tree of about ten inch diameter and two and a half yards long, there moved a piston, the disk of which in order to secure perfect exclusion of air was pasted over with feathers and a kind of varnish composed of oil and rosin. The bamboo tube in question, called passiong, was fixed underneath the cylinder and the air was forced through this. The rod of the piston, eight to ten yards long, was fixed to a long bamboo, which being placed horizontally considerably lessened the labor of working it. This kind of bellows was called bapoetang, and the workmen in order to obtain the required temperature made from forty to fifty pulls a minute.

"When the oven was filled the fire was kept up, a fresh supply of ore being thrown in from above as the contents decreased by combustion. But in order to supply the necessary fuel at the same time, they added ten parts of charcoal to one of fresh ore. They opened the alier hourly for the removal of the slag, but instantly closed it again with wet clay.

"At night the oven was cooled down, the alier opened and the iron thus obtained removed by means of large wooden tongs with iron points. The iron, now a shapeless tough lump of a brownish-red appearance, was then thrown down on the floor which had been previously covered with pounded slag and was belabored with wooden hammers into the form of a cube, weighing about sixty pounds. Each of these was afterwards divided into ten equal parts and hammered and purified from slag until fit for the forge. That is the whole process of manufacture. I may add that the iron from the Kapoeas regions is considered of the best quality, which means a great deal, considering that Borneo iron is celebrated all over the Indian Archipelago. The weapons made of it are highly prized everywhere, and I myself have seen mandauws and swords from Nagara, where the best arms of all are made, with which a nail of seven to the pound was cut through without doing any damage to the edge of the weapon. I have now told all I know and trust I have satisfied the curiosity of our Walloon."

The latter laughed and answered thankfully:

"I shall be able to sleep at last, good-night! By-the-bye, what is the Dayak for iron?"

"Sanaman, and the ore they call batoe sanaman."

"Many thanks, good-night."

Shortly after midnight Wienersdorf was aroused by a Dayak who beckoned him to come outside for a minute where Hamadoe was waiting to speak to him. He found her crying bitterly. Silently taking him by the hand she conducted him to the abode of Harimaoung Boekit, her brother, whom he found raving in a paroxysm of fever. A profuse perspiration covered the brow of the patient, his respiration was rapid and stertorous and in his delirium he spoke of nothing but Johannes' threat of sending the fever home to him. This incident, so constantly repeated by the sick man, spread among the Poenan companions gathered around his bed, and murmurs of dissatisfaction, nay even threats were heard amongst them. To play upon the credulity of a primitive race is rather a dangerous experiment.

Hamadoe, full of alarm at the condition of her brother, had thought it wise to summon her Dohong, having full faith in the omnipotence of the art of healing possessed by the whitefaces. Wienersdorf being thus created physician felt the patient's pulse, looked at him with a sage and dignified air and applied his hand to his forehead, arms and chest. At length he ordered the body of the Poenan to be bathed with vinegar and water and cold compresses to be applied to the head, with the satisfactory result of reducing the temperature of the patient and of soon restoring him to consciousness. He further prescribed an infusion of akar pahit, the root of a native plant and a very good substitute for quinine, with the addition of some honey, and ordered his patient to take a draught of it occasionally. Whether from the effect of the medicine or from natural reaction the patient soon fell into a healthy slumber. Wienersdorf then went to inform Johannes of what had taken place and was surprised to find his information received with a burst of laughter.

"I don't see anything to laugh at," the Swiss said, "the situation is too serious. Believe me I have heard the most horrible threats uttered against you for sending the fever to the Poenan chief and you know best what sort of people they are."

"Don't feel alarmed, my worthy Swiss! I will soon make it right again. When next they call you in professionally, send for me and I will accompany you."

Early in the morning the Dohong was sent for again, and accompanied by Johannes he soon entered the sick room, where he found preparations being made for incantations to remove the disease by the aid of the priestesses.

"For Heaven's sake," the Dohong cried, "stop this noise; it will make him worse."

Upon seeing Johannes the patient displayed an angry countenance and reproached him with ingratitude.

"I pardon you," he said, "for Dohong's sake, but they have

taught you this ingratitude in Bandjermasin. What have I done to you to be treated so badly?"

"Only a mistake, my friend," Johannes answered. "I was tipsy last night when the fever seized me. I had taken too much toeak and I intended to send the fever to the Commander of Kwala Kapoeas. It seems that I have made a serious blunder and mentioned your name instead. But you will see that I have the power of removing the fever as well as of sending it."

And taking a handful of rice from a cocoanut shell which he had brought with him he strewed the grains around the bed of the patient, chanting in a loud voice: "O strewn grains, enter the house of the Sangiangs together; enter noiselessly, ye golden grains, into the home of the Sangiangs!"

Then passing his hand over the forehead of the patient and gesticulating as if casting away something, he said:

"At last it is over. One hour hence the Commander of Kwala Kapoeas will have the fever as badly as you have had it. Remain quiet now, drink the obat—medicine—which Dohong will give you. In about half an hour's time you will experience some singing in the ears but don't feel alarmed, it will be the sign of the disappearance of fever for Kwala Kapoeas."

With solemn steps he quitted the apartment. Wienersdorf now produced a bottle containing a solution of sulphate of quinine and gave it to the Poenan to drink.

Without moving a muscle the latter swallowed the bitter draught, wiped his lips with the back of his hand, but assured his doctor that he had greater confidence in the magical performance of Johannes than in all the bitter drugs in creation.

A quarter of an hour afterwards he had fallen into a deep slumber.

Previous to his departure from Kwala Kapoeas, Johannes with his accustomed foresight had requisitioned some quinine from the doctor's medicine chest and this drug was now rendering him good service. Dalim, however, warned him against making similar experiments upon the natives.

"Threats," he said, "have been heard and suspicions have been muttered. Some of the people spoke of the danger of receiving total strangers like yourselves in the kottas. Up to the present they have confined themselves to murmurs. But only let them broach the word antoeën and every mandauw will be unsheathed and you will soon be weltering in your blood, your heads in the hands of the Poenans."

"What is the meaning of the word antoeën?" Schlickeisen asked.

"It means the power of changing into an evil spirit in order to steal the soul of a man and thus to make him ill," was Dalim's reply.

"I thought stealing a man's soul was killing him?"

"Yes, but death only results when the soul remains away too long. With the Dayak illness is simply considered a temporary absence of the soul from the body and healing is therefore the restoration of the abstracted soul in due time. Our priestesses are quite experts in these matters. If you like I will tell you a legend relating to the subject."

The four Europeans hereupon refilled their pipes and placed themselves round the Dayak, who commenced his narrative:

"Once upon a time there lived a family of Dayaks who, while digging a hole in the ground to fix a stake for one of their houses in course of erection, found a large red water-snake which they killed and relished for their dinner. The snake, however, called Lendong, belonged to the family of Naga gallang petak and was a favorite with Mahatara. According to Dayak tradition the first living being created by Mahatara was a great water-snake upon which he gradually deposited mud and sand and thus made it carry the earth. Hence the name Naga gallang petak, or snake serving as the foundation of the earth. Each of its motions caused the earthquake. The part of the world towards which its head pointed had prosperity—that towards which its tail pointed misfortune.

"The God, incensed at the foul slaughter, turned everyone of those who had partaken of the snake into an antoeën. The father of the family was created chief of the antoeën and received the horrible title of radja antoeën batoelang dohong, or king of the antoeëns with bones like warriors' swords. Thenceforward all that family remained antoeëns.

"I may add for your information, that once a person is suspected by the Dayaks of being an antoeën, his life is not worth a day's purchase. Not only for the public safety is it considered compulsory to destroy him, but the one who kills him is looked upon as a hero, to whom everybody owes obligation and gratitude. I have good-naturedly advised you not to pretend to be capable of causing illness to anybody."

"No indeed, never more," Johannes said solemnly. "But can this joke with the Poenan lead to any evil result?"

"As long as the Poenan remains free of fever, it will not. All danger then will be passed, for the only peculiarity of the antoeëns is that they can never themselves undo the mischief which they cause."

"My worthy Helvetian!" Johannes said, addressing Wienersdorf, at the same time handing him a small paper parcel, "here are ten more grains of quinine, let your brother-in-law swallow them by all means, for his recovery is a serious consideration to me now."

The second dose however was not necessary. After having peacefully slept till an advanced hour of the day, the Poenan had awaked, and feeling perfectly well had taken his mat and spread it under the shade of a large tree outside the house.

He was now lying there drinking in large draughts of the fresh air. When he saw Johannes and Wienersdorf approach he arose and cordially shook hands with both; but his manner towards the former showed that he felt a certain reverential fear for one who at his own will could create and cure disease.

Harimaoung Boekit fortunately remained free from fever, whereby Johannes' prestige became increased in no small degree. There was nothing now to interfere with the prosecution of their journey. The deserters therefore pressed for a speedy departure. The Europeans were becoming desperate, when fortunately something unexpected occurred to put an end to their embarrassment.

A djoekoeng from the deputies arrived one morning with the message that although the Dutch Government had accepted the submission of kotta Djangkan, the Commander himself would come with a steamship to fetch the new chief and conduct him to

Bandjermasin, there to take the oath of allegiance. This steamer might be hourly expected. Hairmaoung knew that if the Commander should arrive before his departure he might prevent the emigration of the tribe and therefore their best course would be to depart forthwith. Everything was made ready with despatch and all hands were busy in the final preparations.

The last night passed at kotta Djangkan was of marvellous activity, and when day at last broke forth all was ready for departure. Only the guns which for safety had been left in the batteries over night had to be embarked. The lusty arms of our Europeans soon settled this difficulty, and a leave-taking commenced which promised to be interminable, until Johannes, pointing his finger towards the south, suddenly cried out:

"Banama Asep! Banama Asep!!" a fire ship, a fire ship.

A cloud of smoke was indeed seen above the edge of the forest towards the south. All instantly took their places in the boats and in less time than it takes to narrate, the ten rangkans, containing one hundred and sixty five persons, the grand total of the emigration, had left the shore with all their goods and chattels. The oars clave the waters forcibly and the light vessels sped onwards. A hurrah was given by the travellers and responded to by those their late companions, and the kotta which had so hospitably received our adventurers was left behind.

The country gradually became wilder, the banks loftier, sometimes hanging over as if threatening death and destruction.

The river still preserved its unruffled surface, indicating the evenness of its bed. Although the stream rushed along with increased speed it continued to be perfectly navigable; here and there whirlpools were to be observed as the water rushed over detached pieces of chalk, but these could be avoided with care. The Kapoeas was still a stream in which a small steamer, drawing six feet of water, could find no difficulty in manœuvering. After a couple of hours' towing they reached Batoe Sambong. Amai Kotong went ashore here for a few minutes to take leave of the Chief of the Kampong, with whom he had lived in peace for many years. The inhabitants of the kotta, interested in the travellers, came out in a body and offered them cakes and tocak, both of which were gratefully received not only by La Cueille but also by the women, who according to their limited powers had taken their share in the rowing.

This pause on their journey did not occupy more than half an hour, but it seemed an age to Johannes, who did not feel safe until they had passed that barrier for steamers, the first cataract. Once beyond that, an hour or so would be of little importance as the fugitives could be no longer overtaken. Until then his motto was: "Forwards! forwards!!"

At a short distance from kotta Sambong they passed a solitary cliff of chalk about fifty feet high, to which Johannes drew the attention of his companions. Seen from a distance it appeared to resemble the form of a gigantic woman in a kneeling position, wearing a cloth around her head. Against the foot of this rock the Kapoeas beat with violence, scattering around wild mountains of foam as if furious at the barrier which forced it away from its course to seek a new direction. Johannes informed his friends that the neighboring kotta had taken its name from this stone: Batoe Sambalajong, abbreviated into Batoe Sambong.

"What is the meaning of Sambalajong?" Wienersdorf asked.

"Sambalajong is the name of a white head-dress worn by widows. As that stone bears some resemblance to a widow in the native mourning it is called batoe sambong, which may be translated widow's stone.

The cry of "halt" was now heard from the foremost rangkan. They had arrived at Kiham Hoeras, the first cataract. A subdued murmur, increasing more and more as they advanced, had been heard for a considerable time, but it had scarcely been heeded by the Europeans who were intently listening to the legend of Batoe Sambong. The narrator now ceased talking and the tiktak caused by the movement of the oars in the rowlocks being also suspended, the majestic sound of the waters broke upon their ears. Looking up they beheld the river shooting downwards from on high in a magnificent cascade. The lower part of the fall consisted of massive rocks assuming the most fantastic shapes. At the more elevated part this chalk formation was broken by plutonic diorite, whose dark blue seams appeared between the white chalk on the surface. Here and there were scattered huge black masses of stone which seemed to have broken from the cliffs and to have been weather-beaten into the nearly globular shapes they now possessed. The whole of the upper part of the cataract presented to the eye an agglomeration of similar masses scattered about in the wildest manner. The impressions created by this scene of nature in her sublimity was most powerful. The Europeans looked on in much admiration while their rangkans almost danced on the foaming waters; they could scarcely find words to give utterance to their thoughts.

"It is magnificent," Wienersdorf said, deeply affected; "see over there how beautifully these black and white layers of stones are intermixed; look, a mosaic like that over yonder I defy any artisan to excel."

"Observe that limestone beyond; does it not look as if carved? Only see how beautiful and white it stands out against that black background; it is like a gigantic piece of lace-work."

"Only a little less fragile than your Brussels or Mechlen lace," Johannes added.

"Look," Wienersdorf continued enthusiastically, "at those high steep banks, in which chalk and diorite stones almost struggle for supremacy. Observe how they are clad in the loveliest soft green of gigantic ferns, crowned by the sombre foliage of the majestic primeval forest like the proud gothic arches of a mediæval cathedral. See, higher up, where the trunks lean over bending their branches, interwoven by the creepers and forming a low cave from which the white foaming waters escape as if from the mighty urn of the god of the stream."

"And yet how still all seems, does it not? Nothing, absolutely nothing but the noise of the fleeting waters; not the sound of a bird or animal breaking this dead silence. Life seems almost extinct here."

"Shut up!" was Johannes' gay remark. "Morbid imagination, my boy, nothing else. Our poet is absolutely seeing solitude where none is to be found. The thunder of the cataract deafens all or you would soon hear the harsh cries of the hordes of gray-

KIHAM HOERAS AND ITS PASSAGE.

green paroquets inhabiting the tops of yonder trees. You might hear the piercing cries of that herd of deer now grazing on the tops of the cliffs; you would hear those small bakais or monkeys flying about with their long tails through the branches of the trees, fern leaves and creepers which overhang the abyss, whistling their lively 'kirah, kirah.' By heavens, no! life is far from extinct here. On the contrary it shows itself in its most powerful aspects everywhere around you, even in the waters, where you may find the finest salmon disporting themselves. Presently, when we shall have mastered this wild stream and travelled upwards, all this life will disappear as if by magic. Then you will find all blank and quiet about you just as you have pictured it to yourself. Do not, however, blame nature for the change, but only men."

While our deserters were thus philosophizing the Dayaks had taken steps to accomplish the difficult and dangerous ascent of the kiham. Women and children stepped on shore and began to climb the cliffs which formed as it were a flight of steps leading to the higher territory whence the Kapoeas descended. The four deserters, armed with their unerring rifles, and five Dayaks with their lances and mandauws, served as a convoy to the fair sex, all the while keeping an eye upon what was going on on the river.

The rattan ropes cut at soengei Dahasan and soengei Basarang and the chains found in soengei Naning were now produced and tied together. This long cable was drawn up by eight men, who while performing their task had successively to spring from cliff to cliff, to wade half through the water and swim across some smaller branches of the river. After two hours of hard work the upper end of the cable was attached to a strong tree standing on the bank above the stream while the other end was thrown across the river to the canoes. Two Dayaks now posted themselves at the tree to guard the cable while six leaped into the river and allowed themselves to be carried away by the strong tide, grasping the cable as they sped along with astonishing rapidity. They repeatedly disappeared beneath the foam of the whirlpools, and the hearts of the Europeans beat faster as they witnessed each submersion, but they soon saw the long woolly hair of the swimmers reappear on the surface as they rose up gleefully and swam rapidly onwards.

The object of this manœuvring was to ascertain whether the cable had became entangled amongst the trunks of the trees or rocks, thereby imperilling the drawing up of the canoes. Although the cable was fully six hundred yards long the expert swimmers reached its lower end in a few seconds, when they wiped their faces as if nothing had happened. Five of the men now took their places in each of the rangkans, one of them steering while the four others took hold of the cable to draw the boat up against the terrific tide. The dangerous journey was undertaken by one rangkan at a time in order to prevent accidents arising from the breaking of the cable or upsetting.

Thanks to the skill of the Dayaks and Poenans the rangkans completed the ascent without any misadventure. The cataract now formed a formidable barrier between the Dutch and themselves and further pursuit was almost impossible.

The cable being wanted for other purposes had to be drawn up again, an operation which took two hours to accomplish. The swimmers had to exhibit their skill again in diving to unfasten it whenever it became caught among the rocks.

The women, owing to the difficult path they had to follow in the ascent of the cliffs, had not proceeded very far, although to these children of nature a walk like this was nothing beyond an ordinary promenade. They reached the top in about half an hour, where they sat gossiping around a tree to which the cable was attached. The younger ones passed their time in merriment while the elders lit several small fires to cook the meals for the company. In the midst of all this female clatter La Cueille's voice was suddenly heard crying out:

"Nom d' un chien! what is there in my neck that itches so much?" And tearing away the rag which protected his neck from the rays of the sun he found it soaked in blood.

"I thought it was perspiration," he cried, "trickling down my neck. Am I wounded at last?"

His companions with several Dayaks approached, but the miscreants simply burst out into hearty laughter. Before the Walloon could get any answer to his appeal for help he passed his hand down his neck and felt some slimy, smooth objects from which he suddenly withdrew his fingers.

"What is this?" he asked nervously.

"Halamantek," was the phlegmatic reply of one of the Dayaks.

"Halamantek! what do they mean?"

"Don't make yourself ridiculous," Johannes grinned. "Halamantek are only forest-leeches and they will rid you of some superfluous Walloon blood."

A sigh of relief escaped the wounded man. On examination it proved that during their stampede through a thick wood not only the Walloon, but all of the company had been attacked by these little reptiles. He, however, from some unaccountable cause had received a double share of their favors.

"The forest-leech," Johannes explained, "is a reptile strongly resembling a thick gray thread about the length of a finger. It inhabits the lower branches of trees and from there attacks its prey, either man or beast. It creeps in some crevice of the skin or dress and greedily begins its meal. Its bite is not painful at first, resembling rather a sensation of itching, but as soon as it has sucked itself full the irritation becomes intense."

"That is exactly what I felt," the Walloon murmured.

In the meantime Moendoet had taken a handful of tobacco, infused it for a couple of minutes in some boiling water and with the lotion thus formed bathed the neck of her sweetheart. The leeches dropped off and their wounds soon healed, to the great satisfaction of the Walloon.

"Henceforth we shall often be plagued with these pests," Johannes said, "and I think it will be wise to have some tobacco water ready in our flasks for possible emergencies."

"Shall we have to pass many cataracts?" Wienersdorf enquired.

"A great many; perhaps four to-morrow. But why this question?"

"Because we shall then have to wash ourselves four times at least with this tobacco sauce. We shall be perfumed like the bowl of a German pipe."

"Very likely," Johannes laughed, "but fortunately we don't

want to make our entré de salon, or perhaps you are anxious lest Hamadoe will be disgusted with you? Don't feel alarmed, she is quite accustomed to tobacco."

By the time the cable had been drawn in, the sun had also finished his course and unceremoniously disappeared in the west behind the forest. Our men and especially the Dayaks and Poenans had had a fatiguing day and longed for some rest. They consequently resolved to pass the night in the immediate neighborhood. The rangkans were tied to a projecting tree, leaving them room enough to float in mid-stream. The women and children were lodged within them, ten of the men occupying one at each end as a safeguard. One of the men in each canoe was told off to mount guard, while the others of the crew were divided into two equal watches, posted along the banks of the river opposite the rangkans.

The four deserters joined this party, two of them in each watch, one to keep lookout while the others rested.

Their precautions were excellently taken and showed the solicitude felt by Johannes for their general welfare. The night however passed by undisturbed. Early in the morning Schlickeisen noticed a creaking sound coming from the forest bordering the banks. He kept a sharp lookout and observed a herd of about fifty deer, led by a handsome buck with a magnificent pair of antlers, coming down the slopes to drink from the crystalline river water. While the herd was drinking their leader stood posted on the top of the bank whence he could overlook the surrounding country. There he remained, sniffing the air and pricking up his ears, offering a fair mark to the Swiss, who proceeded to take good aim and fired. His first movement, however, had alarmed the stag; the noble animal suddenly threw his horns back on his neck, uttered a loud cry and took his first and last leap. Tumbling from the steep height he rolled into the water and would undoubtedly have been carried out of reach had he not struck against one of the rangkans and become entangled among the lines.

The rest of the herd had suddenly disappeared.

The alarm and commotion caused by that shot and its reverberations through the steep banks was great, but thanks to the cool behavior of the Europeans peace was soon restored. The buck was drawn out of the stream, skinned and quartered, promising a delicious adjunct to the ensuing meal. All congratulated Schlickeisen upon his fair shot, but he vowed to be less hasty for the future and never to fire during inconvenient hours.

An hour afterward the flotilla was again en route, making way against the fierce and increasing current of the wild stream.

This day also contributed its share of difficulties. A little beyond Kiham Hoeras, near kotta Hoerakan, the dioritic soil suddenly changed into a coarse yellow-brown sandstone. This friable stone, subject to rapid disorganization, filled the bed of the river to such an extent that in some places no canoe could pass; a rangkan had to be steered with the utmost caution in order to keep within the narrow strip of water which formed the channel. The sand of this stone is easily displaced by the immense force of the fleeting mass of water and here and there forms banks in mid-stream where the tide is slackened and the river shallowed. Sometimes the sandbanks assume the dimensions of islands and are known as karangans by the natives. Harimaoung Boekit informed his friends that these are highly auriferous and that not unfrequently small nuggets are found of a quality considered the best of the Kapoeas regions.

"We ought to try our luck here," La Cueille said.

"Certainly not," Johannes replied; "our way lies forward! We are still too near the Dutch and must place a few more cataracts between them and ourselves."

"And," said Amai Kotong, "neither could we go washing gold so readily. We would soon find ourselves in trouble with the population of these regions. Each kotta has its own grounds and parts of the river, which they would not allow to be poached upon by strangers with impunity."

"Then in heaven's name forwards!" the Walloon muttered.

Besides the wild part of the river close to these islands, they had to mount four kihams that day, some of which gave them considerably more trouble than they had experienced at Kiham Hoeras, so that it was quite four in the afternoon before the tired and exhausted travellers reached kotta Karangan.

This kotta, situated on the left bank of the Kapoeas, was a handsome and strong fortification with a population of over two thousand souls. Our travellers, who had been surprised at the skulls ornamenting the palisades of kotta Djangkan, felt alarmed at the immense number of these ghastly trophies here exhibited. How many human lives must have been sacrificed to supply such a quantity?

Amai Kotong found friends here also and was thereupon unhesitatingly allowed to enter the kotta. The presence of

Harimaoung Boekit and his Poenans, however, excited considerable suspicion and it was only after much trouble and difficulty that they succeeded in pacifying the people and in preventing them from opening hostilities. Johannes repeated the old story already told at kotta Baroe, how they had been commissioned by the Dutch government to open communication with the Olo Otts, and to learn their views. He had also beforehand taken the precaution of planting the Dutch flag on one of the largest rangkans. He now solemnly produced the stamped document taken away from Damboeng Papoendeh, and mentioned that the Poenan chief had been added to his party by the Great Heer of Bandjermasin to make the meeting with the Olo Otts more feasible.

It is doubtful whether the Karangannese altogether believed the story. They certainly looked respectfully at the seal, impressed in red wax, and abstained from all hostilities, but they would not permit one of the company of travellers to enter the kotta except Amai Kotong; to the others they offered their tomoi for occupation. This caused considerable satisfaction, for such a concession indicated that they were considered as friends, and the laws of hospitality being strictly recognized in Dayakland could not be violated in their persons.

Our travellers, therefore, could fearlessly take their rest, having only to guard themselves against dangers from without. They consequently deemed it sufficient for one of the Europeans to keep watch, though two of the Dayaks volunteered to join in the service.

CHAPTER XV.

A DAYAK BREAKFAST—THE HALT ON THE ISLAND—THE BOEHIES—A NEW KIND OF SOUP—THE THUNDER-STORM AND ITS RESULTS—RUMORS OF WAR—A NIGHT ATTACK—THE PARABOH—KOTTA HAMEAK BESIEGED—THE BESIEGERS ROUTED.

SHORTLY after daybreak our travellers were again ready to continue their journey. At the moment of parting Johannes distributed twenty parcels of tobacco amongst the most influential inhabitants of kotta Karangan; to the wife of the chief he offered a necklace of handsome beads, part of the goods purchased from Baba Poetjieng, a courtesy which was highly valued and served to remove all lingering suspicion. In recognition of this present the hostess offered to each of the party some bundles of Ketan rice wrapped in pisang leaves, accompanied by a large piece of Kalamboe-ei, or bakatak, and a stiff dram of doubly distilled toeak.

La Cueille was delighted with the liquor; he smacked his lips and suspiciously wiped his mouth before he began his breakfast. He knew the sticky rice and with a little salt and grated cocoanut he found it very palatable. But he looked suspiciously at the other viands with which they had been presented. He smelt them and the aroma tickled his olfactory. He took a bite and found the taste more delicious than the smell. He banished all thought of pileworms and snakes and set himself to make a hearty meal, when Johannes asked him whether he knew what he was eating.

"I don't care," the Walloon answered, "it is very nice!"

"As long as you like it I am satisfied. I also find it nice though rather dirty."

With his mouth half filled the Walloon looked up at Johannes.

"And what may it be after all?" he stammered.

"The Kalamboe-ei is a snail of the size of your fist with a beautiful shell."

"And the other?" he asked in utter despair.

"The bakatak is a green frog found everywhere along the borders of the rivers. Here, take a draught and wash it down."

As he spoke thus, he handed him a small bamboo measure of gin. At one gulp the Walloon swallowed it down, exclaiming:

"Ah! ha! That is better. I will eat ten more snails for another dram."

"I believe you, my lad," Johannes smiled, "but ten of these snails would ruin your digestion. Besides, you have quite enough courage now, so you had better finish your rice."

Breakfast being completed they all resumed their places in the boats and with a loud hurrah the fleet of rangkans was again set in motion.

The stream grew gradually wilder and the passage more difficult. They had only three kihams to surmount, but the river itself became narrower and more shallow as they advanced, although the force of the current diminished as each affluent was passed.

Towards the afternoon the flotilla was moored near an islet, or rather a sandbank, which, appearing above the surface only at low water, consisted of blinding white sand intermixed with small round pebbles. It was, however, delightfully shaded by the trees lining the sides of the river, which had here become rather narrow, and therefore offered a charming resting-place. The travellers had scarcely stepped ashore to stretch their cramped legs when a whole troop of "boehies" was seen gambolling among the branches of the high trees. Boehies are black and gray apes noted for their long tails. Curious like all quadrumana they approached the edge of the forest and stared at what the travellers were doing on the island. Gradually gaining confidence they came nearer, making the most curious summersaults in their progress, while some of the younger ones risked themselves amongst the lower branches, hanging down by their tails and balancing themselves so close to the heads of the men that they could almost touch them. When their confidence had advanced thus far, Harimaoung Boekit whispered something to the Europeans who kept their guns ready loaded with shot and slugs, while the Dayaks seized their blow-pipes. The gay colony of monkeys, ignorant of the danger awaiting them, still continued their acrobatic performances above the heads of the men. At a given signal the rifles were discharged and twelve boekies fell mortally wounded. The cries uttered by these wounded animals were heartrending. Their companions disappeared with the speed of lightning. But not all of them; a mother seeing her young one fall under the fatal lead, and being herself unhurt, pounced down to grasp her dying infant, pressed it to her bosom and before any one could prevent her leaped into the river, dived, gained the shore and disappeared in the thick foliage. Another of the wounded did not fall, but spasmodically supported itself by its hind legs on the branch where only a short time before it had been gaily disporting. For a moment only it remained hanging there and they could almost touch it. With tears in its eyes it pressed its hands upon its chest, from which the blood trickled down between its fingers. It had received a gaping wound; its groans were agonizing; its looks expressed melancholy reproach, its whole appearance was so pitiful that not one amongst the Dayaks nor even the wild Poenans had the courage to attempt the capture of the animal. At last the poor creature collected all its strength, grasped the branch with its hands, raised itself and sat down. It then plucked some leaves and green sprigs, chewed them and applied this self-made poultice to its wound. Then it kept quiet for a few minutes as if to take breath, after which, supporting itself by its tail and three hands, the fourth covering the wound, it gradually withdrew and disappeared amid the dark umbrage of the forest.

The Europeans after witnessing these two scenes felt shame and regret at their share in the battue. But before they could find time to give expression to their feelings the Dayaks approached the wounded monkeys, mandauw in hand, and killed them all, regardless of their pitiful cries. A horrible scene now ensued. Every Dayak seized an animal, hastened to rip it open and to rout about with both hands among the yet warm viscera, as if in search of something. In the intestines of some animals, but especially in those of the boehies, a green stone of the size of a large pea is often found, to which the whitefaces used to ascribe an extraordinary medicinal power in former times. It was imported into Europe under the name of bezoar stone, and rivalled in value the most precious jewel. At present its old fame has totally disappeared amongst the whitefaces, but among the natives of the Indian Archipelago it has retained a certain value, and when large commands as much as eighty dollars in Batavia and Singapore.

Our travellers were extremely fortunate on the present occasion. It sometimes happens that a hunter may kill three and even more boehies without finding a single batoe galiga, as the natives call them. They had now killed twelve monkeys and had been rewarded with eight stones which, although not all equally large, were worth fully sixty dollars each. Harimaoung Boekit smilingly collected them, put them in the hollow of a bamboo tube and offered them in token of gratitude to the preserver of his life and as a testimony of his affection for the future husband of his sister.

"That greases the wheel!" La Cueille muttered, "if every shot would only yield that amount! By George! I shall keep a sharp lookout and every boehie I see shall be mine."

"You may spare yourself the trouble," Johannes answered, "this species of monkeys is not quite so abundant. It sometimes takes a great deal of trouble to get one in view. Now that this rifle fire has sounded amongst them I would bet that you would have to wait months before seeing another."

"I have plenty of batoe galiga at soengei Miri," Harimaoung Boekit assured Johannes. "When we get there I will exchange them for the guns you took away from kotta Djangkan. I should like to have them mounted on my kotta."

"We will talk about that when we are there, my dear Amai," was the reply. "Perhaps in addition to the guns we may also throw in the rifles."

"I begin to believe," the Walloon interrupted, "that we won't reach home empty-handed."

"Possibly, but before all, let us try and get home, anyhow. I can assure you we have not come very far yet in that direction."

The Walloon heaved a deep sigh.

During the time occupied by this conversation the women had busied themselves in preparing the meal. In every direction small fires were burning and the atmosphere was so perfumed with the smell of the viands, that despite their hurry all became anxious to satisfy the cravings of their stomachs. At last the whole company, divided into small parties, sat or rather lay down around the mats upon which the various dishes were spread. There were heaps of steaming rice, boiled nearly snow white and perfectly dry. Numerous saucers and leaves stood close by filled with delicacies. The venison of the buck shot by Schlickeisen that morning, appeared under different disguises and was thoroughly enjoyed by all. On the mat occupied by the Europeans there was a brass pot covered with a wooden lid. At first it had escaped their attention, but now that their appetites had been somewhat sated their curiosity became excited.

"What might that contain?" La Cueille asked.

"Only soup," Johannes replied, "they have heard that in

Bandjermasin it is generally eaten and the women have prepared it as a surprise for us."

"Soup?" Schlickeisen asked. "Well, you ought to have told us of it before, when we might have begun our meal with a plateful. But, no matter, it will be equally acceptable now," and drawing the pot towards him, he removed the lid and greedily inhaled the delicious aroma of the concoction. He dipped a spoon in it and was on the point of filling a cocoanut shell when he suddenly dropped the ladle, took a wooden fork, and with it fished up something which on being exhibited caused all excepting Johannes to fall back in disgust. Fixed between the prongs of the fork there was something not unlike the dissected head of an infant to which, when lifted out, there were attached two arms with well-shaped hands. Speechless and horror-struck, Wienersdorf and the Walloon kept staring at Schlickeisen, who, almost paralyzed, stood there with the fork in his hand.

"What is the matter now?" Johannes asked.

"Don't you see?" was the panting reply of La Cueille.

"What? This soup? Certainly I see it, and very nice it smells."

"They mean to make cannibals of us!" the Walloon cried. "Never! never!!"

"Cannibals?" Johannes asked innocently. "Now don't play the fool with me," and pushing Schlickeisen aside he filled his cup with the highly flavored soup, brought it to his lips and emptied it.

"Ha!" he said, stopping for breath, "delicious!"

"How could you!" Wienersdorf remarked. "Has man become totally wild in this country?"

"How could I do what?" Johannes asked surprised.

"Swallow that human soup!"

"Human soup?"

"Yes, human soup; don't you see that baby which Schlickeisen has fished up?"

Johannes had gained his end; those stupid Europeans were nicely sold. He burst out laughing.

"Ha! ha! ha! human soup. You never get such fare in Europe, not even in the best Parisian restaurants. Capital!" he roared. "I shall laugh myself to death."

And snatching the fork from Schlickeisen he produced the entire mass of flesh from the pot, exhibiting besides the parts already seen, two long legs and a tail a yard long.

"A monkey!" La Cueille gasped.

"One of the boehies killed a little while ago. The women quietly immersed this animal in boiling water to remove its hair, and then made it into a delicious soup."

The Walloon and the two Swiss still hesitated, but Johannes tried to reconcile them to this new fare by explaining that the monkey is one of the cleanest and daintiest animals in creation, feeding entirely upon vegetable diet.

"Now compare this to the pig and the fowl," he continued, "so highly valued by you all, I really do not see what there is against eating an ape."

"But the likeness! It almost seems like eating your own brother."

"Mercy!" Johannes resumed smiling, "that is an argument overlooked by Darwin while endeavoring to make his celebrated theory acceptable. I mean the horror men have for eating monkey flesh under the impression that he is consuming his own brother. I am happy to say that we Dayaks do not despise the monkey as food, although we are unacquainted with the taste of human flesh."

But Johannes might have talked till doomsday, he could not convert his mates. The soup remained untouched by the Europeans. He however enjoyed his share of it and helped himself to one of the monkey's legs, which he ate with great satisfaction.

Dinner being finished the journey was continued. Since their departure from kotta Djangkan, the country had gradually become more rugged and they had approached a range of hills between which the Kapoeas made its way. They now perceived lofty mountains in the north and north-west, the tops of which were clearly defined in the distance. Johannes pointed out to his companions that they would have to traverse those mountains in order to reach the Chinese sea. But he added: "We are only commencing to see its southern slopes. God only knows when we will be able to descend the other side."

They rowed with all their might until about three o'clock, when Amai Kotong signalled them to halt. They had now arrived opposite the mouth of the soengei Samoehing, which, after a short consultation, they entered. Johannes asked Harimaoung Boekit his reason for so doing, as they had full three hours to spare and in that time might perhaps reach Toembang Roengoi.

Without a word of reply the Poenan pointed towards the

sky in the north which was getting rapidly darker, presaging a thunder-storm. Dalim told the Europeans that a soho, or flood, called bandjer amongst the Malays, could be extremely dangerous sometimes, for the waters rise suddenly and run with irresistible force. Vessels caught by the soho are frequently carried away and are exposed to the danger of foundering in one of the whirlpools, or of being shattered against the cliffs of the kihams. As soon as they entered the mouth of the soengei Samoehing they landed and drew their boats as high on the shore as possible in order to place them beyond the reach of the flood. They were still occupied in this work when a noise like distant thunder was heard approaching nearer and nearer. The Europeans really believed it to be thunder, a conviction which seemed to be confirmed by the increasing darkness of the sky and the large drops of rain that began to fall. Dalim, however, called the deserters aside and together they mounted the hill which separated the Kapoeas from the Samoehing. There they had a magnificent view over the whole river. Perfect silence reigned everywhere; not a leaf moved, not a blade of grass vibrated, not a bird twittered nor a moth took wing. The clouds heavily pressed downward on the earth causing an insufferable heat, a feeling of depression under which the whole universe seemed to labor. Nothing but the still distant roar was heard gradually approaching nearer and nearer.

"Look! Look!" Schlickeisen cried, pointing to the upper part of the stream in anxious astonishment, whence with a roar like thunder there advanced a wall of water from twelve to fifteen feet high, as if about to overwhelm everything—hill and wood and travellers. Rushing forward and carrying every obstacle before it, it hurried on like a perpendicular cliff, foaming and seething as if discharged from some subterranean volcano. Under the irresistible influence of the waters rocks groaned as if wrenched from their base; trees were uprooted and carried away; large masses of stones became dislodged from their encasements of clay in the banks and fell into the surging flood, being kept afloat for a moment by the immense power and rapidity of the stream.

The appearance of this wall of water lasted for an instant only, but when it had passed our travellers like a shadow, the surface of the river had risen some fifteen feet and kept rising still, so that where only a few moments before a crystalline stream had sped over its bed of clear white sand and pebbles, nothing but a roaring and seething yellow turbid mass of water was now to be seen.

Our Europeans had looked on at this phenomenon with the highest admiration, but before the swift-moving wall of water had entirely disappeared from view their attention was diverted by the storm which suddenly burst forth in all its majestic grandeur.

First there shot forth a blinding dart of lightning, rapidly followed by a rattling peal of thunder which was only the forerunner of incessant discharges breaking forth from almost every point in the firmament. At the same time the wind rose and blew with violence, uprooting trees and spreading destruction in every direction. The roar of the rushing stream, the crash of the rattling thunder, the creaking of broken branches, the crash of falling trees, the howling of the wind, the anxious chirping of the birds, the frightened cries of apes, all these combined to form a sublime harmony which at once filled the heart with terror and with admiration for nature as seen in this conflict of the elements.

The clouds became blacker and heavier and drooped down to the earth as if incapable of retaining any longer the burden with which they were weighted. The rain then descended in regular torrents which, carried along by the gale, formed an undulating curtain that arrested the view along the horizon and concealed objects which were almost near at hand. Vast streams of water collected from every side and following the slope of the territory discharged themselves into the river.

Dalim and the Europeans quickly descended the hill to join their companions. Arrived in the kampong they found everything and everybody in the wildest commotion, for the rise of water had been so great and rapid as to compel them to bring the rangkans higher up the shore. The Europeans joined in the task, and assisted by four pair of strong arms like theirs the boats were soon carried beyond the reach of danger.

The storm continued with unabated fury for a considerable time, after which it gradually disappeared in a south-westerly direction. The flashes of lightning became less vivid; the thunder gradually decreased in volume and the intervals between its peals grew longer. The gale also gradually abated, the rain dwindled into a fine drizzle and the clouds began to separate. The blue sky became once more visible and, gilded by the setting sun, seemed to announce that nature had finished its battle. The river alone remained boisterous and wild, but before the sun had totally disappeared beneath the western horizon that also had ceased to rise. By nightfall the travellers felt certain that the flood was subsiding, and guarded by their outposts they all retired to rest full of confidence.

Next morning the whole kampong was ready betimes to continue the journey, and our travellers were soon on their way. Rounding the first angle of the stream they observed a considerable fortification called kotta Samoehing, whence cries of alarm and loud beating of drums were heard to proceed as soon as the inhabitants perceived the approaching fleet of rangkans. Johannes hoisted the Dutch colors while Amai Kotong despatched words of salutation. When the Samoehingese heard the old chief their nervousness abated, and their cries of alarm ceased. Upon stepping on shore Amai Kotong learned that a report was current of the defeat in the Kapoeas country of the Doessonese under Tomonggong Soerapatti.

That celebrated Dayak chief was now said to be waging war with the inhabitants of soengei Sirat. He had not yet been seen in that neighborhood, but alarming reports were prevalent of the intentions of this disreputable fellow who was bent upon destroying by fire and sword all the inhabitants of the Kapoeas. A council of war was held consisting of Amai Kotong, Harimaoung Boekit, Dalim and the Europeans with the Chief of the kotta Samoehing, whose name was Amai Pari. They assembled in the tomoi to deliberate upon the measures now necessary to be taken.

"You will have to return whence you came," Amai Pari said.

"Yes," replied Amai Kotong, " to kotta Djangkan."

"How strong do you think these Doessonese are?" asked Johannes.

"I hear about twelve hundred men."

"Have they fire-arms?"

"Only a few rifles, perhaps six or seven; but they have four small pieces to bombard the kottas."

"How many do we muster?"

"Counting every one," said Amai Kotong, "we muster eighty-four men fit to carry arms."

"And how many rifles have we?"

"I believe six-and-forty."

"And," said Johannes in a fierce rage, "do you propose to return to kotta Djangkan to be captured by the Dutch? Do you desire to see Harimaoung Boekit in fetters? to see him condemned to penal servitude as an inveterate head-hunter? Tell me, Amai, are we old women or do men's hearts beat within our breasts? No! by Mahatara and all his Sangiangs! not one step backwards. With forty-six rifles in the hands of men like us we can traverse the island from one end to the other. I for one would like to meet this Soerapatti should he dare to encounter us."

Johannes stood, bravely handsome, like a bronze statue of disdain. Harimaoung, carried away by these stirring words, unsheathed his mandauw with his right hand while with his left he grasped Johannes' arm.

"No!" he exclaimed, "not one footstep backwards. On the contrary forward to meet those old women of the Doessan." His enthusiasm seemed infectious, for not only Amai Kotong and Amai Pari but the whole assemblage broke out in one loud cry: "Forward!"

An hour after breakfast the fleet was again in motion. They

moved on uninterruptedly, nothing occurring to retard their progress or to excite suspicoin. They did not meet a single djoekoeng on the river, nor did they see a human being on the banks from whom any information could be gleaned. It seemed as if this part of the river had become depopulated.

At four in the afternoon when the fleet, to which the Samoehingese had now joined themselves, arrived at the mouth of the soengei Sirat, nothing of a suspicious nature had been yet observed. Some of the Poenans stepped ashore to reconnoitre the territory as they intended to pass the night there, but they soon returned with the report that on the northern bank of the soengei, about two hundred steps from the shore, a distinct trail had been discovered in the long grass, indicating that a large number of men had recently passed. Harimaoung Boekit and Dalim, as true forest spies, at once set out to examine the trail while Johannes, Schlickeisen and Wienersdorf with the Dayaks accompanied them as covers, armed with rifles.

The reconnoitring party soon returned; it had been ascertained that the trail was quite fresh and left by a numerous band who had travelled from west to east, as proved by the footsteps observed in the spots bare of grass. They had followed the trail for about a thousand yards, where it emerged into the Kapoeas and turned towards the north. On this sandy soil it became so clearly defined as to leave no doubt of the presence of a large number of people at no great distance. Harimaoung Boekit also fancied that he had heard some human voices coming from that direction. Be that as it may, the greatest precaution was undoubtedly necessary. They therefore resolved to hide their rangkans behind a sharp curve in the southern bank while four Dayaks armed with rifles were posted in some trees to guard the upper stream. Half of the men would keep awake, rifles in hand, and be prepared to act energetically in any emergency. At the place where they had moved their rangkans some huge trees were felled along the banks which, with the shrubs, would form an obstruction difficult to be passed without challenging their attention. Our travellers would soon become aware of the necessity for these precautions.

About midnight one of the sentries observed something float by in the soengei strongly resembling the trunk of a tree. He thought it might be a crocodile, and he therefore whistled softly to draw the attention of the men in the canoes, fearing lest the monster should utilize the opportunity by pouncing upon some unlucky member of the crew to disappear with him in the dark depths of the river. After giving his warning whistle the sentry noticed that the tree or crocodile was moving towards the shore and was followed by about fifty similar objects. Their movements by no means resembled the noiseless motion of a crocodile, besides which the presence of so many following the first was opposed to the habits of these animals. He therefore became certain that there was something in the wind. He discharged his rifle, and his companions hearing the signal also opened fire. The shots had hardly sounded in the midnight silence when a savage yell was heard from behind the obstruction. Several figures now appeared trying to break through the barrier, a few of them succeeding. Fortunately the night was not dark, the air was calm and the stars shone brightly, partly illuminating the scene. Nothing could be observed of what was going on behind the obstruction, but every figure that surmounted it became distinctly apparent against the faintly lit background and was exposed to the well-aimed bullets of the four Europeans. The Dayaks, who had also been entrusted with rifles, began under the influence of their native impetuosity to open a deafening discharge. The Europeans, more collected, only fired whenever they saw a dark figure hurrying towards the river, and they rarely missed their mark. The two Swiss took no share in the firing but carefully reserved their ammunition for moments of imminent danger. Their precaution was not in vain, for suddenly a large number of assailants succeeded in creeping through the obstruction and, mandauws in hand, rapidly sped toward the river to throw themselves on the rangkans. The women commenced to shriek and were almost mad with despair, but the two Swiss now joined in the struggle and firing calmly and deliberately made a couple of the assailants bite the dust at each discharge. Their rifles sounded regularly and did good execution among the Doessonese who approached the river. A few of them, however, managed to creep through the fire, threw themselves into the river and grasped the rangkans, which they tried desperately to capsize. Now arrived the turn of the Dayaks: their mandauws cleft some skulls and lopped some hands, sending the dissevered fingers in the laps of the women. A few shrieks, a few groans, some death struggles, and the work was done. The assailants dropped into the stream to become, whether dead or wounded, a prey to the crocodiles.

All was now quiet along the banks of the river, so quiet that one could hardly have credited that only a few moments before a struggle for life and death had taken place on this spot. The

Swiss hastened to reload their Remingtons and all prepared for further emergencies.

Four rifle shots were suddenly heard, followed by cries of terror. They came from the four sentries who were still seated in the trees and who were now being attacked. Our travellers could distinctly perceive figures climbing into these trees, greatly endangering the safety of the sentries whose heads the assailants were bent upon securing. Upon seeing this Harimaoung Boekit and his Poenans quietly took to the water, and when they had reached the shore the Europeans fired into the trees, aiming at those of the enemy who were uppermost. This caused them to tumble from their perches and in their fall to dislodge all who were following them. The Poenans now came into action.

With loud cries they threw themselves upon the terrified enemy, wielding their mandauws vigorously and unsparingly. Hoarse shrieks of despair, terror, rage and disappointment were heard during this fight with the naked weapon. After a short interval the Poenans returned to their boats, each bearing at least one reeking human head in his hands while several carried two or three. A loud hurrah from the throats of all the Dayaks, women as well as men, greeted the conquerors. But no sooner had this welcome been given than renewed cries of alarm were heard and the sentries pointed towards the river as the spot whence danger now threatened them. Four rangkans heavily manned were seen coming down the soengei, making for the vessels of our travellers. They were received by the Dayaks with a well-sustained rifle fire in which the Europeans soon joined. Courageous as the Doessonese were, such a shower of bullets proved too much for them. They soon counted many dead and wounded and attempted to retire. As soon as they commenced their retreat, which was somewhat retarded by the strong tide, Johannes collected all his armed men and made them fire a few volleys. The other three Europeans calmly took aim, fired with deliberation, and by their clever marksmanship sent death and destruction among the hostile vessels. Three of the rangkans made good their retreat, but the fourth seemed to find some difficulty in contending against the current. Despite the desperate attempts of the crew it remained almost in the same spot swaying backwards and forwards. One after another the oarsmen were being shot down, when, as if to embrace their only remaining chance of escape, the survivors leaped into the river to save themselves by flight, leaving the rangkan to float down with the strong tide. At sight of this the Poenans could not be restrained. In the twinkling of an eye they had boarded the rangkan, decapitating every dead and wounded man found therein. The bodies were then thrown into the water and the captured vessel towed on shore as an accession to their own fleet.

Eight-and-twenty heads had been captured and the greater part of the men were soon busy cleaning them. The spectacle was something horrible to the Europeans; for a moment they were spellbound by the sight, but then they made haste to leave the dreadful scene.

The night passed undisturbed and at daybreak half of the Dayaks and all the Poenans went ashore, decapitated the enemies found dead or wounded near the barrier and threw their bodies into the river. The number of skulls now captured amounted to thirty-nine. On reconnoitring both banks of the soengei they concluded that they had been attacked by two distinct sections of the enemy, one of them being the party whose trail they had discovered on the previous day. If both assaults had been simultaneous the result might have been most disastrous.

It was henceforth necessary to be doubly watchful. They had tried conclusions with the enemy and although they had sustained no loss, the experience gained taught them that they had to deal with a courageous and enterprising foe. Johannes consequently arranged that the rangkan containing himself and his companions should form the advance guard; the Europeans were no longer to take part in the rowing, but were to keep a sharp lookout with Dalim and Amai Kotong in order to be ready with their unerring fire whenever necessary. Harimaoung Boekit and his Poenans would form the rear guard, to which he added a few more men carrying rifles, wherewith to discharge alarm or signal shots when required. That these precautions were not taken too soon was speedily proved.

It was about nine in the morning; they had rowed on unflaggingly and up till now nothing had been seen of the enemy. Suddenly Dalim uttered a low cry and pointed towards a man, who, nearly hidden by the trunk of a tree, was busy apparently cutting down some rattan ropes with his mandauw.

"Parabah!" Dalim cried terrified.

"Row quickly!" Amai Kotong commanded, as a warning to the rangkans following his.

The man on shore had already cut through one rope. He remained looking intently at the rangkans and when he saw they had come sufficiently near, he raised his arm to cut through the second rope. But in order to do this he had to expose himself; his form was only visible for a short time, but that was long enough for the two Swiss to discharge their rifles with unerring aim. Pierced almost exactly in the same spot by two bullets, the Doessonese made a summersault and fell dead. One of his companions appeared from behind the tree to complete the projected work, but before he had moved two steps he shared the same fate. The same thing occurred with a third and a fourth of them. A fifth crept along the ground and thus escaped the observation of the firing party. He got to the rope, which was wound round the tree four or five times about five feet from the ground, and in order to reach it he had to raise himself on his knees. He then grasped it with his left hand and lifted the right to deal a smart blow to the tightly strung rattan, when again two shots were fired. These completely smashed his left fist, but at the same time one of the bullets almost severed the rope.

"Row for your lives!" both Amai Kotong and Dalim yelled.

The rangkans almost fled onwards, lashing the water into foam. For a moment only they saw the top of one of these giants of the forest wave backwards and forwards. The huge trunk bowed, righted itself again, then bowed again to fall with a noise like thunder, covering the river with its branches and foliage and scattering the water high in the air in wild spray that enveloped everything in a misty veil. The rangkans had fortunately passed the spot where the tree fell; by only a few seconds they had escaped destruction, for if overtaken by the fallen giant, they must inevitably have been crushed and their living freight hurled into a watery grave.

"That was a narrow escape!" La Cueille cried.

"Well may you say so," Johannes smiled satisfactorily. "But look out; you now see what sort of dare-devils these beggars are. It is one of the usual tricks of war among the Dayaks. Whenever they expect an enemy by the river, they prepare for him by cutting through the base of the trunks of the very largest trees found along the banks. They then retain them in their natural position by means of rattan ropes which are severed at the precise moment that the enemy is opposite to them. The trees then fall and either crush the advancing boats or interpose an impenetrable obstacle to their further progress. Six men are generally placed on watch near the ropes, and these, as a rule, keep themselves hidden. Once the ropes are cut they fly as fast as they can and watch the result from a distance.

"I heard Dalim cry out parabah! What does this word mean?" Schlickeisen asked.

"It is the name given to the dodge of letting these trees fall."

"It is cleverly planned, I must say!" La Cueille observed. "If you were to get such a tree on the top of your head you would scarcely require a new hat, would you now? But we shall have to keep our eyes open, without doubt."

"That we shall," Johannes answered, "but I have decided to let a dozen men march along the banks of every river over which we may have to travel, with orders to keep about twenty yards ahead of us and to examine every tree. This will render any accident impossible and at the same time do us good service otherwise."

"And in what manner will it serve you otherwise?"

"First of all, our men will disperse or shoot these liers-in-wait. They will then search for the half-cut trees, which are not difficult to discover when you are ashore; then, waiting until all our rangkans have safely passed the spot, they will cut the rattan ropes and let the trees fall over. Thus our rear will be protected, both against the Doessonese, who may get reinforcements along the soengei, and against the Dutch whenever they put themselves upon our track. There will be no serious difficulty in putting this plan into execution, for, as a rule, only a few men are placed to watch the parabah and these will soon be driven away by our rifles."

They now travelled onwards cautiously but rapidly. Two trees on the point of toppling over were all they discovered, and as Johannes had predicted a couple of shots sufficed to drive the watchmen away, and a triple obstruction was thus thrown across the river completely blocking all access from the lower districts.

Shortly after noon they sighted kotta Hamiak, where events were taking place not of an encouraging nature. A desperate fight was going on at the time. The inhabitants were in a state of siege. They could be seen peering over the tops of their palisades, here, like everywhere else in Dayak land, surmounted by many human skulls, and throwing anything accessible at the heads of their assailants, who were trying to scale the barrier at various points. At a small distance from the kotta the besiegers had two small guns planted behind an entrenchment formed of twigs, but their balls produced little or no effect against the strong ironwood palisades. The artillery, it seemed, was more intended to frighten the inhabitants and drive them away from the defence than to do any material damage. The Doessonese had also brought together a large heap of dry wood, piled it against the palisades and set fire to it. The fire had already burnt for a considerable time, but the wall had not suffered much, though it would soon begin to be dangerous for the besieged.

The travellers arrived under the steep banks of this sharply-curved soengei. They had been unobserved, and from behind the thick shrubs growing along the banks were able to watch the movements of the enemy. After Johannes had studied the position for a moment, he beckoned Harimaoung Boekit to approach, pointed towards the thickly growing shrubbery in the distance, running very close to the rear of the assailants, and whispered something in his ear. The Poenan chief grinned, collected his followers, stepped ashore with them and disappeared behind the foliage which concealed the banks of the soengei. Johannes then called his companions together, selected about thirty armed Dayaks, including Dalim, and made straight for the Doessonese. Meanwhile the flank attack concerted with the Poenan chief was put into execution and threw the besiegers into confusion, and the whole band took to flight. In an incredibly short time the immense army which had besieged kotta Hamiak had been dispersed and driven into the forest.

When the Doessonese had thus disappeared the warriors of our travelling company fraternized with the inhabitants of the kotta. The rangkans were brought forward and the women and children allowed to step on shore. The old drama of horror was again enacted. The men of the kotta, as well as the Dayaks of the rangkans and the Poenans of Harimaoung Boekit, busied themselves decapitating the fallen enemies, dead or wounded. The lives of some few whose injuries were not severe were provisionally spared; a more terrible fate awaited them, however.

While disposing of the dead enemies by simply throwing them into the soengei, it was discovered that five Poenans and six Dayaks of the company had fallen, and that the Sirattese had lost four of their number. But what caused the utmost grief was the death of Amai Mawong, chief of the kotta Hamiak. He had always been a personal enemy of Tomonggong Soerapatti, and the attack just repelled was the outcome of Soerapatti's undying hatred against him.

The body of the beloved chief was carried inside the kotta and laid out for exhibition until the funeral could be solemnized. The Poenans and the Dayaks of the kotta. Djangkan made the necessary preparations for burning the bodies of their companions on the following morning, a ceremony practised among some tribes whenever time and·opportunity do not serve for the celebration of the customary funeral obsequies. Eight prisoners had been taken and these were now secured in cages, fettered with strong irons, until the next sunrise should summon them to a horrible doom.

During the fight Schlickeisen had received a severe cut over the left arm. This Wienersdorf now carefully examined. He found that although the wound was formidable from having caused considerable loss of blood, it had not penetrated deeply and was therefore not dangerous. A poultice was applied to it to remove all inflammation. This done, Johannes made due arrangements for their safety during the night and all retired to rest.

CHAPTER XVI.

CREMATION—THE SLAUGHTER OF PRISONERS OF WAR—A PRISONER OF WAR SAVED—COUNCIL OF WAR—SCARCITY OF WATER—HAMADOE THIRSTY—WIENERSDORF ATTACKED BY AN ORANG OUTANG—ON THE KAHAJAN—A BLOODY BATTLE—SCHLICKEISEN LOST.

NEXT morning all the inhabitants of the kotta, as well as the Poenans and Kapoeasese, were busy preparing for the burning of the bodies of those fallen companions who did not belong to kotta Hamiak. A sanggarang, or richly-carved flag-staff, was erected in the centre of the square of the fortification. A wooden bird with its wings extended was fixed on the top of the mast, and immediately below the bird an earthen pot with its bottom cut out was suspended. Under this pot a piece of wood was nailed to the sanggarang, extending five or six inches on each side of it, and to this eleven lances were tied, spread out like a fan. These were to represent the number of bodies, not counting Amai Mawong and the Sirattese, whose funeral would take place later. The Dayak believes that the souls of the sanggarang, of the bird, the pot, and the lances, when in the kingdom of souls, are transformed into numerous necessaries for the use of the deceased.

As the deceased had fallen by the hand of their enemy, a triangular pole was planted at the side of the sanggarang, crowned with a skull of one of their foes. On the sides of the pole they had made seven oblique notches to receive sticks projecting about four inches, upon which curiously folded palm-leaves were hung as ornaments.

In front of these masts were erected the sapoendoes, those fatal posts to which the prisoners were to be tied, while in front of these again a large mound of earth was heaped up four feet high, eight feet wide, and fifteen feet long. After the soil had been thoroughly stamped down, the pamahei, funeral pyre, was built on the top of it, consisting of alternate layers of dry wood and small baskets of rosin.

All the preparations being complete, the inhabitants of the kotta gathered around the pyre and the bodies of those fallen were arranged on the top of it clad in their full war costumes. The rosin at the bottom layer was ignited and thick clouds of smoke followed by great flames soon shot up high into the air. The prisoners of war were now fetched from their cages and tied to the sapoendoes. Their aspect betokened the deepest misery. Their matted hair fell around their shoulders and the ewahs which formed their only garments were hanging from their loins in tatters. For the rest, their appearance was calm and peaceful; not defiant, but yet not downcast. As soon as they were tied to their respective stakes the priestesses began their incantations as a sign that all was ready for the commencement of the degrading ceremony.

Some of the men posted themselves near the pyre and blew poisoned arrows into the rising smoke to disperse evil spirits, but the majority of them made a wide circle around the poor victims. High up among the trees a number of hungry vultures had collected with an instinctive knowledge of what was going to take place.

Amai Kotong now stepped forward; he raised his lance and slightly wounded the first of the prisoners in the shoulder. He was followed by Harimaoung Boekit, the Poenans, Kapoeasese and Sirattese, each of whom in his turn gave a prick and passed on to make room for others to succeed. When all had had their turns the same order was resumed and the round recommenced. The blood flowed abundantly and as it congealed in large clots was eagerly devoured from time to time by the vultures.

The intense agony felt by the martyr elicited not a single cry from him, but the descent of the birds to devour his blood seemed to cause him the most poignant anguish. That he should behold while living the fate that awaited him after death was a martyrdom so terrible, so inhuman, that only the imagination of fiends could have conceived it. It was hard enough to be fasttened to a stake unable to defend himself from certain death, while full of vital power and clinging to dear life despite its trials and miseries. But to be reminded of the inevitable by every thrust of the lance, by each descent of the vultures upon his oozing life's blood, formed a climax of anguish that must have wrung the heart of the sufferer. Nevertheless, though exhibiting signs of mental perturbation, he stoically abstained from uttering a sound to gladden the souls of his tormentors. At last there came an end to his martyrdom; death supervening from loss of blood. His executioners then quitted him to repeat the same operations upon their next victim, leaving his still warm body hanging in its fetters to stiffen on the stake.

Now came the turn of the vultures and a scene ensued too horrible to depict. Seven more human bodies were massacred that day with the same tortures and under the same terrible circumstances.

The four Europeans, anxious to escape from this horrible scene, had at first sought refuge in a corner of the square remote from the place of execution, but the wind brought to them the sickening fumes of the burning flesh; they then removed to a shed on the opposite side, where they tried to divert their attention from the horrors then in progress by cleaning and repairing their own rifles as well as those used by the Dayaks. Alas! those horrors they were powerless to prevent.

Johannes with a great deal of trouble had succeeded in begging the life of one of the wounded Doessonese, who was accordingly spared and given to him as his own hireling. He was a youth of about twenty, of quiet appearance, but displaying great firmness of character. He had only received a slight scalp wound, but being stunned he found himself locked up a prisoner of war. When released he was at first shy and frightened. He could not understand how any one should be so interested in him as to spare his life and wish to save him, all from a feeling of compassion. But after the four Europeans had spoken to him in a friendly and encouraging manner, when he saw how carefully they dressed his wound and shared their food with him, the icy crust of his reserve gave way, rendering him both curious and communicative. He asked several questions.

all of which Johannes frankly answered. After having fully gained the confidence of the prisoner they learned from him that Soerapatti with twelve hundred men had started from soengei Lahej, first to take revenge upon Amai Mawong and then to ravage the Kapoeas and Kahajan districts with fire and sword. He had left his son Goesti Kornel in charge of two hundred warriors before kotta Hamiak, with strict injunctions to destroy that fortification and to bring him the skull of its chief. He himself with the other part of his army had advanced upon the Kahajan, the first object of his journey being to attack kotta Oepon, whose chief was Tomonggong Toendan, one of his principal enemies. The prisoner further informed Johannes that several of Soerapatti's warriors were armed with rifles, and that he also carried three or four pieces of artillery, captured some years before from the Dutch.

All these were important communications not to be neglected. When evening had set in and most of the male inhabitants of the kotta were seated together, dissecting the skulls of the slaughtered prisoners of war, Johannes presented the spared Doessonner with a mandauw, gave him a basketful of provisions, conducted him outside the fortification, pointed toward the east, pressed his hand cordially and set him free. The Doessonner did not need to be told twice that he was at liberty, but taking the hand of his benefactor he placed it on his own head and bent his neck before him in silent reverence. Then without hesitation he made his way towards the thick wood, in which he soon disappeared like a ghost. Johannes now re-entered the fortification and immediately summoned Amai Kotong, Harimaoung Boekit and the son of Amai Mawong to inform them of what he had heard and to consider what was now to be done. His reports awakened the utmost alarm, for the route taken by the Doessonese was exactly that which Harimaoung Boekit intended to follow himself. They found that they must alter their plans entirely.

"The course we have to follow is quite clear to me," said Harimaoung Boekit. "Going forward we shall either meet with the chief army of our enemies or with one of its flanks. Now we are much too weak to think of meeting them in the field."

"Is there no way out of the difficulty?" Johannes asked.

"Yes; to get ahead of the Doessonese," was Harimaoung's reply.

"Would that be possible?"

"Yes; with a great deal of speed and exertion. You see," continued the Poenan, pointing towards the west, "soengei Miri lies over there, but we'll have to go in that direction," indicating the south-west. "We will follow soengei Sirat until it reaches soengei Mantarat, then sail up the latter as far as the kotta of that name. We will then disembark, drag the rangkans over land into soengei Minjangan, where we will set them afloat and sail down the stream into the Kahajan."

"Beautifully planned," cried Johannes. "But first of all what is the distance between soengei Mantarat and soengei Minjangan?"

"When a person bathes in the former, his hair will not have dried when he reaches the latter."

"Yes, yes," said Johannes smiling. "I know that calculation

of time. Your long hair tied in a firm knot and protected by a head-dress in the bargain does not dry very rapidly. Let us assume that it would take five or six hours. What is the character of the country we should have to traverse?"

"It is very rugged and steep, but not difficult. I have frequently travelled the entire distance. Once arrived at Boekit Riwoet we gradually descend."

"But shall we arrive at Oepen Batoe before Tomonggong Soerapatti?"

"That is not quite certain; perhaps we shall if we make haste."

"Suppose we find Oepon Batoe already besieged?"

"Naughe," I don't care, was the easy reply of the Poenan. "I will call together the tribes of the Upper Kahajan and then we will see who cries king."

"If that is the case we must not lose an hour," Johannes decided. "To-morrow morning at daybreak we must be on our journey again."

The Poenans and Kapoeasese when under the controlling influence of the Europeans were very punctual.

As soon as daylight began to appear in the east the camp was in commotion, and half an hour afterwards the rangkans left the shore. The inhabitants of kotta Hamiak, with tears in their eyes, took leave of the friendly travellers who had arrived so opportunely to aid and succor them in their recent extremity.

The journey up the mouth of the soengei Mantarat, which they reached about ten o'clock, was not very eventful. The rangkans sailed up the rivulet and reached the kotta shortly after noon. There nothing whatever was known about the enemy.

Our travellers occupied themselves in making six wooden rollers wherewith to facilitate the transit of their rangkans over the hills dividing the Kapoeas and the Kahajan. They then selected six of the strongest and largest vessels, partly unloaded them, pulled them on shore and placed them on the rollers. That effected, they loaded them again, adding as much of the cargo of the canoes to be left behind as they could conveniently receive. They also prepared large ropes of rattan and other creepers to be used as cables. By the time all these preparations were completed, evening had set in, and worn out with fatigue everybody retired to rest, under the protection of the sentries.

At daybreak the journey was continued; the number of men capable of bearing arms now amounting to seventy-two. Johannes arranged his men, directing ten of them armed with their rifles to serve as an advance guard. Then followed the six rangkans, each impelled by nine strong pairs of arms. Behind these came the women and children, protected by eight men carrying rifles and forming the rear guard. At first the travelling colony advanced rather rapidly. But the slopes became steeper and more rugged and the difficulties greater in consequence, especially as the heat of the day became more intense. There were times when they were forced to pause, panting for breath. Worst of all were the insects, such as beetles, ants, and other nuisances against which they had to battle. Everybody was completely exhausted.

In the middle of the afternoon, after surmounting a considerable eminence which by its steepness had greatly fatigued the travellers, Harimaoung informed them that with this height their greatest difficulty had been overcome. But no one could

MOVING THE RANGKANS OVERLAND.

be coaxed into moving a step further; they all longed for rest. They therefore resolved to seek shelter in a small wood situated at the top of the hill and to pass the night there. But before they could retire to rest Johannes ordered the six rangkans to be arranged in the shape of a hexagon, enclosing a space large enough to contain the whole company. He also had some young trees cut down to form along the corners of this artificial palisade a barricade which it would be difficult to penetrate.

The women busied themselves in preparing dinner, stimulated by the appetites of their lords and masters. But when they came to wash and boil their rice, the staple constituent of a Dayak meal, water was wanted. No one had thought of this. From the moment they had left soengei Mantarat not a single brook or rivulet or spring had been met with. They were in a sad strait, when a few Dayaks and Poenans, acting on their instinct, penetrated the wilderness whence they soon brought some pitcher-plant cups containing the purest water.

This treasure trove was received with loud acclamations, for every one was thirsty and wished to refresh himself with a hearty draught. But the quantity was insufficient for boiling the rice. They would have to be satisfied with some dried fish, and for the rest they must pull their waistbands a little tighter and in that way control their appetites. Very few bright faces were seen, the children especially clamoring for food and exclaiming how hungry they were.

Dalim, who as a miner at Pengaron and Kalangan had gained considerable experience, took his mandauw and disappeared in the adjacent forest, whence after a short absence he returned carrying a large parcel wrapped in leaves.

Having reëntered the enclosure he squatted himself down, spread a few leaves in front of him, opened his parcel and produced a dark-gray substance not unlike dirty pipe-clay. When Harimaoung Boekit saw it he exclaimed, "Ramon petak kinan," eatable soil, and seating himself near Dalim commenced to share his meal. They both seemed to enjoy the strange food as a welcome addition to their ration of fish. They then called the children and gave them each a large slice to allay their hunger. The Poenans, learning from Dalim where he had obtained his supply, sped thither in all haste to return soon with provision for the whole company. The two Swiss and the Walloon looked at this peculiar food with great suspicion, but when they saw Johannes take kindly to it and heard from him that it was a species of edible soil, their appetites urged them to try it. Although not absolutely pleasant to eat, being almost tasteless, it could not be considered disgusting. A few grains of salt and a sprinkling of pepper assisted deglutition. They could not eat much of it, however, as it was rather indigestible. The meal being cleared away the Europeans remained chatting about the wonderful island whose very soil is food for man. The learned Wienersdorf, holding a piece in his hand, broke out in the following explanation: "Ramon petak kinan is an amorphous substance, very brittle and easily pulverized. See, it can be cut with a knife and its incised surface exhibits a scaly structure of a spongy dark-brown color. It has a faint bituminous smell and adheres to the lips. Its taste—"

"We have learned," interrupted La Cueille, "and it is not very pleasant. In the name of the saints, cease your prating. It is enough to turn one sea-sick. Nom d' une pipe! how provoking these savants are! You had better tell us whether we shall have to eat this stuff much longer."

"No, no! my worthy Walloon," said Johannes, "you will have to eat it only once more for breakfast. I hope by this time to-morrow we shall be encamped at soengei Minjangan, where our women will be able to boil their rice as usual."

"Thank heaven!" La Cueille muttered. "Only fancy being compelled to consume this muck for several days."

"You would not get thinner, I assure you. On the contrary it would give your skin a fine glossy appearance. Hence they frequently mix it with the food of horses and dogs."

In the meantime the day was drawing to a close. The sun was gradually disappearing behind the margin of the forest when Hamadoe beckoned Wienersdorf to come to her. She was suffering intensely from thirst and begged her lover to procure her some water. Wienersdorf, accompanied by La Cueille and Dalim, entered the forest to seek more of the pitcher-plants with their valuable contents. In order to gather as many as possible, they separated from each other to prosecute an independent search. As a means of communication they were to call and respond to each other with the cry of the takekak. Their quest proved most successful. In a very short time each had found ten cups. Wienersdorf had already given the original taaaaak kakakākāk, when something weighty fell from a tree just in front of him. He stooped to see what it was and to his astonishment perceived, lying in the tall grass, what looked like a hideous child covered with red hair. It did not move, but remained rolled up like a huge ball: its legs drawn together, its face peering from between its elbows, and its stomach protruding above its contracted knees. He at once concluded that it was a monkey.

"It is rather a large one though," he muttered.

While stooping over the animal he felt something jump on his back and grasp him by the neck. Then came a rapid succession of blows, as if administered by a professional cudgeller.

"Himmels kreuz donnerwetter!" exclaimed the Swiss, terrified.

He endeavored to rise but was unable to do so; the load on his back was too heavy and the hand at his throat squeezed like a vise. All his efforts to shake off his assailant proved ineffectual. The cudgelling continued with increased force. At length his strength gave way. Breathless and nearly suffocated he just had power enough to cry:

"In God's name, help." Then he sank down and became insensible.

Upon recovering consciousness he saw the solemn face of La Cuielle, who was bathing his forehead and temples with the contents of the cups. When the Walloon saw him open his eyes he uttered a shriek of joy.

Wienersdorf extended his hand to him. The Walloon seized it and pulled him up on his legs. The Swiss was unhurt: his limbs were sound, though sore from the thrashing. At a little distance from him lay his assailant, whom Dalim was busy tying.

The Dayak and the Walloon upon first hearing the cries of the

Swiss had hurried to his aid, and upon seeing the struggle in progress Dalim had exclaimed in accents of terror:

"Kahio!"

He immediately cut a large branch, made it into a cudgel and requested La Cueille to do the same. They then approached the fighters as quickly as possible and Dalim began to belabor Wienersdorf's assailant with all his might. The ape had not before observed their approach, but he now left the Swiss and made for his new enemies, cudgel in hand. The fight did not last long, but yet long enough to prove that, armed with the most original weapon, man was not equal to the animal, which, like a trained fencer, avoided the blows of his opponents, and succeeded in regaling them with a thrashing they would long remember. At last Dalim managed to catch hold of the stick of the monkey and grasped it firmly. La Cueille, who up till now had been unable to join in the combat, owing to the rapidity of the movements of the combatants, then dealt the monkey a blow on the head which rendered him insensible immediately.

"Kahio!" Dalim cried again, pointing to the animal.

"Orang outang!" La Cueille said.

"Kahio!" the Dayak repeated.

"Orang outang!"

This quarrel was only brought to an end by Wienersdorf who now began to move about, groaning slightly. The ape also commenced to move and tried to rise. But Dalim threw himself upon the animal, dealt it a few more blows, and finally tied its hands and feet. Wienersdorf in the meantime had gained his legs, assisted as we have seen by La Cueille. Many of their cups of water had been spilled, trodden upon, or run empty, but they managed to save the valuable contents of about twenty. They now resumed their return journey, taking the animal with them.

They found that she was the mother of the young monkey which had fallen out of the tree before their battle, for as soon as they were brought near each other the little one hastened to seek its natural refreshment from the udders of the imprisoned animal.

At sunrise the fatiguing journey was resumed. The travellers had now to draw the rangkans over a range of hills, which did not take long. This done, the country became less rugged and they consequently proceeded much more rapidly. The slopes grew more gentle and the vegetation assumed a character which interposed little difficulty to their progress. Travelling being thus much easier the party was able to reach the borders of soengei Minjangan in the afternoon. But the day was already too far advanced for the immediate resumption of the journey, as the navigation of the rapid stream might be perilous after dark. They therefore made preparations for an early start in the morning, and went to their needed rest.

When travel was resumed next day the rangkans almost flew onwards. While passing down cataracts especially, their speed was terrific, for besides the rapidity of the stream in these parts, the helmsmen urged the rowers to exert their utmost vigor as necessary for the safe steering of the vessels over those seething waters. Amid loud yells one rangkan after another shot down the rapids, frightening the Europeans to death. The thought of possibly coming in contact with the rocks rising from the waters at almost every point caused them to shudder. But the helms were in safe hands, the oarsmen were wary and obedient, and the vessels safely reached the Kahajan River.

It was now about midday, and steering due north the rangkans at once sailed up this magnificent stream. At about three the travellers reached kotta Dewa, where Amai Kotong and Harimaoung Boekit landed. They found all in the greatest confusion, for an invasion by Tomonggong Soerapatti had just been reported. This intelligence determined them to travel all night, as the moon was shining brightly and there would be no danger in a nocturnal voyage over the broad and slowly moving stream.

It was about eight in the morning when the travellers saw, far away on the left hand, rising perpendicularly from the bed of the river, a colossal rock with a rounded top. This was the end of their night's journey. The rangkans, though propelled by the utmost exertions of the oarsmen, proceeded but slowly through the foaming waves which dashed against the perpendicular sides of the rock, here four hundred feet high. As soon as they had passed a little beyond the western side, there was a basin with a white sandy bottom, in which a tomoi had been built as a landing-place for canoes. Upon approaching the travellers observed three large rangkans already moored at this pier. They were empty; their caretakers having taken to flight upon seeing the strange vessels. But their appearance was sufficient to create a panic among the travellers.

"Olo Doesson, olo Doesson!' men from the Doesson, they exclaimed, causing no little confusion among the women and children. Harimaoung Boekit, however, addressed a few words to them and succeeded in calming their agitation. The women and children were all removed to two of the rangkans and their places in the vacated boats occupied by men. The rangkans containing the women, who by the way could manage the oars with equal facility, crossed over to the right bank and floated down the river some distance. The other two rangkans carrying the armed men including our Europeans landed at the tomoi. Not a soul was to be seen there. They cautiously examined the small buildings but could find nothing. The men now carefully entered the path and made their way up a steep clay hill in which there were occasional depressions. At last they caught sight of the rock upon which the kotta was situated. About fifty paces further they came upon a party of sixty Doessonese grouped together and engaged in an attempt to climb up to the plateau upon which the kotta was built. Against the rock there were several lofty trees, and in them notches had been cut to form a primitive staircase, up which about twenty men were mounting to the upper edge of the cliff. When Johannes, who had again assumed the command, saw this troop he ordered his men to halt and to direct a platoon fire into the midst of the group. The two Swiss followed their old tactics, carefully saving their ammunition for more opportune moments. La Cueille and Johannes opened fire upon the climbers, carefully selecting those who had mounted the highest. The result was astonishing. Those who fell bore down all beneath them in their fall. The consternation thus caused became further increased when the unerring bullets of those two marksmen were sent in the midst of the gathered

Doessonese, among whom they did more damage than all the noisy shooting of the Dayaks, and a large number of dead and wounded men soon covered the ground. After the first moments of surprise the most courageous amongst the Doessonese stepped forward intending to throw themselves upon their assailants, but as they approached a vigorous rifle fire shot them down. They then made a desperate assault, some of them actually landing amongst their besiegers, but the two Swiss soon settled their fate with their repeating rifles. The havoc caused by these rapid and successive shots made a lane through the ranks of the Doessonese, separating the foremost warriors from the main body. A terrible panic now seized them. Wild with terror and despair they hurried down a path which led to the edge of a precipice forming part of the chief rock overhanging the river. The fugitives here came to a momentary pause, but when the rifle fire sounded behind them in all its fury they threw themselves headlong into the river, with the view of swimming to the opposite bank. Many of them were drowned, while those who escaped a watery grave were afterwards followed and hunted down like wild animals.

After this drama had been played out the Poenans and Kapoeassers were about to decapitate the dead as well as the wounded Doessonese, when suddenly a fearful yelling was heard from the top of the rock. Although nothing could be seen, Harimaoung Boekit assured his friends that he knew perfectly well what was going on above. The Doessonese were making the chief attack on the eastern side with the main body of their army, but in order to compel their enemy to divide their forces had planned the scaling of the rock on the northern side by a comparatively small number of braves. This bold feat would have certainly proved successful, but for the accident which brought the adventurers just to the very spot.

Johannes hereupon led his men to a prompt execution of the plan he had formed to aid the defenders. He threw his rifle across his shoulders and began to climb the notched trees, which gave access to the upper edge of the rock from that side. The Kapoeassers and Poenans followed him, uttering deafening hurrahs, and in less than a moment they were seen dangling between heaven and earth, high above the abyss. After this difficult scaling, which took them about half an hour to accomplish, the valiant climbers were all at the top. Schlickeisen, whose wound forbade all exertion, had exchanged his Remington for the rifle of La Cueille and joined by four Dayaks who had been severely wounded, now returned to the rangkans.

As soon as Johannes was at the top he collected his men, tired as they were, and spoke a few words of encouragement. The wooden palisades which protected the kotta on that side were not high, because any attack from that direction was improbable. Johannes therefore leaped over the low barrier accompanied by Harimaoung Boekit to survey the kotta and ascertain the position of affairs. A heavy battle was in progress on the east of the fortification. The besieged were defending themselves desperately against an enormous number of Doessonese, and were so busy in conflict that he and the Poenan had been able to enter unobserved. In a single moment he saw the critical position of the garrison. Not a shot was fired here; everything was done with the naked sword. The assailants had already climbed the palisades at certain points and secured a firm footing on the ramparts. The most desperate effort to drive them back proved utterly ineffectual. New assailants were arriving every moment and they would soon be strong enough to throw themselves bodily in the interior of the kotta, when the doom of the garrison would be speedily sealed by the outnumbering hosts of the enemy. Johannes therefore hurried back to summon his companions, while the Poënan chief boldly advanced to attack the assailants and thus convey to the inhabitants the information that help was near. Suddenly a shot was heard and a Doessonese who was just appearing above the palisades to leap inside the kotta, fell backwards mortally wounded. A second and third shared the same fate. The Europeans, like fate's inexorable executioner, shot every Doessonner whose head appeared above the palisades. In the meantime the other Kapoeassers had signalled the inhabitants to clear the way for them to operate, and a heavy and continuous rifle fire was discharged amongst the troop of invaders who still retained their defiant position on the ramparts. Volley after volley was poured in, and a sortie made by the besieged to attack the flank of the enemy. The invaders wavered and dispersed; the vast army of Soerapatti flying down the hill to collect and rally at its base.

The withdrawal of the besiegers gave the Europeans time and opportunity to survey their position. Kotta Oepon Batoe might be called strong, nay, very strong, against a native enemy. With proper vigilance it was almost unassailable on two sides. The plateau upon which it was built was naturally divided by a cranny in the soil into two parts. A crystalline spring arose from this cranny, the water of which, rushing down the hollow, formed a foaming and turbulent torrent. For the rest, the whole plateau was bestrewn with huge blocks of rocks. Two of these especially drew the attention of La Cueille. They were enormous tabular stones, flat, but very massive, situated about a few yards from each other. Each of these rested upon a much smaller stone of a globular form, supported in such a manner that the whole of this colossal mass might be set in oscillation at the slightest pressure of the hand. The Walloon thought this very peculiar, pressed and pressed again, but could not accouut for the mobility of the huge piles. He stooped down and saw that both stones were elevated about three feet above the ground. He further noticed that they stood outside the ramparts, immediately on the edge of the plateau above the slope of the hollow just described. He bent over the edge of the declivity, but only saw a vast funnel-shaped shaft, through which the torrent streamed downwards. An idea struck him; he called Johannes, whispered a few words in his ears and both set to work to roll a large boulder underneath each of the two movable stones. Thus the two oscillating colossal masses were firmly supported. They then excavated the soil beneath these stones, filled the holes thus made with about twenty pounds of gunpowder obtained from the chief of the kotta, and having inserted a fuse they closed the mines with heavy lumps of rocks. This done, La Cueille led his port-fire between the palisades to the interior of the kotta, where he concealed it under a couple of fagots.

They had barely finished these preparations when a deafening noise announced the renewal of the attack by the courageous besiegers who were shortly seen rapidly mounting the heights from the eastern side. The rifles were speedily discharged, but the enemy being well covered by the edge of the hill the result was trifling. In less than a moment they had appeared above the plateau and commenced the storming of the fort, utterly defiant of death. It was a real troop of heroes. But all their bravery could not break down the defence. Each head as it appeared above the palisades served as a target, and if occasionally a single one escaped from the well-aimed bullets to succeed in leaping into the enceinte, he was met by the lances and mandauws and mercilessly killed. In the meantime the rifle fire was uninterruptedly sustained through the loop-holes and caused heavy losses among the assailants. These still persevered, determined not to give way, displaying a devotion worthy of a better cause. Encouraging each other and hurling contemptuous epithets at the besieged, they mounted the parapet again and again, always with the same fatal result.

While the whole garrison of the kotta were devoting their attention to the repulse of this attack, La Cueille, who seemed to have his own plans, was directing his regards to another point. His bullets were still speeding forth, but his thoughts were elsewhere directed. At last he fancied that he heard some noise on the north side. He then quickly repaired to the exterior of the kotta, crept like a snake along the plateau as far as its edge, and looking over saw a dense mass of men silently mounting the hill through the cranny. He had guessed rightly; the real danger lay here. The assault from the other side was only a feint, a brave sacrifice of heroes, in order to give their companions time and opportunity to accomplish their chief attack. As quietly as he had gone, La Cueille crept back, called Johannes and Wienersdorf, and ran to the kitchen to get a piece of burning charcoal, with which he set fire to the match. For a moment only, the Europeans saw the spark run along the ground to disappear through the palisades. They waited impatiently, but saw nothing more. The foremost of the enemies were already visible from the edge of the plateau. These leaped up, followed by others, until a hundred men were assembled on the top. Merciful Heavens! could the port-fire have become extinguished? that would be terrible. The Europeans opened fire upon the besiegers, but the number of the enemy became larger every moment, and they began to distribute themselves all over the plateau. The situation was becoming perilous, when, hark! there was a report so loud, so terrific, that for a moment besieged as well as besiegers stood motionless and horror-stricken. A fearful tongue of flame shot up from the ground as if a crater were opened; a thick cloud of smoke mounted to the sky, and one of the oscillating stones, lifted as if by magic, was seen to rise, drop from its support, topple over, and disappear thundering down the abyss. Before the assailants had time to account for this phenomenon, a second explosion took place and also hurled the other stony mass to the bottom. La Cueille's mines, well laid and efficiently charged, had succeeded wonderfully. The huge piles rolling down the declivity caused terrible havoc among the climbers, dispersing them like chaff before the wind. Those already at the top fled in terror, their panic extending to the army engaged in the feigned movement on the eastern side. The terrible destruction of their brethren filled them with consternation and led to the abandonment of their siege.

When the defenders of the kotta were able to estimate their losses they discovered that they had suffered considerably. Fourteen of the Kahajannese were found dead among a much greater number of Doessonese, and nearly twice as many were wounded. Not one of them hesitated to admit that, but for the timely arrival of our travellers, the result would have been immensely more fatal. La Cucille especially came in for a large share of admiration. He was a man who could dispose of thunder and lightning, making them rise from the earth to hurl upon their enemies mighty rocks which could only be lifted by Sangiangs. The Walloon, not being of a proud disposition, took this admiration with becoming modesty, though he was by no means disinclined to pose as a hero.

The Poenan chief now sent a couple of warriors to hail the rangkans which contained the women, while Johannes and a few Dayaks descended by means of the notched trees to fetch Schlickeisen and the four invalid Dayaks. Arriving below at the landing-place of the tomoi, they found that the rangkans in which their friend had been left, had disappeared. Four decapitated bodies of the Kapoeassers were lying on the bank, half in the water, with Schlickeisen's gun near them, but of the Swiss himself there was not a trace.

*

CHAPTER XVII.

PURSUIT—A BAND OF DOESSONESE SURPRISED—ON THE TRACK OF SCHLICKEISEN—HE IS SAVED—HARIMAOUNG BOEKIT MAKES A DISCOVERY—THE JOURNEY RENEWED—GOLD HUNTING—LA CUEILLE MAKES A FIND—BARTER WITH THE OLO OTTS.

THIS was indeed a terrible blow to Johannes. In nervous haste he examined the tomoi and the whole of its limited extent, without discovering anything further. He therefore rapidly ascended the Oepon Batoe and informed his companions of their misfortune. They all received the news with the deepest consternation, but Wienersdorf especially, with tears in his eyes, lamented the sad fate of his friend and countryman. It was certainly possible that he had saved himself by taking to the water. He was an expert swimmer, Wienersdorf said; but Harimaoung Boekit pointed to the wild and boiling stream and suggested that no human being could possibly swim across that torrent without being crushed to atoms a hundred times over, against the sharp and jagged rocks visible everywhere around. A third idea to which the Europeans clung, was that he had been carried away alive. This last would involve a terrible fate. They knew by experience how the surrounding natives treated their prisoners of war. And when these Doessonese, who might be classed among the most cruel tribes of Borneo, should discover that their prisoner was a whiteface, what hope would remain to him? The idea alone was enough to terrify them. And yet Wienersdorf desperately stuck to this hypothesis. At least it left him and his friends the hope of being able to render some assistance—possibly to save the lost one. He therefore urged this opinion with all earnestness. Johannes also felt inclined to believe that. Schlickeisen had been taken prisoner, and true to his loyal nature he at once commenced to work for his deliverance. The first things to be determined were, which band of the enemy had captured him and whither he had been carried.

Harimaoung proposed to start for soengei Miri by the overland route. He and Amai Kotong called their warriors together, provided them with an ample supply of rice and as soon as the sun disappeared beneath the horizon the little troop of Dayaks and Poenans, accompanied by three Europeans, silently descended the hill and marched towards the north. While descending La Cueille had ample opportunity to notice the terrible effect of his recent stratagem. Human bodies completely flattened out were seen buried in the deep and hard ruts made by the rolling blocks of stone. Here a fractured skull, there a ripped chest or gaping abdomen, further on dissevered hands and feet—everywhere blood. It was a fearful sight. Even the hardened senses of the Dayaks were moved, and with looks of horror the woodmen turned aside to hasten on their route.

The path at the foot of the hill ran almost parallel to the

Kahajan. They marched on unflaggingly that night and the whole of the following day, without discovering any trace of the enemy. At sunset they halted at a convenient spot to take a few hours rest, after which the march was resumed with renewed energy.

The moon was shining brilliantly, considerably lessening the difficulties of marching through a tropical forest by night. The path, however, was so narrow that only one man could pass at a time, so that they were compelled to travel in Indian file. Fallen trees were lying about everywhere. In many places they had to cut a way through the thorny creepers, a work which, besides damaging their clothes, occasioned them many disagreeable pricks.

About midnight, when they were marching along a grassy lawn dotted with large umbrageous trees, one of the Poenans warned them to keep silent. Through the midnight calm he had heard at no great distance some suspicious sounds which he believed to be human voices. Harimaoung Boekit softly whispered a few words to his companions, then he and six of his warriors threw themselves on the grass and cautiously crept along the ground. The rest of the travelers remained perfectly still for a quarter of an hour in an excited state of expectation. Of a sudden some cries of terror, rage and despair were heard which were succeeded by utter silence. Then the Poenans reappeared, two of them carrying human heads and the four others dragging behind them two gagged prisoners. These men at first refused to answer any questions. Johannes then gave them to understand that he would employ means to compel them to speak. One of them hurled some offensive epithets at his captors and in return received between his eyes a blow which set him spinning and almost stunned him. They then became more docile and bit by bit revealed that they belonged to a marauding band and knew nothing of the proceedings of their compatriots in that neighborhood. They had, however, been informed that many of their people had perished in an explosion at the Oepon Batoe and that all the inhabitants of the kotta had been killed at the same time. The Doessonese they had heard had secured many heads and had also captured a whiteface. Our friends listened breathlessly to this last item of intelligence, though it caused Harimaoung Boekit to stare with astonishment. Johannes then calmly enquired how this whiteface could have come here in these remote regions.

"Djaton tau," I don't know, was the reply; "but we have seen him. He was lying in a rangkan, tied hands and feet. His jacket had been torn off. His face and hands were brown like ours, but his chest and back were white. He had dyed his skin with katiting."

"And what have they done with him?" inquired Wienersdorf, hesitatingly, as if afraid to put the question, "Have they killed him?"

"No: many pleaded to have him killed, but it was resolved to carry him before Tomonggong Soerapatti, who will, without doubt, deliver him into the hands of the Dutchmen at Bandjermasin, with whom he wishes to make peace."

"Is the prisoner unhurt? And where is he now?" were the important questions of the Swiss.

The prisoners hesitated, looked at each other and remained silent even after Johannes had repeated his question. But La Cueille applied his rattan to their backs with such vehemence that their obstinacy was soon subdued. They then stated that at sunset they had seen the rangkan which contained the white man lying close by the bank of the river, the oarsmen evidently intending to rest at that spot for the night.

The pursuit was immediately resumed in the hope of capturing the vessel. A quarter of an hour later, upon approaching the banks of the Kahajan, they caught sight of the rangkan. When its crew became aware of their presence they hastily pushed their boat from the shore and made for the opposite bank. A couple of bullets were sent after the flying vessel, but it rapidly disappeared from view among the dark shadows of the thick forest. Directly after the discharge of their guns, however, they had distinctly heard a cry, "Help! help!" This not only convinced them that they were on the right track, but also assured them that their abducted companion was still alive. A council of war was now held. The Poenan chief assured his friends that he was acquainted with a by-way which would speedily bring them to a spot above stream in advance of the fugitives. Once there they could await the approach of the rangkan and act according to the circumstances. Before starting, however, they had to obey a cruel necessity. The two Doessonese prisoners had been brought in their train. To take them further would not only retard their journey, but also considerably increase their danger. Wienersdorf proposed to set them free, but his counsel was overruled, as they would certainly bring a whole troop of their brethren in pursuit.

La Cueille's suggestion was that they be securely tied to trees and left to the mercy of fate. This was objected to as unnecessarily cruel. Nobody might pass to liberate them and they would die a painful, lingering death. Johannes solved the difficulty by whispering something into La Cueille's ears, to which the Walloon responded by a nod of affirmation. The march was continued, La Cueille being intrusted with the care of the captives. He allowed the troop to pass on in advance, led by Wienersdorf and Johannes; he and his prisoners bringing up the rear. They had thus proceeded only a short distance when two shots were heard in succession and the Walloon came hurrying forward with the information that his prisoners having tried to escape he had been compelled to shoot them down.

They now marched on with increased speed and at daybreak found themselves near a little hill situated like Oepon Batoe on the bank of the river, which hurried by below this point in a wild cataract. This was Kiham Batoe Naroi, the most difficult as well as the largest fall on the Kahajan, though owing to the breadth of the stream by no means the most dangerous. Harimaoung Bockit here divided his little band into two companies. The smaller one mounted the heights and remained concealed in a recess of the rocky wall which commanded the curve of the river for a considerable distance. The other division was posted at the foot of the hill in order to cut off the retreat of the Doessonese, the men being instructed to keep themselves hidden behind rocks and shrubs until the moment for action should arrive.

As the Poenan chief had foreseen, a considerable time elapsed before the expected rangkan came in sight. The spies reported that it was manned by twenty oarsmen, but that nothing could be seen of the prisoner. As the boat approached, however, they distinguished Schlickeisen lying at the bottom in a most deplorable condition, tied hand and foot and perfectly naked. The rangkan made for the intricate passage of the kiham. Here in the country of their enemies, the Doessonese could not venture on land in order to guide their boat with a cable; they must row through the rapids despite the extreme difficulty of the feat. The rowers manipulated their oars magnificently and guided their craft with marvellous skill, now urging it forward calmly and steadily, and deftly keeping it afloat in the raging flood until all the difficulties of passage were successfully overcome. One more leap forward and the rangkan would have floated on calm water, when lo! a shot was heard. The foremost rower dropped his oar and fell back among his companions mortally wounded. Another and another shot, always with the same fatal result. Wienersdorf had put aside all his humane compassion: his sole aim was the deliverance of his faithful companion. Not a bullet must be thrown away, for the shot that failed to reach its mark would certainly imperil the safety of his friend. Kneeling down like a bronze statue he supported the stock of his rifle against his shoulder and aimed as if his whole existence, yea, his very soul, depended upon the line which his bullets must follow. The index of his right hand moved mechanically in manipulation of the trigger, and bullet after bullet carried death to the crew of the rangkan. Four of the oarsmen had been killed before the men could realize their position. They had not heard the noise of the firing, owing to the roar of the waters, but when they saw several

RESCUE OF SCHLICKEISEN.

of their crew writhing in their last agonies, they looked anxiously around and discerned the thin clouds of smoke rising along the dark wall of the rock. The Captain of the rangkan endeavored to preserve some order among his men by shouting, "Beseai bewèi," row firmly, and the boat shot forward on its course. But when directly afterwards three shots sounded in rapid succession and three more of their men fell backwards, their courage began to fail then.

They reversed their oars, and carried away by the fearful current the rangkan shot back towards the kiham. It was now the time for Johannes and La Cueille to play their parts in the fusillade. Their aim was not quite so unerring as that of the Swiss, nevertheless their bullets did such terrible execution among the Doessonese that the survivors leaped into the water even before reaching the bottom of the fall and tried to save themselves by swimming. This was the moment for which Harimaoung Boekit had been anxiously waiting. Ordering the men armed with rifles to keep up a heavy fire on the fugitives, he and his Poenans leaped into the river, swam to the deserted rangkan and drew it safely to the bank, where Wienersdorf already stood to receive them. Having moored the boat, they hastened to seek Schlickeisen and found him stretched at the bottom of the craft naked, senseless, and apparently in a high state of delirium. His neck and breast were covered with hundreds of minute wounds, all of which were greatly inflamed and stained with some blue pigment. Wienersdorf divested some of his companions of their head-cloths, which, after an effectual washing, he steeped in the cold river water and applied to the forehead and wounded breast of the sufferer.

They now took counsel together as to the immediate disposal of the sick man. The most alluring plan was to sail at once for soengei Miri to which they were already so near, but the captured rangkan could only accommodate thirty persons, while their party numbered fifty. After some deliberation it was agreed that Amai Kotong and a few of the Kapoeasese and Poenans should travel overland, while the rangkan, freighted with the others of the party, should sail down the Kahajan.

The cold applications prescribed by Wienersdorf for the inflamed wounds of his compatriot gave him effectual relief. Johannes and La Cueille constructed a covering of branches and leaves to shelter the patient from the rays of the burning sun. Shortly after their departure Schlickeisen opened his eyes and looked around; but when he tried to move a cry of pain escaped his lips. His companions bent over him, renewed the cold applications, gave him water to drink and by nursing him with all possible care rendered his sufferings sensibly lighter. When they found that his fever had abated they bathed his entire body with the cool river water. This process removed the blue pigment with which he seemed to have been painted all over and laid bare his white skin, in which innumerable little punctures were discovered. Harimaoung Boekit opened his eyes in astonishment when he saw the skin of the European. He bent over the patient and examined him minutely, at the same time casting an enquiring glance at Johannes, La Cueille and Wienersdorf. They all understood this look and felt that some violent revolution was taking place in the mind of the Poenan. Wienersdorf immediately tore open his jacket, and in the circle of these four men huddled around the patient, exposed his own shoulder to the Poenan chief. When Harimaoung saw the white skin from which the katiting had become wholly effaced, he murmured:

"Olo bapoeti!" a white man.

The son of the forest sat for a moment as if paralyzed, covering his eyes to hide the violent emotion raging in his soul. But the conflict was only momentary. The adventure upon the raft in lake Ampang came before his eyes. He remembered how Wienersdorf and Schlickeisen had saved him at kotta Djangkan when tied, like a wild animal, he was being dragged away by his foes. Wiping his forehead as if to remove an unwelcome thought he lifted his head, cast a look at Wienersdorf and taking him by the hand, whispered almost inaudibly:

"No matter, thou art my elder brother."

"And they?" asked the Swiss, pointing to the other Europeans.

"My younger brothers," said the Poenan, shaking each of them by the hand.

A sigh of relief escaped the breast of Johannes, who had looked upon the scene with a throbbing heart. It was now hurriedly arranged that the Europeans should still preserve their disguise before the others of the band, reserving the narration of their history for some future time.

All now turned their attention to the condition of Schlickeisen. Harimaoung Boekit informed his companions that he was in no danger from his wounds. He had only been tattooed. This proved to have really been the case. When the inflammation subsided Schlickeisen related all that had befallen him. After the disappearance of his company up the rock, he and the four wounded Dayaks had been overtaken by a troop of Doessonese coming down the river. They had suddenly appeared and their attack had been so wholly unexpected, that before the Dayaks could defend themselves they were decapitated. Schlickeisen owed his escape from the same fate to the fact that while struggling his jacket became torn and discovered his white skin. His assailants exclaiming " Olo bapoeti!" threw themselves upon him, pinioned and led him away prisoner. He heard his captors speak of carrying him to Soerapatti, who would deliver him up to the government at Bandjermasin, in the hope of thus securing a peaceable footing with the Dutch. Naturally they had no idea that their prisoner was a deserter from the Dutch army. But the proposal to spare this prisoner—a white man; the thought that so valuable a skull should escape them, almost infuriated these wild savages, until by way of a joke, some wag suggested that they should tattoo him and then offer the Dutch government a tattooed white face. One of the company then produced a pantoek, or needle, and immediately commenced to prick small wounds on the skin of the captive, designing the usual fantastic figures. These punctures were made by placing the point of the needle in the skin, forcing it in by gentle taps. The wounds were then washed with hot water to produce a copious hæmorrhage, and afterwards with melon juice, an application which made the patient roar with agony. When the wounds became swollen and inflamed they were smeared with a thick solution of indigo. The sufferer was then left in the most agonizing pain, exposed to the full force of the sun's heat without any covering. He suffered terrible thirst, yet no one offered him a drop of water. A febrile condition necessarily ensued, rendering him wholly insensible. Thus had he lain the whole night until frightened out of his lethargy by a succession of rifle shots. He had then called aloud for help, but tortured by the most excruciating agony he had again lost consciousness. When recovered from this insensibility it was to find himself surrounded by his friends.

"You have escaped through the eye of a needle," said La Cueille, "but it is a pity that those fellows did not paint you all the way down. You would have looked very much like wall paper; just like that Poenan over there. How handsome you would have been? Ah, won't the young ladies of Switzerland admire you!"

The sufferer smiled feebly at this remark. His friends renewed the cold applications, and presently he fell into a sound sleep from which he did not awake until the rangkan arrived at Oepon Batoe. He now felt so much refreshed that he was able to step ashore without assistance. The punctures were still somewhat painful, but the inflammation had totally subsided and there was no sign of fever. The circles and lines on his body remained, however, a fixed picture for the remainder of his life.

After a short interview with their women and children the party prepared for the resumption of their journey, and before the evening had set in they were all under way.

Forty-eight hours afterwards the fleet of our fugitives was lying moored to the pier of kotta Rangan Hanoengoh, and the travellers stepped on shore. The journey would have been accomplished much more quickly if their passage along soengei

Miri had not assumed the character of a real triumphal procession. Our friends had been compelled by the natives to make frequent delays. Everywhere they were received with the greatest enthusiasm. The number who pressed around La Cueille to admire the man who made mountains vomit fire, was at times so great as to endanger the modesty of the Walloon.

Shortly after their arrival Wienersdorf had an interview with Harimaoung Boekit, during which he related his whole history; explaining also the causes which had driven him and his companions to desert from Kwala Kapoeas. It was thereupon determined that the whitefaces should still keep their nationality a strict secret, the Poenan chief declaring that the value of European skulls in these regions was too high to justify their risking the consequences of a disclosure. They then proceeded to converse about the proposed marriage, which Harimaoung now wished to see concluded. True, he had discovered that the man was a whiteface! But had he not drunk that man's blood? Were they not now brothers? Aye, the whiteface had saved his life more than once, and he was bound to him by a sacred tie. He finally determined to refer the matter to his sister and to suffer her to decide. Hamadoe at once declared that she loved the European and was ready to follow him wherever he went, prepared to share his weal and his woe. Harimaoung's only answer was to draw the devoted girl into his arms to kiss her passionately in endorsement of her decision.

It was now arranged that the marriage should take place as soon as possible in order that the Europeans should prosecute their journey to the north without delay. But the ceremony could only take place at new moon, and that phase of lunation had just been passed. Thus five-and-twenty days would elapse ere the ceremony could take place. That time would, however, give full opportunity for preparations on the grandest possible scale.

La Cueille's projected marriage was abandoned, the young lady objecting to leave her tribe and kindred forever to follow her husband to his distant home. That was requiring from her too great a sacrifice, especially after the appearance of another swain. A celebrated head-hunter presented himself to the capricious damsel. Besides his hand and heart he offered a magnificent string of skulls, and she at once accepted him, vice La Cueille—deposed.

When the Walloon heard of his deposition, he bethought him of the words of a French king well acquainted with female fickleness, and thus gave expression to his feelings: "Souvent femme varie, bien fou qui s'y fie."

All this while Johannes was chafing at this enforced interruption of his journey for so long a time as three weeks. When, however, he saw that the delay was unavoidable, he applied himself to the utilization of this enforced leisure by reviving his plans to improve the financial condition of the company whose president he still considered himself. He reminded the Poenan of his promise to trade with them for the bezoar stones, and after a little bargaining received two hundred of them in exchange for the small guns carried off by the deserters from Kwala Hiang. Harimaoung Boekit also stipulated that the Europeans should mount the guns on the batteries of his kotta, and should further instruct his Poenans in their proper use. All willingly promised assistance, La Cueille undertaking to be chief instructor of the school of artillery.

The bezoar stones received in exchange for the guns were really very fine. Some of them were of extraordinary size and would realize a considerable sum at Singapore. When the Europeans came to estimate their value, they cordially commended the good management of Johannes in arranging their business so advantageously. The small heap of greenish-gray peas lying before them in a cocoanut shell represented about twenty thousand guilders. Johannes further informed them that he had sold the rifles captured at Kwala Hiang for one hundred thäels of gold dust.

"Hurrah!" cried the Walloon, "that is six thousand guilders. I have a good mind to open a gun factory here. These hundred thäels added to the bezoar stones give a total of over twenty-six thousand guilders. We are getting on in the world."

"Ah," said Johannes smiling, "that is not yet all. I have agreed with Harimaoung Boekit and Amai Kotong to go gold digging to-morrow morning. We shall find ample employment at that work as long as we remain in this place, and according to what I hear I expect it to turn out a very profitable game. Then besides there is all our merchandise to dispose of. Only leave everything to me and see how well I shall manage."

Next morning our adventurers started gold digging operations. Before setting out Harimaoung Boekit made them promise to observe all the usual formalities in order to evade the vengeance

HUNTING FOR GOLD.

of the sarok boelau, especially as he personally did not wish for a second attack of fever. The customs prescribed were as follows: During the time that they were employed in gold digging they must never approach a coal fire—must never seat themselves with legs hanging down—but always cross-legged—must scrupulously abstain from touching iron or steel, and finally must never, when bathing, turn against the stream. To all these instructions our friends promised to conform and they started on their new enterprise. They sailed down soengei Miri on a raft for a short distance and soon arrived at their destination. The raft was then moored by means of a ladder let down to the bottom of the river and there secured by means of heavy stones. Provided with wooden basins they went down into the stream, descended to the bed of the river and filled their bowls with auriferous sand, which they immediately conveyed to the raft for examination. The bowls were of the size of a large plate, about fifteen-inch diameter, scooped out in the centre.

The work, being strange to the Europeans, was at first awkwardly executed. There was many a laugh and joke at their expense when through some clumsy movement they suffered the stream to sweep away the entire contents of their bowls. They gradually became more expert and after their first success became infected with gold fever. Thus they labored all the day without cessation and when at nightfall they were forced to suspend their operations, Harimaoung proceeded to weigh the day's collection. He found that they had gathered half a thäel, which he valued at about thirty guilders.

"That is not much," said the Poenan, "but when my brothers

are a little handier at the work the result will be more satisfactory."

Nevertheless, the result was sufficiently remunerative to make the adventurers enchanted with gold washing. La Cueille especially was awfully excited. He talked of nothing but gold-seeking, and even in his sleep was haunted with the wildest dreams about the precious metal.

The labor was continued for several days consecutively, and as predicted by Harimaoung Boekit with constantly increasing success. There were days when the collections amounted to five thäels. The gold was generally found in the shape of a fine, soft powder, but occasionally it was met with in the form of scales, threads or small nuggets. The larger nuggets, never exceeding the size of large peas, were rarely found, though Harimaoung Boekit informed them that some time ago nuggets one inch in diameter had been taken.

La Cueille as a professional miner was naturally more observant than his companions. He noticed that gold dust was invariably found in proximity to a glittering white sand.

One day when through a lazy fit of the natives the Europeans were doomed to inaction, La Cueille was wandering about the neighborhood when he stumbled over a hole hidden by some foliage and nearly dislocated his ankle. The hole was simply a fissure in the yellow clay soil of the bank of a small rivulet. Upon extricating his foot he found it quite covered with the white sand. He enlarged the fissure with his hands, removed the foliage and proceeded to work downwards. The excavated sand exhibited unusually rich traces of gold. La Cueille therefore hastened for his basin, but also brought with him his spade and pickaxe, having a presentiment that he would be amply rewarded for a little extra labor. The result was marvellous: the deeper he penetrated into the soil the more auriferous grew the sand, until he finally arrived at a layer of blinding white sand, from the midst of which the precious metal shone forth as if all the treasure of the world had been stored there. He filled his basin and hastened to the brook, where, after a hurried washing, he found collected in the hollow of his dish several nuggets the size of a pea. He pursued his operations and soon discovered that the deeper he penetrated the rarer became the white sand, but the larger and more numerous grew the nuggets, until at the bottom of the hole he found a few as large as a bean, and of the purest quality. Beneath this layer there was only, however, gray clay, without any trace of gold. The Walloon now became almost mad with joy as he gazed upon his treasure spread out before him and glittering in the rich sunlight. He danced around it in the most fantastic manner and in his excitement displayed the most childish folly. He carefully covered the little heap with leaves and branches and hurried to the kotta to inform Johannes of his find. They sallied forth together provided with a sack to bring home the booty. When secured and weighed it was found to represent four hundred thäels, or about forty pounds of pure gold.

"I never expected to be so lucky," exclaimed La Cueille. "Let me see, four hundred times sixty guilders."

"Exactly twenty-four thousand guilders," said Johannes. "That is a handsome haul which you made there. I heartily congratulate you."

"And added to the other twenty-six thousand of the bezoar stones—that makes exactly fifty thousand guilders."

"To which you may safely add another ten thousand, as the yield of the gold dust already found and which we may yet find, besides a little barter I am thinking of doing."

The Walloon was excited with joy and exclaimed:

"Over sixty thousand guilders, and divided into four equal shares—will give more than sixteen thousand to each person."

The others nodded an assent: then taking the Walloon's hand they pressed it warmly. La Cueille had shown himself to be a faithful companion, for he had never thought of appropriating the gold to his own use, although he alone had found it.

"I knew," said Johannes, "that I was not mistaken in him."

Wienersdorf, who had been meditating, now remarked: "It is all very well that La Cueille has found this gold, but how are we to carry it away with us?"

"Pray don't trouble yourself about that," rejoined Johannes.

"Not trouble about it?" asked Wienersdorf. "Perhaps you mean to forward it by railroad or express!"

"Ah, it will take some time yet ere the whistle of the locomotive will be heard in these parts. But listen! We will carefully separate the nuggets from the gold dust. For the former we will make leathern belts doubly lined. Each of us will carry one of these belts filled with about eight pounds of gold. For the gold dust we will make four walking sticks or leaping poles, employing for the purpose Dayak blow-pipes. Let me, however, advise, if you pay visits on the road never to leave your walking cane behind you."

"By George, no," said La Cueille, "especially as we could not advertise them in the morning papers, offering a reward to the honest finders. But a belt around one's waist weighing eight pounds, and a walking-stick of two pounds' weight in one's hand, will be no treat in addition to the burden we shall have to carry on our journey."

"Quite so. Besides your rifle and cartridge-box you will have to carry on your back a basket of provision and reserve ammunition. But all this we will arrange hereafter. If, however, you imagine that our possessions are to be easily transported you are greatly mistaken. That train about which Wienersdorf joked just now is not ready yet, therefore you will be compelled to carry your treasure yourselves."

"So you see again that nothing in this world is perfect," said the Walloon.

"Now that I am a rich man, I naturally long for others to do the work for me."

Johannes now thought of finding some means for disposing of the goods which he had procured from Baba Poetjieng, from Bapa Andong and from kotta Baroe, with the view of trading with the Olo Ott. Now that they had amassed a considerable fortune this barter seemed unnecessary, but Johannes was anxious to witness himself and to show his companions the Dayak manner of doing business. He therefore talked the matter over with Harimaoung, who found the plan perfectly feasible. Everything was therefore prepared for the trading expedition and one fine morning our four white friends, accompanied by Dalim, Harimaoung Boekit and Amai Kotong, sailed up soengei Miri in a rangkan chartered for the purpose. The journey was rather a long one. On the third day the travellers reached soengei Danom Pari, where they landed at a gigantic and umbrageous tree near the brink of the river. At the foot of the tree they spread mats, upon which they placed heaps of salt, glass beads, articles of clothing—such as jackets and ewahs made of coarse linen or bark; about twenty mandauws, several pieces of iron, a few dozen rudely manufactured knives and numerous parcels of tobacco made into little bunches. All these were laid out separately on the extemporized stall. Some edibles were added consisting of cakes. The drinkables were represented by a huge jar of toeak.

"I should not object to stand sentinel over that jar," said La Cueille.

"For fear of its running away?" asked Johannes, smilingly. "You had much better leave it alone, for the jar would not be able to take care of you and, I assure you, you require to be taken care of in these quarters. We are in the domains of the Otts, of whom I will tell you more by and by."

When the goods had been all displayed, Harimaoung Boekit took a metal gong, suspended it from the branch of a tree and with a piece of wood struck several blows, the echo of which was heard all over the forest. They listened attentively for about ten minutes and hearing no response the Poenan repeated his strokes on the gong. Then from a distance a number of similar sounds were heard; they were muffled as if they had proceeded from a hollow tree. Harimaoung Boekit now bade his companions re-enter their rangkan, struck another blow on the gong and the whole party rowed down the river a mile and a half, where they halted and waited in mid-stream.

"I am blessed if I see how we are ever to get our goods back again," said Schlickeisen.

"Don't be alarmed," replied Johannes, "only wait."

They had not to wait very long. A couple of hours afterwards the gong sounded and the rangkan obeyed the signal by sailing up the soengei to the original position.

They returned to their stall and inspected its condition. La Cueille made the first discovery; he cried out in dismay:

"Look here, our toeak jar is empty!"

But his astonishment as well as that of his companions became greater still when they proceeded to take stock of their goods recently submitted to their invisible customers. Next to each article offered for trade there had been something placed as its proposed equivalent. One or more bezoar stones, some heaps of gold dust, tiger skins, were thus offered in exchange for a mandauw, a dress, a knife, some tobacco or glass beads.

"But what next?" asked Wienersdorf.

"Let us look well and estimate the value of the things," said Harimaoung. They then carefully went over their stock and its proffered price and found that most of the articles offered in exchange exceeded in value the wares disposed for sale. The salt especially seemed to be in the highest demand by the Olo Ott, for the largest heaps of gold dust were tendered on barter for that commodity. As our traders were satisfied with their prices the Poenan collected all the things left by the Olo Ott and had them conveyed to his rangkan. The stall containing their own goods was left intact. Harimaoung then struck his gong violently as a signal and proceeded to take it down and convey it to his canoe, when the journey homewards was at once commenced. On making up their balance-sheet, Johannes perceived that for the rubbish offered by the Europeans for traffic they had received one hundred bezoar stones, about six thäels of gold dust and a large number of tiger skins. These last were ordered by Johannes to be converted into jackets which would be of great service to them during their projected march through the wilderness.

"By jingo," said La Cueille, "this is profitable business. It beats the wholesale merchants hollow."

"But suppose," asked Wienersdorf, "the Otts had not left sufficient value for our goods, what should we have done?"

"In that case," answered Dalim, "we should have simply removed our goods and left theirs."

"And suppose they had taken away our goods without leaving anything instead?"

"Such a case has never occurred," Johannes explained. "The most implicit confidence is observed in this mode of barter without the parties being known to each other. It did once occur that some Malay merchants, in removing their property, took away some of the articles offered in exchange by the Otts. But they had scarcely gone half-way up the soengei ere they were overtaken and made to pay for their dishonesty with their lives."

"You say that the traders never see each other? Is that really the case?"

"Always. Whenever the Otts show themselves, it means war and one of the parties is sure to be annihilated."

"What kind of fellows are these Olo Otts?"

"Ah! now you ask me more than I can answer. I have never seen them myself; but ask the Poenans and you will hear that they are half monkeys and have tails."

"Tails!" echoed La Cueille, quite amazed.

"Yes; tails, my worthy Walloon," said Johannes smiling. "Don't forget that you also once had a tail: at least your forefathers had; and if———"

"Your forefathers, perhaps, not mine," was the angry rejoinder of the Walloon.

"And," continued Johannes calmly, if you only examine the end of your spinal column you will find that the last vertebra feels as if it had been broken off. Some savants might attempt to prove that that is only the result of our habit of sitting down, by which the original tail became worn off. This peculiarity they pretend has been since continued from generation to generation. Is not that the case, Wienersdorf?"

"Quite so: Adams, Schlegel, and later on, Darwin———"

"Stop, stop," cried La Cueille, "we don't know any of those gentlemen!"

"And yet it is really a positive fact," continued Johannes, "which many savants have accepted, that here in Borneo tribes do exist rejoicing in the luxury of a tail. According to them this tail is nothing but a small motionless elongation of the spinal column. The bearers of this appendage always carry with them small pierced boards about six or eight inches long, upon which they sit in order that the excrescence may not interfere with their comfort. As for these Olo Otts, they are looked upon as the aborigines of Borneo, gradually driven back into the wilderness by other tribes. They are extremely shy, very treacherous, and head-hunters, and by no means averse to a titbit of human flesh with or without salt and ·lombok. They have no kampongs, neither are they of a social disposition. They live together in families, which are however sufficiently large to form bands of from twelve to fifteen males. Whenever the alarm is sounded on the hollow trees of these forests they speedily assemble from all directions until they muster a couple of hundred valiant men. Houses in our sense of the term they have not. They make a kind of nest in a large tree and live in it. For the rest they move about on the tops of the trees of these woods, with an amount of ease of which we can form no idea. They are only surpassed by the kahios, boehies and other monkey tribes. You may, however, rest assured that from the moment we entered their neighborhood we were not unobserved for a single moment. Even now, though we do not see them, they are nevertheless close around us."

"The deuce they are," muttered La Cueille, "we had better move on a little faster and get out of their way."

They rowed on steadily and the rangkan descended the stream quickly and peacefully.

CHAPTER XVIII.

TRAVELLING APPOINTMENTS—THE DIAMOND OF THE SULTAN OF MATAM—DIAMOND FIELDS—GEORGE MULLER'S DIARY AND SKULL—MARRIAGE CEREMONIES—AGAIN ON THE ROAD—A NOVEL BURIAL-PLACE—ON THE EQUATOR—AN INKY LAKE—THE ASCENT OF BATANG LOEPAR.

ON the following day gold washing was resumed, as our adventurers were anxious to collect as much of the precious metal as they possibly could. They had discovered that there would be no difficulties of transport, the faithful Harimaoung Boekit having volunteered to conduct them under the safeguard of thirty Poenans to the Sarawak frontiers. Wienersdorf and his companions gratefully accepted this assistance and made their preparations accordingly.

One morning when busy at kotta Rangan Hanoengoh preparing ammunition, La Cueille thought he would make some cartridges. They would, he thought, be handier for the use of the Poenans, besides being less dangerous and less wasteful. But in order to make cartridges he must have paper, a luxury not easily found in a Dayak kotta of mid-Borneo. He talked the matter over with Harimaoung Boekit, showing him at the same time one of his cartridges. As soon as the Poenan comprehended what was needed he went indoors and returned with a pile of old books. Most of them proved to be Bibles, printed in the Dayak language, which are largely distributed over the interior of Borneo, though none of the natives know how to read. Among these books, however, the Walloon found a large MS. folio in a most imperfect condition. The volume now consisted principally of blank leaves. Those which had been written upon were torn and battered. There was no title-page to indicate who was the author or owner. While turning over the leaves his attention was drawn to a page half of which was wanting, which however bore these words:

"Oct. 14, 1824.

"I have found that gold appears here as in other districts, in layers—separated from each other according to the formation of the ground, so that in one spot one might meet with a real treasure, while in its immediate neighborhood nothing would be found. The sand containing the gold generally lies upon a layer of light yellow clay and is covered with a darker bituminous clay. The gold dust originates from the friction of the nuggets and laminæ against each other, or against stones, while they are being borne along by the wild rush of the waters. Real mines in which the layers—"

At this point the page had been torn and the remainder was wanting.

"What a pity," sighed the Walloon.

He turned over the page and suddenly his attention was again arrested.

"By Jove, this is interesting, I must read it."

"July 16, 1824. I saw the large diamond of the Sultan of Matam yesterday. By the extraordinary precautions taken, I could perceive that it was the real one; for whenever the Sultan distrusts a foreigner he shows him a fine djakoet which resembles the great gem. It is a magnificent stone and was found in the kingdom of Landak. It weighs three hundred and sixty-one carats. I weighed it myself. In shape it is a pyramidal dodecahedron or double hexagonal pyramid, broken at about two-thirds of its entire length, perhaps while freeing it from its covering, as often occurs. Its form is somewhat irregular and oblique. It is of the purest water; its light hue somewhat tending toward rose-color being more due to refraction caused by fissures, than to its want of purity. Its longitudinal section is two and one-sixth inches, its lateral measurement one and one-fourth inches. The short side of the pyramid is one and one-third inches, and the longer one one and one-half inches. In Dayak language it is called Sagima, angular; in Malay, Danau Redjo, and it is estimated at a value of five million two hundred and twelve guilders."

"Five million guilders," cried the astonished Walloon. "Five million guilders! What wouldn't I give to find a stone like that! I say, where is Landak?"

"In that direction," answered Johannes, pointing to the southwest.

"Shall we pass there?" asked the Walloon.

"What do you mean?" Johannes replied. "How shall we pass there when we are journeying towards the north?"

"Look here," said the Walloon, showing the tattered book.

"A diamond has been found in Landak valued at five million guilders. Suppose we could find such a stone?"

"Bah! you hope to find a diamond worth over two million dollars! Your aspirations are on the increase. Let us see what your book says about that gem."

Johannes took the manuscript and commenced to read. Having finished the description of the jewel, he leisurely turned some of the pages, becoming gradually more interested in their persual.

"Where did you get this book?" he enquired of the Walloon.

La Cueille related how Harimaoung Boekit had given it to him among other volumes for the purpose of making cartridges. The Poenan was now questioned, and after thinking awhile remembered that he had appropriated it during a head-hunting expedition among the Penhengs. He also informed them that it had been profusely illustrated, but that the children had torn out the pictures.

On further examination Johannes fancied that on the inside of one of the covers, over which a blank leaf had been pasted, he could perceive some writing. He carefully loosened the page and detached it from the cover, when he read the following:

"All my companions have been massacred to-day. To-morrow it will be my turn. God have mercy upon my soul.

"G. M."

Johannes continued for some time gazing at these initials. "Good Heavens!" he exclaimed, "may this not be the journal of George Muller, the savant who was butchered in this country more than thirty-five years ago! This is a real treasure-trove. Yes, undoubtedly it is Muller's diary."

Harimaoung Boekit, who had gone indoors, now reappeared with a rosary of skulls, one of which he exhibited to the Europeans. Its conformation proclaimed that it had belonged to an individual of the Caucasian race.

"Found with the book," said the Poenan.

Schlickeisen and Wienersdorf both implored Harimaoung Boekit to give them that skull, but all their efforts were in vain. The possession of a white man's skull was invaluable to the Poenan; so carefully tying his rosary together he took it indoors and placed it in safety. Johannes, however, took charge of the book to protect it from further mutilation.

Thus passed the days prior to Wienersdorf's wedding. He had been longing to possess his beloved Hamadoe, and Johannes had been equally anxious to see the journey resumed.

The day of the full moon arrived at last, and early in the morning Dalim and Johannes commenced to prepare the bridegroom for the marriage ceremony. According to Dayak custom he had first to bathe in the river. Then he was painted with katiting and afterwards rubbed over with boengkang, the fat of a black cat, until his skin shone like a polished door-plate. The nails of his hands and feet were then gilt and on his forehead two broad red stripes were painted, which appeared like fiery eye-brows, overriding the brown ones which nature had given him. He was now dressed in a karoenkoeng, or suit of rattan armor, and on his head was placed a cap of monkey skin, ornamented with two handsome feathers from the tail of the rhinoceros bird. The ewah, thrown around his waist, was made of very fine beaten bark and was considered to be of rare excellence. Dalim then clasped around his loins the state mandauw of Harimaoung Boekit and supplied him with a shield upon which a monstrous crocodile was painted. His toilet was then complete.

"You do look fine," exclaimed La Cueille. "I should like to have you at the fair at Jupille. What money I should make by exhibiting you as a wild Indian."

Wienersdorf was just ready when three deputies, relatives of the bride, appeared and solemnly asked him whether he was prepared to fulfil his marriage contract.

"I should think so," La Cueille answered, "he is boiling over with impatience."

The answer having been formally given in the affirmative, each of the deputies received a present of gold dust from the bridegroom, who immediately accompanied them to the residence of the bride. The other Europeans and several attendant Dayaks followed in solemn procession.

The entire population of kotta Rangan Hanoengoh had assembled in a shed facing the house of Harimaoung Boekit. Here they were joined by numbers of the inhabitants of other kottas who had come over to witness the ceremony. The bride, dressed in a long silk cloak and wearing a saloi embroidered with gold, was modestly seated among twenty of her young companions. Bride and bride-maids had all ornamented their luxurious hair with flowers.

As soon as the bridegroom entered Amai Kotong, as the oldest of the company, arose and solemnly invoked Mahatara and all the

Sangiangs, but especially Kadjanka, the ruler of the moon, imploring them to guard the young couple from all trouble and misfortune. He then loudly proclaimed the possessions of both parties, employing the most marvellous exaggeration, in recognition of the Dayak idea that the Deity, like earthly beings, is more propitious towards the rich than the poor. He next mixed in an earthen vessel the blood of a buffalo, a chicken, a woodpigeon and a pig, and invoked the Sangiangs to contribute to this mixture some blood from their karbauws of chickens, etc. In order to make the ceremony more impressive this invocation was repeated by the eighty-four priestesses present, and was accompanied by fearful yells and loud beatings of their katambongs.

Amai Kotong having thus acquitted himself of his part in the ceremony, six of the oldest men of the tribe came forward with a new invocation, which being duly recited, was paid for by the bride at a cost of two dollars' worth of gold dust to each elder.

Hamadoe and Wienersdorf were then ordered to seat themselves on a garantong or metal plate, facing each other. The bridegroom was made to uncover the upper part of his body while Amai Kotong assisted the bride to do the same. These preparations concluded, Amai approached carrying a jug filled with blood. He dipped his first and second fingers and the thumb of his right hand in the gore and invoked again the blessings of the Sangiangs on the bridegroom and his bride, as he besmeared their forehead, shoulders, wrists, etc., with the contents of the jug. This process was repeated by each of the six elders.

Wienersdorf then shared among the relatives of the bride the gifts which he had prepared for presentation. Harimaoung Boekit received a magnificent jacket of scarlet cloth, with a broad gilt collar. Amai Kotong and the others were presented with handsome ewahs.

With these presentations the ceremony closed for the time and the noisy multitude betook themselves to the refreshment department, which had been most liberally provided by the Poenan chief.

At the approach of evening, while the guests were still regaling, the husband and wife were separated. According to Dayak custom they must not meet each other again on the wedding day. The bride was led away by her companions, and the bridegroom was left with strict injunctions not to sleep, lest nightmares should visit him. He therefore rejoined his friends and shared their festivity.

As soon, however, as the sun began to reappear on the horizon, the bride was brought out by her companions. She and her husband entered a djoekoeng and rowed into the middle of the stream. Arrived there, she gave the light vessel a sudden jerk which precipitated Wienersdorf into the water. This immersion of her husband accomplished, she assisted him to re-enter the canoe and they rowed back to the shore, where they were received by the shouting priestesses. These priestesses then proceeded to strew rice upon the heads of both bride and bridegroom, subsequently introducing a chicken which they set to pick up the rice. This was intended to symbolize the removal of all misfortunes from off the heads of the newly-wedded pair. Toeak was now served around, and after a parting glass all departed to their respective domiciles, leaving the new husband and wife to the enjoyment of each other's society.

The marriage had been solemnized and now there was nothing to prevent our adventurers from prosecuting their journey. It was therefore resolved to start as soon as the final preparations could be made. A couple of days sufficed to complete all arrangements, and at daybreak of the third day the journey was resumed. The party consisted of Mr. and Mrs. Wienersdorf, the three other Europeans, Dalim and his companion of Kwala Kapoeas, and Harimaoung Boekit, who, faithful to his promise, would with a few of his followers accompany the travellers until they should be out of danger. For their reception a large rangkan had been provided, manned by a crew of forty Poenans, who were to serve first as oarsmen and later on as carriers of the goods and chattels. Under the impulse of so many oars the vessel, though carrying so many persons, moved briskly toward the north. As long as the kotta remained in view the occupants of the rangkan exchanged loud hurrahs with their late friends, who finally fired a salvo from the six guns which had been mounted on the ramparts by La Cueille. This salute was intended as a recognition of past favors and also as a proof of the efficiency of the artillerists offered to their departing instructor. The Walloon, however, seemed dissatisfied.

"No. 1 of the second gun," said he, "handles his sponge awkwardly—the fellow should know better. No. 4 is careless in closing his vent. There will be an accident some day."

Rising in the boat he was about to call out to the men who were serving the guns, when the rangkan suddenly shot around an angle of the stream and the kotta disappeared from view.

The journey was continued up the soengei Miri, which was found to be navigable for two more days, after which it became so shallow that further progress had to be abandoned. At nightfall of the second day they landed and camped, making all arrangements to continue the journey by land on the following morning.

"Shall we not see something of the Otts?" asked Schlickeisen. "We are now in the country, are we not?"

"Let us hope that we shall not be favored with a visit from them. To see them means a fight for life," said Harimaoung. "You may, however, be sure," continued he, "that they have seen us and that we are still being watched by them; but they know me and we have never had any dispute with them."

"Yet must we be on the watch," thought Johannes. He therefore divided the band into two sections, to keep alternate guard during the night. The hours, however, passed undisturbed and at daybreak the Poenans shouldered their baskets, in which the provisions and ammunition were stowed away. The four Europeans also carried baskets, the burden not proving unfamiliar to them in consequence of their old experience with the knapsack. But besides a supply of cartridges, their baskets contained their gold dust and bezoar stones. Even Hamadoe had prepared her basket, duly freighted with her trinkets, but when she took it up she found it empty. Wienersdorf had unpacked it and added its contents to his own burden. She protested, but was soon silenced with a kiss, after which she patiently submitted.

The Europeans cheerfully seized their canes, loaded with gold dust, slung their rifles over their shoulders and manfully took the road. A couple of Poenans moored the rangkan in a small creek and there left it without any doubt of its perfect safety.

"Shall you find it there when you return?" Wienersdorf asked his brother-in-law.

"Certainly; theft is unknown here. The only article that I have to guard is my head."

The Swiss soon discovered that their direction lay toward a very lofty mountain visible on the north-west. They learned, on enquiry, that this was the Boekit Doesson. It was not a mountain range, but more like an elevated plateau which formed the base and starting point of the numerous peaks constituting the central highlands of the country. The road—if the track formed by human feet among the luxurious vegetation could be so called—was not difficult. It undulated between gently inclining hills and only tried their powers when it became intersected by the innumerable brooks which rushed through the deep hollows of the clayey soil. Here, however, they generally availed themselves of the opportunity to take a bath in the clear fluid, a refreshment which neither gave trouble nor caused delay to the sparsely-clad travellers. During these ablutions careful watch continued to be kept; one-half of the men enjoyed the bath, while the remainder rifle in hand remained on guard. Nothing of a suspicious nature was, however, observed; not a human soul was seen. They could almost imagine themselves to be on a desert island. But during one of these halts the travellers found reason to know that they were not unobserved. A fine ironwood tree adjacent to their resting-place had attracted Wienersdorf's attention. He approached it to gaze upon the giant which, rising like a column, proudly erected its magnificent crown of rich foliage one hundred and fifty feet in the air. A couple of squares formed by vertical and horizontal cuts in the trunk, led him to fancy that the bark had been removed by human hands. He noticed also that the new growth over this area was of later date than the surrounding bark. He stood there looking a little longer and then drawing his knife he commenced to carve a colossal W in the middle of one of the squares, intending to add the initial of Hamadoe's name and to enclose both in the figure of a heart. While thus occupied a whistling noise caused him to look around, when he saw a small arrow enter the tree between his head and hand. With the quickness of lightning he drew back, presented his rifle, and fired into some shrubs behind which he perceived some movement. All his companions hurried toward him in alarm, when he pointed to the little arrow sticking in the tree. The Europeans presented their rifles to clear the ground with a prompt volley. Harimaoung Boekit, however, interposed, depressed their rifles and uttered a cry, followed by a few words in another language not intelligible to his companions. The Poenan then remained for some moments in an attitude of expectation, his countenance betraying the deepest anxiety. At last a few hoarse sounds were heard in reply, whereupon Harimaoung's face cleared up and he assured his friends that all danger was passed. The people living here were Ott Njawongs, a tribe with which he was on friendly terms, but he begged that the tree on which Wienersdorf had commenced to carve his name should be no further molested.

A Sign of the Enemy.

"What a queer notion," growled La Cueille, "to cut one's name on a tree in the depth of a wilderness."

"What is the matter with that tree?" asked Wienersdorf.

"The Otts have buried one of their people inside that tree," explained Dalim. "They burn the bodies of the dead, wrap the ashes and half consumed bones in a shroud, bore a large hole in an iron-wood tree and place the parcel inside. They then close the orifice with rosin and bees-wax and cover it with moss. Nature in a very short time restores the bark and the marks gradually disappear. No one would think that that magnificent tree with its slender trunk and broad crown forms the grave of a human being."

"A new model cemetery," observed the Walloon.

At the close of the second day the travellers arrived at the foot of Boekit Doesson, which the Poenan chief intended to climb on the following morning in order to look for some landmark by which to regulate his course.

The two Swiss, hardy mountaineers of the Alps as they were, were not satisfied to be left behind and insisted upon making the ascent with him, while La Cueille and Johannes also begged to be permitted to join the party. It was then decided that the whole company should join in the climbing excursion.

The journey was undertaken next morning. Their way led at first through forests of bamboo interwoven with rattans and other creepers, which covered the high trees and formed an almost impenetrable net-work, greatly impeding their march. But the higher they went the lighter this vegetation became, until ultimately it disappeared altogether.

It was about half-past ten when the travellers reached the broad, gently-curved summit, which crowns every mountain of the Bornean central highlands. They were to rest here for a couple of hours. While, therefore, Harimaoung took his observations, Hamadoe, assisted by the Poenans, prepared a simple repast. The rest of the troop dispersed over the summit to look for rajoh, a fine specimen of moss found in the highlands wl ich is highly prized by the Dayaks.

The Europeans were charmed with the view spread out before them; they gazed with rapture upon the panorama and feasted their eyes upon the magnificent tropical vegetation above which they seem to be suspended. While most of the party were thus wrapt in admiration, Johannes was observed to be making notes on his pocket-book. " It is just seventy days since we left Kwala Kapoeas," said he.

"Is it as long as that?" rejoined La Cueille. "Let me see; we quitted the fort on the tenth of January, did we not?"

"Yes, and to-day is the twenty-first of March, making exactly seventy days."

"The twenty-first of March!" said Wienersdorf, struck by the date. " Then the sun must enter Aries to-day and be exactly above the equator. Wait; I will soon find out in what latitude we are."

Cutting a fine young cedar of about ten yards in length he removed all its branches and planted it upright on a smooth bit of turf. He then took his compass and verified that the short shadow of the pole pointed due east and west.

" Error is impossible in these latitudes," said the Swiss meditatively. "But——that could be accidental. Perhaps there is a little local attraction which makes the needle deviate. I shall soon see."

"What are you muttering about?" asked La Cueille.

"Silence!" was the laconic reply of the Swiss, while he continued to watch the shadow cast by the pole. It grew gradually less and at last disappeared altogether. For a moment no shadow was to be seen.

"Mid-day!" cried Wienersdorf. "I have the pleasure of congratulating you, gentlemen, upon being at the equator."

Schlickeisen approached to look and, truly enough, no shadow could be seen. The Boekit Doesson therefore was exactly on the equinoctial line.

"So that I am now sitting on the equator?" remarked La Cueille.

"Yes, my boy, you have that distinguished privilege."

"I say, what joy that would cause at sea! Neptune would come on board to greet us, and there would be drinks all around."

"And so shall there be here. We will bid farewell to the southern hemisphere with a hearty cheer," Johannes said, and jumping up he produced from one of the baskets two bottles of gin which he proceeded to dispense among the company. The Poenans were delighted at the treat and joined their leeeeeh lelelele ouiit to the hurrahs of the Europeans, who shook hands with each other and exchanged congratulations on their lucky escape.

"But we are not yet out of the woods," was the pessimistic remark of Johannes. "The worst is yet to come."

From Boekit Doesson Harimaoung guided the travellers in a westerly direction, keeping the crest of Boekit Lientang, which rose high above the surrounding hills, for his beacon. Thus they reached soengei Malahoei, which they crossed on an extemporized raft constructed of bamboos, which were found growing here in abundance. After the passage of the river their march was toward the north-west, until at nightfall they approached some huts, situated near a cataract, Kiham Toeak, on the soengei Nanga Boenoet. Harimaoung Boekit was well known here and knew all the inhabitants intimately. He entered one of the huts and without much trouble succeeded in purchasing for a few thäels of gold dust a rangkan capable of receiving the entire company.

At break of day, twenty-four hours later, our travellers found themselves at the mouth of the Blitang, up which they rowed into Danau Loewar, the largest of a group of lakes situated at the foot of the Batang Loepar mountain range.

When the rangkan had gone half way across its occupants caught a glimpse of a range of mountains bordering the northern horizon.

"There!" cried Johannes, " Once there and we are free."

The Europeans, powerfully affected, gazed at this mountain range, drawn like a dark blue ribbon against the light azure of the sky. For some moments none of them could speak. All the dangers and privations which they had encountered in getting this far seemed to pass before their eyes and they sat solemn and silent. At last Schlickeisen asked:

"What is the name of those mountains?"

"Batang Loepar," Johannes answered.

"How high do you consider them to be?"

"The English reckon the highest peaks to be between six and seven thousand feet."

"When we are once up there shall we have a long way before us?" asked La Cueille.

"In order to reach Jupille? Yes, a very long way."

"No; stupid," rejoined the Walloon, "I mean before we reach the sea-shore?"

"That, I don't know; I have never been here before."

This question, when put to Harimaoung Boekit, still remained unanswered.

The Poenan chief only shook his head and smiled. He was unskilled in the calculation of distances.

"How black the water of the lake looks," Schlickeisen remarked, "we seem to be sailing on ink."

"Yes," answered Wienersdorf, "I noticed the same on the Blitang. On this lake, however, I find the drearily tinted water to be a mirror fitted in a becoming frame. Observe its placid surface. Even under the sun's rays it is a jetty-black, while before us in glowing contrast is the dark-green foliage of the mountain slopes. Mark too, yonder, the gradual transition of gentle glades into rugged steeps, furnishing a combination of beauty and sublimity rarely met with anywhere."

It was indeed a lovely view. The beautiful mirror of water stretched itself far to the south and south-west. Mount Tomodok was visible in the west; the Batang Loepar range gradually rose in the north, and the acuminating peaks of Sareboe Saratoes were piled one above another, to be overtopped in the distant background by the summit of Japoh Poerau, called by the English Boekit Tebong, glistening like silver under the tropical sun.

"A glacier!" exclaimed the Swiss in their own language, pointing to the glittering summit. "Shall we have to climb that?"

Harimaoung Boekit shook his head, implying the negative, and pointed towards the north. Their disappointment at having to leave unvisited that snow-clad summit seemed a little surprising to their companions.

It was mid-day before our travellers reached the northern shore of the lake. They immediately seized their burdens and resumed their journey on foot.

The rangkan having been carefully concealed under the direction of Harimaoung in a spot where he could find it on his return, the Poenan and his men hastened to join their companions on their march.

Their path at first led through a marshy tract surrounding the lake, but this, after half an hour, was left behind and they approached the first slopes of the mountain. Travelling was now tolerably easy. They could perceive that considerable traffic existed along this road, although neither man nor habitation was to be seen. They stepped on bravely and made such rapid progress that when evening approached they had already reached the highest point of the pass over Batang Loepar. Here, under the shadow of the trees, they made their bivouac and the whole of the company excepting the appointed sentries left on watch were soon lost in profound slumber.

CHAPTER XIX.

DESCENT OF THE BATANG LOEPAR—A BORNEAN WATERFALL—THE FRONTIER PASSED—SIMANGANG—PARTING—ON BOARD THE FIRE-FLY—A SARAWAK FORT—AT KOETSHIN—ON BOARD THE RAINBOW—AT SINGAPORE—DEPARTURE FOR EUROPE.

WHEN the travellers awoke in the morning and the mist had been dispersed by the first rays of the sun a magnificent view rose before their eyes. The southern slope of the mountain which they had ascended the previous day was covered with high woods. The summit which they had surmounted was clothed with magnificent specimens of the intertropical flora of the higher zone. When, however, they approached the edge of the northern slope it appeared as if the luxuriant vegetation hitherto seen had suddenly departed in order to exhibit nature in her wildest and most fantastic form. Wild was the true word wherewith to describe the country in which they had arrived. All around were piles of gigantic rocks which threatened to interrupt all progress. Through these obstacles, however, they found tunnels cut and passages hewn out which barely offered standing room. Yawning around them were dangerous precipices and fathomless abysses beneath which mountain torrents roared like thunder, though the eye could not distinguish them through the vast depths. At other places rocks rose almost perpendicularly into the sky as if threatening death and destruction to the passer-by. And yet amid this chaos formed by the terrible forces of nature our travellers occasionally came upon verdant oases, gentle slopes crowned with short, fine grass, from out of which arose plumed cedar trees, forming a lovely picture that carried back the Swiss to the memories of their Alpenweide with its firs and pine trees.

On entering one of these oases the travellers noticed a cascade falling from an adjacent cliff. With insatiable delight the Swiss looked up at the dark-blue diorite of the rock whose edges were sharply defined against the soft azure of the skies. They watched the falling torrent—a fluttering robe which the water-nymph sent floating in the expanse. The soengei Oendoep, as this stream was called, arrested in its course by huge masses of rock, threw its water from a height of about four hundred feet. Beautifully shaded in greenish-blue, its principal branch would have reached the bottom of the valley over the perpendicular wall of the mountain like a crystalline stream, but half-way down its course was arrested by a projecting mass of stone upon which it descended with the noise of thunder; then beaten into foam it rushed downwards on its way to the valley—a milk-white ribbon, silvery bright. The other branches of the Oendoep wildly separated themselves from the edge of the cliff; the torrents were speedily met by stony crags and rocky pinnacles to which they seemed to cling for a moment; then they broke into millions of bubbles which shone like fire under the rays of the tropical sun and disappeared forever.

The four friends with Hamadoe' approached as near to the fall as was possible, and as if by instinct chose for their point of observation the spot where they could observe the magnificent rainbows formed everywhere around by the reflection of the sun's rays. They drew yet nearer and each became surrounded by a double rainbow, which while they remained in its immediate neighborhood seemed to move with them backwards and forwards and to follow every change in their position. Their hair, skin and garments became covered with minute particles of water, each of which, like a diamond, shone with the incomparable brilliancy of prismatic coloring.

"Beautiful! Magnificent!" the young wife exclaimed, "are such scenes also met with in your country?"

"This is undoubtedly very grand," replied her husband; "but Switzerland can also boast of her cascades. We have the Rhinefel at Laufen, the Staubbach in the valley of Lauterbrunnen and the Giesbach near Lake Brienz."

"Where the whitefaces amuse themselves by painting the waterfall. Is it not so?" remarked Johannes jokingly.

"What do you mean by painting?" Schlickeisen asked.

"Have I not read somewhere that nature in your country is found too poor and requires Bengal fire to make your waterfalls attractive?"

"Well, they do certainly illuminate the Giesbach; and whenever you come to Europe, if you find yourself in Switzerland, just go to that same fall and pay your six francs to see it at night."

"I should be very sorry indeed," said Johannes, somewhat disdainfully.

"And pray, why?"

"Because nature is in my opinion too exalted to be desecrated by such mockery. But to change the subject, let us, while impressed with the grandeur of this cataract, shake hands and bid each other God-speed."

"With all my heart," responded La Cueille. "I like wishing good-luck, because it is usually accompanied by a dram."

Johannes took from one of the baskets two square bottles. He poured out a stiff dose for each of them. Then raising on high his cocoanut drinking-cup, said:

"Men and brothers, this morning we have crossed the Batang Loepar mountains. That range marks the frontier between Dutch territory and Sarawak. We are over that frontier now and stand in the domains of Rajah Sir James Brooke. Brothers, I drink to Rajah Sir James Brooke, who established upon the most inhospitable coast of Borneo the colony which will now receive us after a long and weary pilgrimage. Hip! hip! hurrah!"

"Hip! hip! hurrah!" the Europeans cheered.

"Lēēēh lèlèlèlèle ouiiiiit," yelled the Poenans.

The travellers now cast their eyes over the country into which they were descending. However wild the upper slopes of the Batang Loepar must have been, here below them lay a carpet of the loveliest verdure, in the midst of which a silver ribbon was seen winding its course from south to north. Harimaoung Boekit explained to his frinds that the stream they saw was the soengei Oendoep. He also pointed out to them a spot on the horizon standing out beautifully white against the green background.

Wienersdorf took his glasses and looked.

"Those are white men's buildings," he exclaimed in a voice trembling with emotion.

"Thank Heaven!" said Schlickeisen.

"Benie soit la très Sainte Vierge de Jupille," added La Cueille, devoutly uncovering his head.

"Yes!" Wienersdorf continued, still looking through the glass. "They are dwellings efficiently lime-washed. There is also a fortification. It appears to be a square-bastioned redoubt. I can distinguish a flag on the flag-staff—a field of gold with a cross dividing the field into four equal squares. The perpendicular bar of the cross is red and black; the horizontal one is half red and half black."

"That is probably the Sarawak flag," said Johannes.

"That place is called Simangang," Harimaoung explained.

The travellers now quickly descended to the plain and before evening set in they arrived at the Sarawak fort. The garrison were turned out; but as soon as the party approached within hailing distance, Schlickeisen, who spoke English fluently, advanced alone, leaving the others behind. He shouted out his request for an interview with the authorities and was accordingly carried into the presence of the Assistant President and Military Commandant. When that official learned from him, that among the approaching travellers there were four soldiers who had deserted from the Dutch army his lips curled into a smile. It tickled Mr. Spencer's fancy that those stupid Dutchmen had been tricked. After inspecting the visitors he graciously gave his permission for the Europeans to enter the fort, but Harimaoung Boekit and his Poenans, he ordered, must remain outside.

"You are just in time," added he. "To-morrow morning the Firefly sails for Koetshing and you can continue your journey on board of her. You are certain to find some vessel at Koetshing which will convey you to Singapore."

The Europeans cordially thanked the commander for his reception, but announced their intention to remain outside the fortification.

It would be the last night they should pass with the brave Poenan chief. The morrow would see them on board the Firefly, and the Poenan and his band would immediately start for soengei Miri.

The night was passed in agreeable conversation teeming with reminiscences of the past trials through which they had fought hand-in-hand. Occasionally they became saddened by the thought of their approaching separation, but were soon reconciled to what they all saw was inevitable. At daybreak the Europeans carried the baskets containing their treasures on board the Firefly; Harimaoung Boekit accompanying them to the vessel. When the warning shriek of the steam-whistle sounded, the Poenan embraced his sister and looked lovingly into her eyes as if anxious to read her thoughts. Hot tears streamed down her cheeks as he clasped her to his breast. He then took Wienersdorf's hand and carried it to his lips.

"Paharingkoe Dahong," my brother Dohong, he sobbed. These were the only words which his violent emotion permitted him to utter.

Another tinkling of bells, another whistle. He tore himself from the last embrace of Hamadoe, pressed the hands of his four friends and leaped ashore. The plank was withdrawn from the pier, the paddles began to rotate, and between brother and sister there interposed a gap which increased with every second, until their forms became lost to each other in the morning mist. Then Hamadoe wiped away a tear and whispered in Wienersdorf's ear. "Now, you are everything to me."

The Firefly was a swift steamer and moved rapidly over the wide stream. By sunset she had reached the mouth of the river and the travellers obtained a full view of the ocean. The head of the vessel was now turned westward and before daybreak she entered the mouth of the soengei Moratabas, a branch of the Sarawak River. A few hours later she was at anchor before Koetshing, the capital of the Sarawak country. Our travellers were courteously received by Rajah Sir James Brooke, who listened to the history of their experiences with wrapt attention. He expressed his admiration of their pluck, perseverance, and presence of mind, but at the same time frankly condemned their desertion—designating it as "the faithless violation of a contract which they had made with their government." Yet had he not the heart to deliver up to the Dutch men who had accomplished such a journey, who had experienced such trials and suffered so much, who had risked their lives in order to regain their liberty.

Two days afterward the Rainbow, a fine, bark-rigged screw steamer, sailed for Singapore and our travellers took passage on her. During their stay at Koetshing the Europeans had been endeavoring to cleanse their skin from the stain of the katiting by means of vigorous scrubbing with soap and water. The pigment, however, after disguising them so long a time, refused to be easily washed away, so that they still presented the appearance of Indo-Europeans or half-breeds. Only time, the healer of all ills, would be able effectually to bleach their skins.

The travellers had endeavored to provide themselves at Koetshing with decent apparel. Although magasins de mode are rare in Borneo they had succeeded thoroughly and had been able to substitute for the ewahs, hitherto worn, sailors' Sunday suits, convenient if not elegant. Hamadoe, assisted by Johannes and her husband, had purchased a few handsome garments and dressed in these she looked very attractive. Even Dalim and his companion of Kwala Kapoeas had transformed themselves and now appeared in the elegant attire of the wealthier class of Malays. All of them, therefore, when on board the Rainbow looked neat, clean, and thoroughly presentable, so that no one could have imagined it possible that for the past three months they had been wanderers in the wilds of Borneo.

After leaving port, the weather being calm and the sky unclouded, the vessel steamed close in under the rocks of Cape Datoe. Our adventurers were thus enabled to secure a parting glimpse of the island which they had traversed from south to north and in which they had experienced such vicissitudes. They all looked with emotion at that cape—the young wife especially, who with half-suppressed tears gazed for the last time on the land of her birth and watched it gradually fade away, to disappear from her view—forever.

"No matter; it is the Lord's will." She withdrew her gaze from the horizon and sought comfort of her husband.

Three days afterward the Rainbow dropped anchor in the Roads of Singapore and was soon unloaded. The first visit paid by the deserters was to the Dutch Consulate. The verdict expressed by Rajah Brooke on the subject of their desertion had made a profound impression upon the Swiss. They sought to know the expense incurred by the Dutch Government for every soldier enlisted in its army. When informed of the amount, each of them deposited with the Consul gold dust to the value of one thousand guilders to pay the expense of his own enlistment and to hire a substitute for the unexpired term of his service. They also begged the Consul to take charge of a handsome theodolite, field-glass and sextant and two splendid rifles, to be forwarded to the commanding officer at Kwala Kapoeas, whose name they duly supplied. They also frankly confessed their error in having taken the Colonel's instruments and weapons at the time of their desertion, and hoped that the situation would be accepted and their fault forgiven.

The Consul, affected by their words and actions, became greatly interested in them and gladly placed himself at their disposal to assist them through their present difficulties. Through his aid they disposed of their gold dust and bezoar stones in the most profitable markets. After converting all their valuables into specie they proceeded to a division of property. Dalim and his companion were first liberally rewarded and expressed themselves well contented. The amount then accruing to each of the four companions was twenty-five thousand guilders. With the aid of the Consul the two Swiss and the Walloon had their shares converted into drafts on Europe payable to their respective orders. Johannes, who intended to settle in Singapore, preferred to dispose of his share himself.

The Consul in his generous endeavors went still further. Having found four substitutes to replace the deserters in the Dutch army he wrote to Batavia and obtained their papers with a formal discharge from military service. This took some time to accomplish, but during the three months occupied in its execution Wienersdorf was occupied in preparing his wife for the amenities of western life. His first step was in the direction of her costume. With the aid of one of the principal drapery stores he soon transformed her into a real European lady. He did his work tastefully and well, and Hamadoe looked most lovely in her new toilet. For the rest, being naturally gifted and possessing the rare capacity of adapting himself to any condition, her transformation cost her but little trouble.

At length the papers arrived from Batavia and there was nothing to prevent the Europeans from returning to their fatherland. Before leaving they paid a final visit to the Dutch Consul who had so generously aided them. They thanked him again and again, and as a parting gift offered him the manuscript book received from Harimaoung Boekit at kotta Rangan Hanoengoh, which had presumably belonged to George Muller, massacred in 1825. The Consul gratefully accepted the journal and announced his intention of presenting it to the "Museum voor land en volkenkunde," an institution devoted to the study of countries and their population. The following morning the four friends were standing together for the last time on one of the quays of New Harbor, Singapore—the starting point of the ocean mail steamers. The mail boat Hydaspe of the French messageries imperiales was under steam and ready to sail.

The parting between Johannes and his companions was most affecting. Silently and tearfully they pressed each other's hands. When the boat had steamed into the straits which separate Singapore from Poeloe Pandjang, the three friends were still looking back to the shore and fancied that they saw a handkerchief waving in the distance. Long stood Johannes on the quay gazing at the departing ship, and when she disappeared from view, with a loud sob he cried out after them, "May God be their guide! they were brave men."

VOCABULARY OF DAYAK WORDS.

Akar pahit.—" Bitter root," is the root of a creeper largely found in the marshy lower country of Borneo, and until now the best substitute for quinine.

Alier.—The hole through which the slag is drawn off in the process of smelting ore.

Amai.—Means father, and is the title of the chiefs of the upper country.

Antoeen.—The power of changing into an evil spirit in order to steal a man's soul. See page 254.

Baba and *Kee.*—Are used to designate the Chinese in the Dutch Indies. The former is the more complimentary. Kee is humiliating and almost a nickname.

Badjangkan.—In Dayak, means to occupy a large space. Hence the Djankangese were proud of their name, as indicating the powerful tribe from which they descend.

Badjoe.—Married women and girls always walk about half naked in-doors. When company is expected, decorum requires the lady of the house to put on a badjoe, generally made of blue or red silk, and frequently stitched with gold thread.

Bakatak.—A green frog; used as food.

Baloedoek.—An amphibious animal about a foot long, white and covered with fine scales. Its body resembles a fish and it has the head of a frog.

Bangamat.—Flying dog.

Bapoejoe.—A fish like the perch in shape and size. See page 53 for their habits.

Basora.—A legal action pending.

Batoe galiga, or bezoar stone.—Is found in the intestines of certain kinds of monkeys.

Batoe kasisentoe.—Coal.

Batoe sanaman.—Iron ore.

Benting.—Fort.

Bigal.—A national dance of the Dayaks.

Blako ontong.—Means to beg for good luck.

Boea bakoeng.—See weights.
Boea kajoe.—See weights.
Boehies.—Black and gray apes, noted for their long tails.
Boekit riwoet, or Wind Mountain.—A common name for hills or summits of mountains, especially when standing isolated and consequently exposed to every wind.
Boelau oerei.—Gold dust.
Boengkang.—The fat of a black cat.
Boentoeng.—See weights.
Boetoeng.—The nozle of the bellows used in smelting.
Brini.—See weights.
Brotoali.—A species of cactus from which a decoction is made which is used as a protection against mosquitoes.
Djata.—The brother of Mahatara, the Dayak god, was the father of all crocodiles.
Djoekoeng.—Is a canoe formed by the excavated trunk of a tree. It can contain two or three persons only.
Dohong.—Means "war sword." It usually denotes male bravery and in Oriental language it stands for valorous.
Ewah.—A coarse cloth or piece of bark wound several times around the middle, an end hanging down before and behind. It serves a most useful purpose in protecting the abdomen against sudden chills.
Gantang.—Is a measure calculated to hold about four and one-half pounds avoirdupois.
Hagalangang.—The decision of a case by an appeal to arms. See page 232.
Halamantek.—Forest leeches.
Hambator.—Is the larva of a large beetle found in worm-eaten wood. It is very fat and of the dimensions of a finger.
Ipoh.—A vegetable poison made from the sap of a creeper, in which the Dayaks dip the points of their arrows.
Kadjanka.—The ruler of the moon and protector of newly married women.
Kahio.—Bornean name of the orang outang.
Kalamboe-ie.—A large snail; used as a food.
Kalampoet.—A tree of the rhododendron tribe.
Karangan.—A sand bar of considerable size in a river.
Karoenkoeng.—Suit of rattan armor.
Katiting.—A tree belonging to the Rhizophara.
Kee.—See Baba.

Ketan.—Is a species of rice containing much gluten, which becomes thick in boiling. Eaten with treacle and powdered cocoanuts, it forms one of the delicacies of the Dayaks.

Kiham.—Indicates a spot in the river, narrowed by beds of rock, compelling the waters to rush through a much straitened canal. Generally this is accompanied by a tolerable decrease in the bed of the river.

Koedjang.—Is a tuber, largely found in marshy regions, and especially in the lower country, where, after the rice, it forms the principal food of the natives. In the upper country it is also found in pools and marshes.

Kwala.—Mouth of a river.

Laboerang.—An earthen trough in which iron ore is smelted.

Mahatara and *Hatallah* both signify God. The first is seldom used by the Dayaks when speaking to a European. The latter is never used among the Dayaks themselves.

Mandauws.—The Dayak sword, the blade concave on one side and convex on the other. Is about twenty-one inches long, nearly straight, and one and a half inches broad in the middle and tapering to a sharp point. It has only one cutting edge.

Manjapa.—The administration of oaths.

Maroetas.—A species of quarantine declared against a house, village or even whole district in consequence of infectious disease.

Matta boeroeng.—See weights.

Nagara.—Is a district with a capital of the same name situated in the Malayan districts of Borneo, where the best arms of the whole island are manufactured.

Obat.—Medicine.

Palakho.—A settlement deposited by the bridegroom with the bride's parents, varying in amount according to the wealth of the individual.

Pampahilep.—A forest imp. See page 42.

Pangereran.—A crocodile killer, usually a Malay.

Pantoek.—The needle used in tattooing.

Parabah.—A Dayak stratagem. A tree is cut off but held upright by rattan cables. These are severed at the proper moment and the tree falls upon the enemy.

Radjah balawang boelau, or King of the Golden Gate ; sometimes also called Radja Ontong, or king of misfortune. The residence of this benevolent being is above the residence of the Sangiangs, near that of Mahatara, the supreme divinity.

Radja Ontong.—See Radjah balawang boelau.
Rajoh.—A fine moss found on the high lands of Borneo.
Ramon petak kinan.—Eatable soil.
Rangkan.—Is a large canoe formed by excavating the trunk of a tree. It will carry thirty persons, in some cases even more.
Real.—An imaginary coin among the Dayaks. Its value is about 60 cents.
Ringgit.—See weights.
Rioeng.—Noise.
Riwoet-haroesan.—Breath of the stream; a musical sound formed by the waters of a stream meeting the incoming tide from the sea.
Sadjampol.—See weights.
Sakobang.—See weights.
Salambouw.—A square net with medium sized meshes, spread across a stream to prevent the escape of fish.
Sambalajong.—A white head-dress worn by widows.
Sanaman.—Iron.
Sangiangs.—Heavenly beings, servants of Mahatara (God). Many sacrifices are offered to them.
Sanggarang.—A richly carved flag-staff.
Sapoendoes.—Posts to which prisoners are tied to be tortured to death.
Sarok boelau.—The soul of the gold dust, the Dayaks believing that inanimate bodies have souls.
Sarong.—Petticoat.
Satali.—See weights.
Satilai.—See weights.
Singapore.—Although not a single lion is found in the whole of the Moluccan peninsula, Singapore means lion city.
Sipet is a blow-pipe for poisonous arrows. An iron lance is attached to it so that it may be used for offensive operations.
Siren.—A poison made from the sap of a tree in which the Dayaks dip the points of their arrows.
Soengei.—Stream.
Soho.—A flood.
Takakak.—Is a woodcock of great beauty, crowing its loud taaaak-kekakakak at regular intervals, about 9 P.M., 12 M., and 3 A.M.
Talawang.—Shield.
Tangoeli.—The larvæ of bees stewed in honey.
Tarodjok.—A pair of scales.
Tatoem.—The shriek with which the Dayak lament their dead.

Tempon Telon.—One of the Sangiangs, the Charon of the Dayaks, who carries the souls of the dead through a purifying fire into the Elysian fields.
Thael.—See weights.
Titih.—The funeral knell of the Dayaks. See page 18.
Tobah.—A shrub belonging to the Rhisophores; is universally found in the lower country, while in the upper country it only grows in marshy soil.
Toeak.—A liquor prepared from fermented rice, pepper, betelnuts and sugar.
Toending.—The gilding of the nails and painting the forehead. The dead are thus decorated before burial.
Tomoi.—Somewhat resembles a summer-house, erected near the fortified dwellings in the upper country, to receive travellers. No stranger is ever admitted within the fortification; mistrust is principally the origin of this custom, the natives thus protecting themselves against spies, who, under the mask of friendship, may come to reconnoitre the territory; but this practice also serves to prevent dissensions which may arise from the violation of customs and habits of the inhabitants with which strangers are presumably unacquainted.
Weights.—The standard weight of gold in the interior of Borneo is the ringgit. Two ringgits are about equal to one thael. The ringgit contains two sadjampol; the sadjampol two and a half sakobang; the sakobang two boea kajoe; the boea kajoe two boentoeng; the boentoeng two satilai; the satilai two satali; the satali one and a half brini; the brini two matta boeroeng, and the matta boeroeng two boea bakoeng. A boea bakoeng therefore is the 1-960th part of a thael.

www.ingramcontent.com/pod-product-compliance
Lightning Source LLC
Chambersburg PA
CBHW022121290426
44112CB00008B/756